CULTIVATING KINDNESS

An Educator's Guide

John-Tyler Binfet

Cultivating Kindness sheds light on just how children and adolescents are kind, especially in school. Grounded in psychological and educational research on kindness and supported with illustrations capturing the voices of public school students, this book enhances our understanding of kindness.

Written with educators in mind, *Cultivating Kindness* draws from surveys and interviews with more than three thousand children and adolescents. Author John-Tyler Binfet shares perspectives on kindness from the very individuals we hope will embrace kindness. Interwoven among examples from students are findings from peer-reviewed studies on topics exploring the role of joy and stress contagions on fostering or thwarting kindness, the concept of *kind discipline*, and how to measure kindness in school. This book also includes a kindness checklist to guide educators wishing to implement and foster kindness in their classrooms or schools. In addition to practical scenarios challenging the reader to respond kindly, a repository of kindness resources to support the continued kindness education of readers is also included.

JOHN-TYLER BINFET is an associate professor of education in the Okanagan School of Education at the University of British Columbia.

Cultivating Kindness

An Educator's Guide

JOHN-TYLER BINFET

UNIVERSITY OF TORONTO PRESS
Toronto Buffalo London

© University of Toronto Press 2022
Toronto Buffalo London
utorontopress.com
Printed and bound by CPI Group (UK) Ltd, Croydon, CR0 4YY

ISBN 978-1-4875-0732-9 (cloth)   ISBN 978-1-4875-3602-2 (EPUB)
ISBN 978-1-4875-2502-6 (paper)   ISBN 978-1-4875-3601-5 (PDF)

Library and Archives Canada Cataloguing in Publication

Title: Cultivating kindness : an educator's guide / John-Tyler Binfet.
Names: Binfet, John-Tyler, 1964– author.
Description: Includes bibliographical references and index.
Identifiers: Canadiana (print) 2022024524X | Canadiana (ebook) 20220245339 |
ISBN 9781487507329 (hardcover) | ISBN 9781487525026 (softcover) |
ISBN 9781487536015 (PDF) | ISBN 9781487536022 (EPUB)
Subjects: LCSH: Kindness. | LCSH: Affective education. | LCSH: Children –
Conduct of life. | LCSH: School children – Conduct of life. |
LCSH: Bullying in schools – Prevention.
Classification: LCC LB1072 .B56 2022 | DDC 370.15/34 – dc23

We wish to acknowledge the land on which the University of Toronto Press
operates. This land is the traditional territory of the Wendat, the Anishnaabeg,
the Haudenosaunee, the Métis, and the Mississaugas of the Credit First
Nation.

University of Toronto Press acknowledges the financial assistance to its
publishing program of the Canada Council for the Arts and the Ontario Arts
Council, an agency of the Government of Ontario.

Canada Council   Conseil des Arts
for the Arts   du Canada

ONTARIO ARTS COUNCIL
CONSEIL DES ARTS DE L'ONTARIO
an Ontario government agency
un organisme du gouvernement de l'Ontario

Funded by the   Financé par le
Government   gouvernement
of Canada   du Canada

Canadä

*This book is dedicated to educators around the globe who,
in addition to seeking ways to promote academic excellence
in students, yearn to cultivate kindness in students. May this
book inform your thinking and practice.*

1. What does it mean to be kind? (*Define kindness*).

Kindness is making someone feels like s/he belongs or feels special. Like the world didn't make a mistake.

Image credit: J.T. Binfet

A thousand words will not leave so deep an impression as one deed.

Henrik Ibsen

Contents

List of Illustrations and Tables   ix

Foreword by Kimberly A. Schonert-Reichl   xv

Acknowledgments   xxiii

1 Introduction   3

2 The Interplay between Kindness and Social and
Emotional Learning   20

3 Mechanisms Underpinning the Benefits of Kindness   33

4 Responsive Kindness   59

5 Intentional Kindness   72

6 Quiet Kindness   86

7 Fostering Kindness in Students and in Schools   97

8 Measuring Kindness: How Kind Is Your School?   121

9 Conclusion   135

Appendix A: List of Kindness Publications by the Author   153

Appendix B: Prisma Flow Chart   155

*Appendix C: Search Process to Identify Bullying versus Kindness
Publications across Databases*   157

Appendix D: Social and Emotional Learning Resources   159

Appendix E: Drawing Template for Early Elementary Students   163

Appendix F: Drawing Template Teacher Kindness   165

Appendix G: Kindness Scenarios to Facilitate Discussion   167

Appendix H: Kindness Planning Sheet   171

Appendix I: Curated List of Kindness-Themed Books   177

Appendix J: Resources in Support of Students with Special Needs   183

Appendix K: Sample Teacher Survey of School Kindness   185

Appendix L: School Kindness Scale   189

Appendix M: Curated List of Kindness Resources   191

References   195

Index   211

Illustrations and Tables

Illustrations

1.1. Elementary student helping someone who fell. 4
1.2. A fifteen-year-old boy's definition of kindness. 5
1.3. A ten-year-old girl's brainstormed list of kind acts to do. 8
1.4. A middle school student defines kindness. 9
1.5. An eleven-year-old boy's interpretation of what it means to be kind. 9
1.6. An eleven-year-old boy's definition of kindness. 10
1.7. A twelve-year-old girl's definition of kindness. 10
1.8. Frequency of kindness-themed publications across databases, 2000–2020 14
2.1. A twelve-year-old boy's definition of what it means to be kind. 21
2.2. A twelve-year-old boy's example of kindness to self. 21
2.3. A fourteen-year-old girl describes one of her acts of kindness in response to the prompt "What is an example of something kind you have done at school recently?" 25
2.4. A twelve-year-old girl describes her act of kindness in response to the prompt "What is an example of something kind you have done at school recently?" 25
2.5. A twelve-year-old boy describes his act of kindness. 26
2.6. A twelve-year-old boy describes an act of kindness in response to the prompt "Plan and describe an act of kindness to be done over the course of the next week." 31
3.1. A fifteen-year-old girl reflects on participating in a middle school kindness study. 34
3.2. A fifteen-year-old girl reflects on participating in a kindness study. 34

3.3.   A nine-year-old boy describes his act of kindness at school.   41

3.4.   A seven-year-old boy describes a teacher being kind.   43

3.5.   A six-year-old boy describes a teacher being kind to him.   44

3.6.   Conceptualization of well-being benefits.   48

3.7.   A fifteen-year-old girl shares insights after participating
in a kindness study.   48

3.8.   A fifteen-year-old boy reflects on the quality of his
kind acts.   55

3.9.   A fourteen-year-old girl reflects on her kindness toward a
grandparent in response to the prompt: "Plan an act of kindness
to be done over the course of the next week."   55

3.10.   A sixteen-year-old girl shares her planned acts of kindness.   56

3.11.   An eight-year-old boy illustrates how he is kind to his
brother.   57

3.12.   A fifteen-year-old girl describes her act of kindness
for her grandparents.   58

4.1.   An eight-year-old boy shares his example of kindness
at school.   60

4.2.   An elementary student describes his act of kindness at school in
response to the prompt "What is an example of something kind
you have done at school recently?"   64

4.3.   An eight-year-old student describes physically helping a
teacher.   66

4.4.   A fifteen-year-old boy describes how he is kind to
a classmate.   67

4.5.   A fourteen-year-old boy describes how he is kind to a socially
outcast student.   67

4.6.   A nine-year-old girl draws herself helping the school and her
fellow students.   68

5.1.   A twelve-year-old girl describes her act of kindness toward a
student with special needs.   73

5.2.   A fourteen-year-old girl shares her act of kindness toward her
grandfather in response to the prompt "Plan an act of kindness
that you could do over the course of the next week."   73

5.3.   Self-ratings of face-to-face and online kindness by a middle
school student.   74

5.4.   A middle school student plans his acts of kindness
for the week.   74

5.5.   Kindness gas tank.   75

5.6.   A brainstormed list of possible recipients of kindness.   76

5.7.   A middle school student's act of intentional kindness
for a friend.   76

5.8.   A seven-year-old girl introduces herself to a new student.   80

5.9.   A fifteen-year-old girl reflects on the extent to which
        she is kind.   85

6.1.   A seven-year-old boy shares his act of kindness.   87

6.2.   A twelve-year-old boy describes his quiet act of kindness for a
        classmate in response to the prompt "Describe and act of kind-
        ness that you can do over the course of the next week."   88

6.3.   A middle school student leaves change for a stranger.   88

6.4.   A fourteen-year-old boy's act of quiet kindness toward his sister
        in response to the prompt "Describe an act of kindness that you
        can do over the course of the next week."   89

6.5.   A fifteen-year-old girl gives advice to teachers about how to
        encourage kindness.   90

6.6.   A seven-year-old's illustration of her kind act
        for her teacher.   93

6.7.   A six-year-old boy illustrates listening as his kind act.   94

6.8.   A fourteen-year-old boy describes his kindness to his school's
        recycling club in response to the prompt "Describe an act of
        kindness that you can do over the course of the next week."   95

7.1.   A seven-year-old boy's observation of his teacher being
        kind.   98

7.2.   A sixteen-year-old girl gives advice on how teachers
        can encourage kindness.   100

7.3.   A six-year-old boy's illustration of his teacher being kind.   102

7.4.   A fifteen-year-old girl describes her thoughts on her
        kindest act.   103

7.5.   A fifteen-year-old girl reflects on her participation in a middle
        school kindness study.   104

7.6.   An eleven-year-old girl shares her thoughts on why it
        is important to be kind to oneself.   105

7.7.   A twelve-year-old boy shares how his friends influence his kind
        behaviour.   107

7.8.   An eleven-year-old girl describes how her friends influence her
        kind behaviour.   107

7.9.   An elementary student describes teacher kindness
        as listening.   109

7.10.   A nine-year-old boy draws and describes his teacher being
        kind.   110

7.11.   A seven-year-old girl draws how she perceives her
        teacher being kind.   111

7.12.   An elementary student describes a teacher teaching
        as kindness.   112

7.13. A seven-year-old boy draws his teacher being kind.   113
7.14. A fifteen-year-old girl reflects on the quality of
       her kind acts.   115
8.1.   An eleven-year-old boy shares his strategy for dealing
       with racism at school.   122
8.2.   A fourteen-year-old boy describes a teacher's respect for him
       as an act of kindness.   123
8.3.   A six-year-old boy describes his act of kindness for
       a classmate.   125
8.4.   A fifteen-year-old girl reflects on participating in a middle
       school kindness study.   126
8.5.   A fifteen-year-old boy shares his insights after participating
       in a kindness study.   129
9.1.   A fourteen-year-old boy shares his advice to teachers
       on encouraging kindness.   136
9.2.   A middle school student's definition of kindness.   136
9.3.   A middle school student's act of kindness for herself in response
       to the prompt "Plan an act of kindness to be done over the
       course of the next week."   139
9.4.   A middle school student shares how she is kind to herself.   140
9.5.   A fourteen-year-old girl shares her thoughts on kindness
       to herself.   140
9.6.   A twelve-year-old boy shares his views on being kind
       to himself.   140
9.7.   A fourteen-year-old girl shares that she feels unworthy
       of kindness.   141
9.8.   A fourteen-year-old girl's reluctance to be kind to others.   142
9.9.   A fourteen-year-old boy links his in-class behaviour
       to his teacher's well-being.   144
9.10. A nine-year-old boy recalls kindness from his teacher.   145
9.11. A middle school student rank orders her kind acts and justifies
       her kindest act.   147
9.12. A young student draws her act of kindness aimed
       at helping the world.   149
9.13. A twelve-year-old boy shares his insights on why it is important
       to be kind to oneself.   150

Tables

1.1.   Published Definitions of Kindness   7
1.2.   Questions Driving Research in Kindness   12

1.3. Number of Kindness and Bullying Articles Published
       (2000–2019)   16
1.4. Publishing Trend by Kindness versus Bullying (2000–2019)   16
2.1. Social and Emotional Competencies and Kindness   22
2.2. Reflecting on One's Own Social and Emotional
       Competencies   24
2.3. Illustration of Social and Emotional Skills within and between
       Individuals   24
2.4. Things to Consider When Implementing a Social and Emotional
       Learning Program   28
2.5. Socially and Emotionally Informed Teaching Practices   30
2.6. Recognizing Social and Emotional Learning within
       a Kind Act   31
5.1. Suggestions for Developmentally Appropriate Kindness   77
8.1. Characteristics of Kind Discipline (Adapted from Winkler
       et al. 2017)   130
8.2. School Kindness Checklist   133

Foreword

My contention is, first, that we should want more from our educational efforts than adequate academic achievement and, second, that we will not achieve even that meager success unless our children believe that they themselves are cared for and learn to care for others.

Noddings

If each of us can learn to relate to each other more out of compassion, with a sense of connection to each other and a deep recognition of our common humanity, and more important, to teach this to our children, I believe that this can go a long way in reducing many of the conflicts and problems that we see today.

The Dalai Lama

Be kind whenever possible. It is always possible.

The Dalai Lama

This is the moment to pay attention – a demarked time in our collective history in which the cultivation of kindness, empathy, and compassion across the globe is both necessary and crucial. Rarely before have we witnessed such an urgent need for an explicit and intentional focus on promoting students' social and emotional competencies, including their kindness, in our schools and beyond. I am honored to write the foreword for Dr. Binfet's innovative and groundbreaking book on cultivating kindness in schools because his book serves as a beacon for a movement that is unfolding in education. Indeed, this book reflects a worldwide effort to promote students' kindness and caring in education systems. Dr. Binfet's pioneering book represents an essential step forward for the field through its incorporation of science-based strategies on kindness into schools and classrooms. As we contemplate the future of education, it is imperative, as the epigraphs by Nel Noddings and the Dalai Lama remind us, to create contexts in which kindness and caring are at the fore. In a world where global awareness is just a click away, and where stresses and distractions that new technologies bring abound, a twenty-first-century education that attends to the cultivation of kindness and compassion is essential (e.g., Roeser et al. 2018).

I believe that Dr. Binfet's book aligns with a transformation in education that is evolving across the globe and this time represents an important inflection point in our education systems in which true positive change can occur. This transformation has been catalyzed by pioneering research demonstrating that a high-quality education should not only promote the academic competencies of students such as reading, writing, math, and science, but also cultivate the development of positive human qualities such as kindness, empathy, compassion, and altruism – characteristics that will equip our future generation with the skills and competencies to thrive and flourish in an ever-changing world (Schonert-Reichl 2019; Schonert-Reichl and Utne O'Brien 2012). Rarely since the early twentieth century, when educational influencers such as John Dewey asserted that "the aim of education is growth or development, both intellectual and moral" (Dewey 1964, 213), have we witnessed such increased attention to the integration of the social and emotional dimensions of teaching and learning into the very fabric of education to catalyze transformation of our education system at all levels. There is now widespread agreement among educators, parents, students, and the public at large that a more comprehensive agenda for education is needed – one that includes nurturing the development of positive human traits (Greenberg and Turksma 2015; Jazaieri 2018; Roeser et al. 2018).

In the face of current societal economic, environmental, and social challenges, the promotion of these "non-academic" skills in education are seen as more critical than ever before, with business and political leaders urging schools to pay more attention to social and emotional learning, or SEL. In short, SEL is the process of acquiring the competencies to recognize and manage emotions, develop caring and concern for others, establish positive relationships, make responsible decisions, and handle challenging situations effectively (Weissberg et al. 2015). SEL competencies comprise the foundational skills for positive health practices, engaged citizenship, and school success. SEL is sometimes called "the missing piece," because it represents a part of education that is inextricably linked to school success but has not been explicitly stated or given much attention until recently. Schools in particular have been implicated as contexts that can play a crucial role in fostering these positive human qualities, and pioneering research conducted in the past decade has shown SEL approaches demonstrate promise in achieving these goals (Durlak et al. 2011a; Taylor et al. 2017; Weissberg et al. 2015). Indeed, SEL approaches and programs are being implemented in countries throughout the world (Frydenberg et al. 2017; Humphrey 2013; Torrente et al. 2015). Analogously, large-scale organizations such as the World Bank, the World Health Organization (WHO), the Organisation for Economic and Cooperative Development (OECD), and UNESCO (Chatterjee Singh & Duraiappah 2020) are joining in the call for a more explicit and intentional consideration of social and emotional competencies and social and emotional well-being in both education and health (e.g., OECD 2015, 2018).

Dr. Binfet has crafted a book that fills a critical gap in the work on SEL. By offering the stories of students as a window for understanding and promoting kindness in schools and classrooms, he brings to life the authentic voices of students in a way never before captured in the field of SEL by listening in a way that truly respects what each has to say. Moreover, Dr. Binfet cogently underpins each theme that emerges in the stories of children and youth with solid research evidence. As he notes, although kindness is a component under the larger umbrella of the SEL dimension of prosocial behaviours, the explicit link between SEL and kindness is still nascent.

Similar to the growing empirical research on SEL, there has been a concomitant expansion of interest in the cultivation of kindness and compassion both in the general public (Keltner 2009; Post 2011) and in educational settings (Staub 1988, 2005; Roeser et al. 2018). This growing interest is based on the burgeoning research documenting the benefits of kindness, compassion, and prosociality. For example, empirical evidence demonstrates that being kind and prosocial lowers risk for cardiovascular disease in adolescents (Schreier et al. 2013), improves peer acceptance and well-being in elementary school students (Layous et al. 2012), and is a better predictor of academic grades than standardized achievement test scores in middle school students (Wentzel 1993).

In addition to playing a crucial role in predicting health, happiness, and academic success, there are links between children's kindness and later success in adulthood. In one of the most compelling studies on the long-term benefits of children's prosocial competencies, Jones, Greenberg, and Crowley (2015) examined the degree to which late adolescent and early adult outcomes were predicted by teacher ratings of children's kindness measured many years earlier, when children were in kindergarten, following 753 kindergarten children longitudinally thirteen to nineteen years later. Kindergarten teacher ratings of children's prosocial skills (getting along with others, sharing, cooperating) were found to be significant predictors of whether participants graduated from high school on time, completed a college degree, obtained stable employment in adulthood, and were employed full time in adulthood. Moreover, kindergarten children who were rated by their teachers as high in prosocial skills were less likely as adults to receive public assistance, live in or seek public housing, be involved with police, be placed in a juvenile detention facility, or be arrested. Early social competence inversely predicted days of binge drinking in the last month and number of years on medication for emotional or behavioural problems during high school. Given these findings, the authors emphasize the importance of assessing young children's social and emotional competence early on and contend that these "softer" skills can be more malleable than IQ or other cognitive measures and hence important contenders for intervention. Dr. Binfet's approach to the assessment of children's understanding of kindness clearly aligns with this recommendation.

I have spent more than thirty years of my academic career in the field of SEL searching for the ways to create contexts that promote children's kindness, empathy, compassion, and altruism. Over the years, my colleagues and I have conducted rigorous evaluations of SEL programs – such as the Roots of Empathy program (Schonert-Reichl et al. 2012) and MindUP (Schonert-Reichl et al. 2015). We have consistently searched for and found that SEL programs that focus specifically on promoting kindness, empathy, and compassion lead to increases in students' social and emotional competencies, prosocial behaviours, well-being, and school success, and decreases in aggressive behaviours, such as bullying.

My work on SEL and kindness was instigated by my time as a middle school teacher and a teacher at an alternative high school for youth deemed "at risk" during the 1980s in a Chicago suburb. My students inspired me, taught me, and coached me to learn from them about what it takes to create an educational context in which they could learn, flourish, and be kind. What was missing at that time was the field of SEL and the science behind it. How much I wish I would have had Dr. Binfet's book to guide me! I worked on instinct and had little from which to draw in my teacher training or support from the educators in my school context. Two particular lessons stand out for me in my work as a beginning teacher. First, as discussed by Dr. Binfet in chapter 7, the foundation of learning is the creation of a context that is nurturing, participatory, safe, caring, and kind. Indeed, creating supportive, safe, and respectful school environments in which all children feel they belong is

foundational to teaching and learning. As a new teacher at an alternative high school in my early twenties, this was a hard lesson to learn.
The first months at the school were trying, to say the least. My students
essentially seemed to dislike me immensely (this may have been something to do with the fact that I was teaching reading – a subject in which
many of the students struggled). At first, I was devastated – I worked so
hard – how could they dislike me so much? It was not until I saw this as
their strength – their resilience. They had created an "armour" to protect
their vulnerability – they pushed me away so that I could not hurt them.
It was not until I understood this that I could move past my hurt feelings and recognize that I needed to find ways to engage them in creating
the learning context that included them helping decide on classroom
rules, decorate the classroom, have a voice in assignments, and find
the strengths that each possessed. I learned the simple lesson that "students don't care how much you know, until they know how much you
care." Essentially, what I learned was the key messages that permeated
Dr. Binfet's book: make kindness and compassion the essential ingredi-
ents of teaching and listen to the voices of students – success will follow!

The second lesson I learned was to not underestimate the kindness
that is in each and every student – a theme that resonates throughout
Dr. Binfet's book. During my first December working at the alternative
high school, I went to the other teachers with an idea: let's do a toy collection for "Toys for Tots" – a well-known toy drive for needy children.
We can ask all students to bring in toys to donate. The other teachers
looked aghast when I suggested this. They intimated that our students
would not only have no interest whatsoever in giving to needy children,
but that our students might actually steal the toys from a collection box!
Somewhat discouraged but still determined, I decided not to listen to
my colleagues and instead brought the idea to the students. I told them
about the background and mission of "Toys for Tots" and about the
many young children who might wake up Christmas morning with no
presents. I thought that many of them may have also had the experience
of vulnerability and disappointment. To my utter delight, the students
began bringing in toys and putting them into the big cardboard box I
had decorated with Christmas wrapping! Initially, some of them said
that they were doing it because their moms insisted, but soon many of
the students were bringing in toys. There was an expansive smile on
each and every one of my students' faces when they put a toy in the
box. What I learned is exactly what Dr. Binfet espouses – we should
not underestimate our students' capacity for kindness, and sometimes
kindness will not surface until we afford students with opportunities
to express it.

Dr. Binfet's book clearly distinguishes him as a prodigious scholar who is committed to bridging the gap between theory and practice in the area of kindness, and this book demarks a significant step in his imprint in the field of education. His acumen in translating his extensive theoretical and empirical knowledge in children's and adolescents' kindness and apply it to educational practice is laudable. His work is a prototype for illustrating how research evidence can be applied to educational practice to improve the school and life success of all children.

> No society can long sustain itself unless its members have learned the sensitivities, motivations and skills involved in assisting and caring for other human beings.
>
> Bronfenbrenner (2005, 14)

What kind of world do we want for world citizens of tomorrow? Urie Bronfenbrenner reminds us that learning to care for others is essential for the survival of society, and clearly, schools play a fundamental role in this mission. The field of kindness in education holds much promise in creating a future generation of caring adults and students via programs that promote caring classroom and school contexts that can create a kinder world, and Dr. Binfet is a leader in that effort.

In closing, Dr. Binfet's book is a "must read" for individuals who wish to be a part of catalyzing positive change and have access to the latest information on groundbreaking research and practical strategies for cultivating kindness in an educational system in which administrators, teachers, and students can flourish and succeed. Through engaging dialogue about the science underlying the promotion of kindness, illustrations and stories of kindness from students, coupled with a cornucopia of practical strategies that are clear and easy to implement, Dr. Binfet has assembled a rich and compelling volume that integrates not only the "why" for cultivating kindness, but the "how." Until the educational system can become truly cognizant of the fact that teaching and learning are human endeavours founded in the creation and maintenance of kind and caring relationships – a "system" that recognizes the importance of listening to and respecting the voices of students – we will continue to see a disconnect between education and the needs and well-being of teachers, students, and society it serves. Educators will do well to draw from the impressive evidence base and practical implications outlined throughout. One critical message that I have gleaned after reading Dr. Binfet's book is that it is imperative that we make intentional efforts to integrate kindness into every aspect of our education system to promote children's and adolescents' social and emotional competence, including their empathy, compassion, and altruism. Such efforts must be based on strong conceptual models and sound research. Only then will we be in a position to create a world in which kindness and compassion are at the core.

Kimberly A. Schonert-Reichl
NoVo Foundation Endowed Chair in Social
and Emotional Learning
University of Illinois at Chicago

Acknowledgments

But for the returned phone calls from school administrators, the warm welcome from teachers whose classroom doors were always open, the returned signed consent forms from parents, and the transparency of students who readily shared what it meant to be kind, this book would not have been possible. Thank you to the staff, students, and parents of School Districts No. 23 (Central Okanagan), No. 67 (Okanagan Skaha), and No. 53 (Okanagan Similkameen). Appreciation is expressed to agencies who, over the years, generously funded my kindness research. They include the Central Okanagan Foundation, the University of British Columbia's Office of Research Services, and the Social Sciences and Research Council of Canada's Insight Development Grant program. Last, I am grateful for the student research assistants who worked on projects undergirding the material presented in this book and who put up with my detail- and deadline-driven ways. Thank you all.

CULTIVATING KINDNESS

Chapter One

Introduction

I have long been curious about kindness and in particular about how students demonstrate kindness, especially within the school context. A second-grader's drawing affords us a window into how one young person enacts or brings kindness to life within her school (see figure 1.1). Collecting examples like this is how I uncover what it means to be kind – from the viewpoint of the very individuals we hope will embrace kindness – children and adolescents. Throughout this book, you will be provided with definitions and examples of kindness reflecting the views, beliefs, and perspectives of children and adolescents themselves. Their answers are not always neatly presented and I have not corrected spelling or grammatical errors. What you will get is an honest account of just how they understand and enact kindness. The insights from over three thousand Canadian public school students invite you to learn about what kindness means, how students bring it to life, and how educators can foster it. Understanding kindness, especially from the perspective of students, can transform your thinking about this important topic. Moreover, by the end of this book you are likely to rethink your approach to recognizing and fostering kindness among the young people around you.

This chapter begins by defining kindness, differentiating it from similar or field-adjacent terms such as prosocial behaviour, compassion, and altruism. Next, an overview of kindness across the developmental lifespan is presented to give you a sense of how being kind changes as children mature. How kindness is studied by researchers is explored next, including a review of the types of questions researchers have asked to advance the study of kindness. Then, and taking a broad perspective, an examination of publication rates is presented to illustrate how kindness is emerging as a distinct field of study. This includes an exploration of the contexts across which kindness has been studied. This chapter concludes with an overview of the chapters comprising

Step #1: In the box below, draw a picture of something you have done kind at school recently. What have you done to show kindness at school?

WHO? _____ Self + Friend. _____

WHAT? __ I am helping someone up when They fell __

Figure 1.1. Elementary student helping someone who fell.

Image credit: J.T. Binfet

this book to give you a sense of what you are in for as you dive into and learn about kindness and how it is situated and may be fostered within a school context.

Defining Kindness

As a starting point, a definition of kindness informs our shared understanding of what it means to be kind (see figure 1.2). Let our thinking

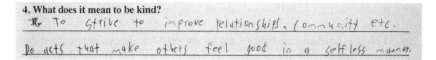

4. What does it mean to be kind?

To strive to improve relationships, community etc.

Do acts that make others feel good in a selfless manner.

Figure 1.2. A fifteen-year-old boy's definition of kindness.

Image credit: J.T. Binfet

here be informed by students' voices. The nuanced definition in figure 1.2 showcases both intra- and interpersonal aspects of kindness. Granted, our definition of kindness will evolve over the course of this book but as a starting point, consider kindness as a term and concept that falls under the umbrella of "prosocial behaviour." Prosocial behaviour is often defined as "voluntary behavior intended to benefit another" (Eisenberg et al. 1999, 1360).

Advancing our understanding of what it means to be prosocial is the work of Kristen Dunfield from Concordia University. Building on the definition proffered by Eisenberg and colleagues (1999), Dunfield (2014, 3) conceptualizes it as behaviour that responds to the *negative* experiences of others. In her model, she offers three categories: (1) *helping* behaviour that responds to an individual struggling to complete a goal-directed behaviour (e.g., "retrieving an object out of reach"); (2) *sharing* behaviour that responds to an individual struggling to access a resource (e.g., "giving up a limited resource"); and (3) *comforting* behaviour that responds to an individual experiencing a negative emotional state (e.g., "offering verbal or physical support"). Dunfield helps us understand how prosocial behaviour might be seen as an overarching term encompassing a variety of kind acts.

Deepening our understanding of what it means to be kind requires differentiating kindness from terms such as altruism and compassion. Although often linked to these concepts, kindness has emerged as its own unique topic of study (Binfet and Passmore 2019; Campos and Algoe 2009; Canter et al. 2017; Cotney and Banerjee 2019; Rowland 2018). As Oxford University researcher Lee Rowland explains, "The essence of kindness, then, is more nuanced than we often consider. It is not a single thing, does not perfectly overlap with altruism and compassion, and has both behavioural and affective components. To fully explore how kindness impacts lives, it needs to be unpacked, its dimensions identified, and its degrees measured" (Rowland 2018, 33). In distinguishing kindness from altruism, Rowland (2018, 33) argues that being altruistic involves an exchange that is "a loss to one individual and a gain to one or more others." This definition differentiates altruism from kindness, because performing a kind act need not involve a loss to the initiator. For example, consider the act of kindness done at the outset of this chapter (figure 1.1) in which a student helps a fellow student who had fallen. Linked to our understanding of altruism and kindness is the concept of compassion – "the act or capacity for sharing the painful feelings of another" (Merriam-Webster 2020). In order to respond to others through kindness, one must perspective-take (i.e., putting themselves in the shoes of the other) and recognize, as Dunfield (2014) argued, a *need* in "the other." This recognition may generate compassion but does not guarantee such feelings will be felt, and even if they are, it does not ensure action will be taken. Recognizing a need in others and feeling compassionate for someone else might be considered the foundation upon which we decide whether or not to enact kindness.

Kindness has also been conceptualized as an interpersonal character strength (Datu and Bernardo 2020; Peterson and Seligman 2004) that contributes to overall well-being. As Datu and Bernardo (2020, 983) describe it, "Character strengths refer to relatively universal, trait-like, and morally valued dispositions in life that can lead to optimal psychological outcomes." Whereas this definition, in part, emphasizes the outcomes that arise from strong character, Shoshani's definition (2019, 86) situates the concept of character within a social context: "Character often refers to an individual's general approach to the responsibilities of social life, which is supported by the acquisition of prosocial skills, knowledge of social conventions, and prosocial emotional reactions to others' distress."

Shoshani's definition of character helps us see clear connections to kindness and to Dunfield's (2014) conceptualization of prosocial behaviour as a response to a perceived negative state in others. Researchers have identified character strength as contributing to resiliency. Shoshani and Slone (2013), for example, argue that character strengths in adolescence serve as a buffer against a host of negative outcomes (e.g., depression, suicide ideation, and substance misuse). In innovative research by Kim and colleagues (2018), kindness has been positioned as a character strength of "humanity" and protects against suicidality in women. Delving further into possible differences in character strengths by gender, a recent meta-analysis by Heintz, Kramm, and Ruch (2019) informs our understanding and thinking here. In their examination of sixty-five studies representing data from over one million participants, overall measures of character strengths were similar for males and females, with the exception of females scoring significantly higher on appreciation of beauty and excellence, kindness, love, and appreciation.

Table 1.1. Published Definitions of Kindness

	Definition	Source
1a	"Kindness is a combination of emotional, behavioural, and motivational components."	Kerr et al. (2015, 20)
1b	"Kind acts are behaviours that benefit other people, or make others happy."	Kerr et al. (2015, 23)
2	"Kindness is a behaviour driven by the feeling of compassion" and when we "act on this feeling of compassion in a helpful and caring way, this behavior becomes an act of kindness."	Long (1997, 243)
3a	"This character strength describes the pervasive tendency to be nice to other people – to be compassionate and concerned about their welfare, to do favors for them, to perform good deeds, and to take care of them."	Peterson and Seligman (2004, 296)
3b	"Doing favors and good deed for others."	Peterson and Seligman (2004, 296)
4	"Voluntary, intentional behaviors that benefit another and are not motivated by external factors such as rewards or punishments."	Eisenberg (1986, 63)
5	"An assertion of self that is positive in feeling and intention."	Cataldo (1984, 17)
6	"An activity that promotes positive relationships."	Layous et al. (2012, 1)
7	"Enacting kind behavior toward other people."	Otake et al. (2006, 362)
8	"A motivation that is sometimes inferred from the fact that one person benefits another."	Baldwin and Baldwin (1970, 30)
9	"Kindness, from the perspective of young children, is an act of emotional or physical support that helps build or maintain relationships with others."	Binfet and Gaertner (2015, 36–7)

Definitions of Kindness

Close scrutiny of the published definitions of kindness reveals definitions reflecting adult perspectives and definitions not specific to educational contexts (see table 1.1). Understanding how children and adolescents define and enact kindness, especially within the school context, is important for a number of reasons: (1) it allows educators to gauge if definitions and acts of kindness align with their expectations;

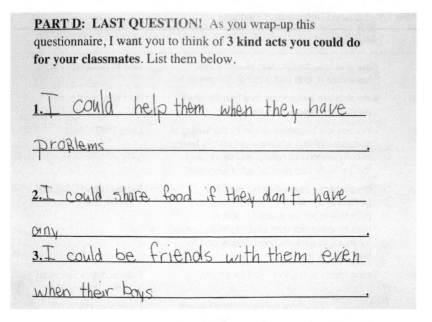

PART D: LAST QUESTION! As you wrap-up this questionnaire, I want you to think of **3 kind acts you could do for your classmates**. List them below.

1. I could help them when they have problems.

2. I could share food if they don't have any.

3. I could be friends with them even when their boys.

Figure 1.3. A ten-year-old girl's brainstormed list of kind acts to do.
Image credit: J.T. Binfet

(2) it informs pedagogical practices – are the instructional steps taken to nurture kindness in children and adolescents effective?; and (3) it provides a window into positive dimensions of development and affords insights into pillars of social and emotional learning, such as perspective-taking, interpersonal relations, and care and concern for others, which are social and emotional skills that enhance students' academic success (Durlak et al. 2011).

Captured in table 1.1 and building on my research investigating the insights and perspectives of thousands of children, my definition of kindness is "an act of emotional or physical support that helps build or maintain relationships with others" (Binfet and Gaertner 2015, 36–7). This definition allows kindness to be manifested in a variety of ways and, after reading this book, you will have a clear sense of the different ways through which young people express and enact kindness to others.

A ten-year-old girl's list of kind acts illustrates just how she understands what it means to be kind (see figure 1.3). In her list are examples of generic helping, material-driven kindness through sharing food, and kindness as friendship transcending stereotypic gender barriers.

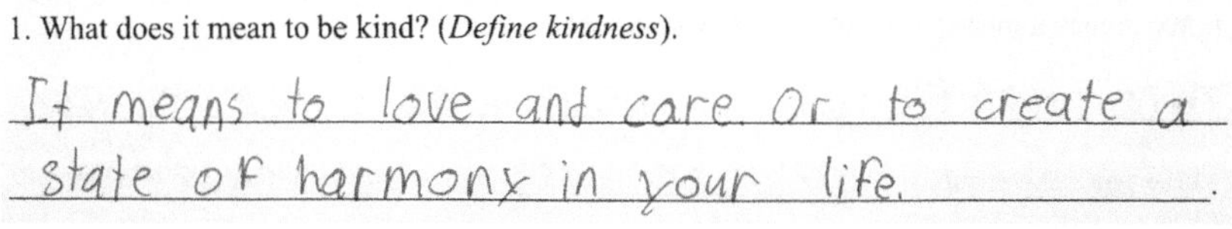

1. What does it mean to be kind? (*Define kindness*).

It means to love and care. Or to create a state of harmony in your life.

Figure 1.4. A middle school student defines kindness.

Image credit: J.T. Binfet

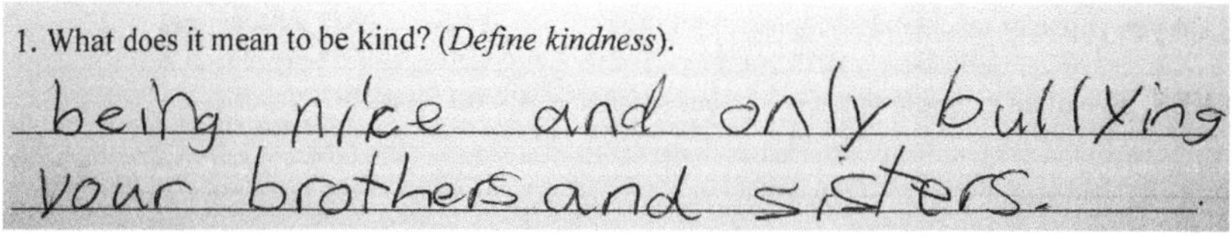

1. What does it mean to be kind? (*Define kindness*).

being nice and only bullying your brothers and sisters.

Figure 1.5. An eleven-year-old boy's interpretation of what it means to be kind.

Image credit: J.T. Binfet

In recent research exploring the definitions and examples of kindness by upper elementary and middle school students, Holli-Anne Passmore and I discovered that students define kindness in both simple (e.g., "to listen," "to be careful with words," and "don't bully") and complex (e.g., "to be sweet, gentle, forgiving, open minded and to be friendly to your friends and family") ways (Binfet and Passmore 2019, 28). A seventh-grader defines kindness as action directed toward others (i.e., "love and care") and benefits to the self from being kind (i.e., "create a state of harmony in your life"). We'll explore this notion further in chapter 3 when we examine the benefits of being kind.

In contrast, as might be expected, middle school students seize any opportunity to showcase their humorous side as a sixth-grader's definition illustrates (figure 1.5).

These examples were generated by students as part of a large study of kindness in elementary and middle schools, which involved surveying 1,752 students about their ideas and behaviours around kindness (Binfet and Passmore 2019). They defined kindness largely in positive terms (e.g., what kindness *was* versus was it *was not*), and there were no gender or grade differences in their definitions: it helped others, showed respect to others, and encouraged others.

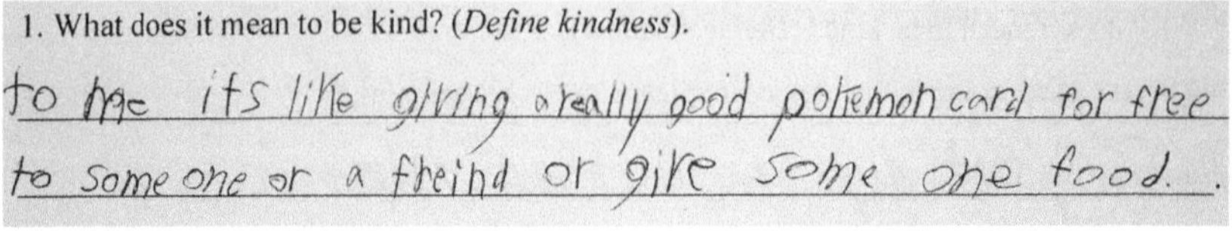

1. What does it mean to be kind? (*Define kindness*).

to me its like giving a really good pokemon card for free to some one or a freind or give some one food.

Figure 1.6. An eleven-year-old boy's definition of kindness.
Image credit: J.T. Binfet

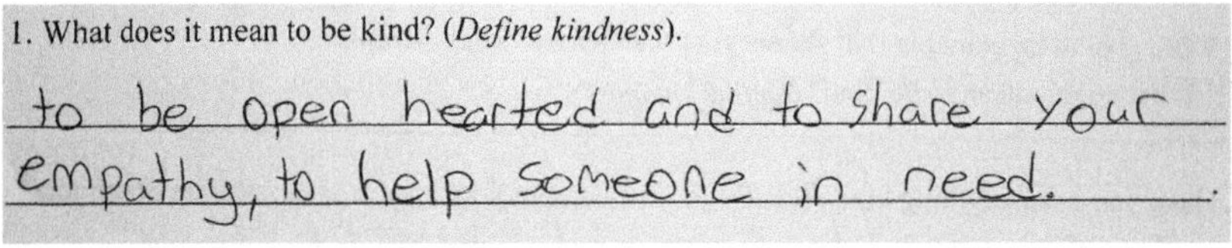

1. What does it mean to be kind? (*Define kindness*).

to be open hearted and to share your empathy, to help someone in need.

Figure 1.7. A twelve-year-old girl's definition of kindness.
Image credit: J.T. Binfet

Prosocial Behaviour across Childhood and Adolescence

Developmentally, prosocial behavior typically increases during early childhood and then decreases during the transition to young adulthood, when self-focused interests become more salient.

Pastorelli et al.

Two student definitions illustrate the developmental trajectory of how children and adolescents understand what it means to be kind and the complexity of that understanding (see figures 1.6 and 1.7). Their definitions align with the work of child developmental theorist Jean Piaget (1932/1964), who argued that children's thinking is initially grounded in a concrete understanding of the world (i.e., a Pokémon card or food – tangible items) and morphs into "formal reasoning" – which is less bound by the concrete and reflects the ability to think abstractly about topics and concepts. Captured in these two examples is the developmental range in reasoning: the first emphasizes kindness as the giving of things and in the second, more sophisticated definition, kindness is described as the sharing of emotion and perspective-taking to offer assistance to others.

Innovative work by Warneken and Tomasello (2006, 2011) helps us understand the origins of prosocial behaviour such as helping others. In their experiments with fourteen- to eighteen-month-old toddlers, they created scenarios to test the extent to which young children help others. Across tasks (e.g., picking up a dropped item, opening a closed cupboard door, etc.), toddlers consistently demonstrated kindness to others, independent of any prompting or reward by the adult caregiver in the room. In summarizing their findings, Warneken and Tomasello (2006) observed that "even very young children have a natural tendency to help other persons solve their problems, even when the other is a stranger and they receive no benefit at all" (1303).

As would be expected, as children mature, a differentiated understanding of kindness emerges (Baldwin and Baldwin 1970; Binfet and Passmore 2019; Lamborn et al. 1994; Nantel-Vivier et al. 2009) and correspondingly, changes are anticipated in how kindness is expressed as children develop. In a seminal longitudinal study in which thirty-two participants were studied from age four to twenty, Eisenberg and colleagues (1999) identified that preschool- and elementary-age children demonstrated kindness by sharing, helping and offering comfort. Layous and colleagues add to our understanding of how older children enact kindness. They asked nine- to eleven-year-olds to perform three kind acts to determine the effects of being kind on well-being and popularity. Examples of being kind for this age group included "Gave my mom a hug when she was stressed by her job," "Gave someone some of my lunch," and "Vacuumed the floor" (Layous et al. 2012, 2).

Although prosocial behaviour increases throughout childhood, this trajectory changes in adolescence. Pastorelli and colleagues (2016) examined the rates of prosocial behaviour throughout adolescence and noted key gender differences in their longitudinal study of 497 adolescents: "For boys, levels of prosocial behavior were stable until age 14, followed by an increase until age 17, and a slight decrease thereafter. For girls, prosocial behavior increased until age 16 years and then slightly decreased" (1086). This declining rate of prosocial behaviour in mid-adolescence for both boys and girls calls for strategies to help bolster this declining pattern of prosociality as adolescents navigate the transition into adulthood. In support, I offer ample applied strategies throughout this book to engage adolescents and to help guide their planning, designing, and delivery of varied acts of kindness.

Trends in Kindness Research

Digging deeply into the published research on kindness allows for observations and identification of trends across studies. Different

Table 1.2. Questions Driving Research in Kindness

Research Question	Researchers
Are there benefits to well-being that arise from being kind?	Curry et al. (2018); Magnani and Zhu (2018); Miles et al. (2021); Rowland and Curry (2018)
Does the number of kind acts affect well-being?	Gherghel et al. (2019)
Does the scheduling of kind acts matter?	Layous et al. (2017)
Can you just recall, or must you do kind acts to receive well-being benefits?	Ko et al. (2019)
Does it matter to whom you are kind?	Whillans et al. (2016)
When asked to be kind, how are children and adolescents kind?	Binfet (2020); Binfet and Passmore (2019); Binfet and Whitehead (2019); Cotney and Banerjee (2019); Paquet et al. (2019)
Do physiological effects arise from being kind?	Nelson-Coffey et al. (2017); Whillans et al. (2016)
How can kindness be measured?	Binfet et al. (2016); Canter et al. (2017); Yurdabakan and Bas (2019)
Are there cultural differences in how kindness is enacted?	Aknin et al. (2013); Gherghel et al. (2019); Shin et al. (2021)
Can kindness be integrated into curriculum?	Binfet et al. (in press); Shapiro et al. (2019)
Does kindness influence perceptions of school belonging and school kindness?	Lee and Huang (2021)
Does showing kindness through spending on others versus oneself increase happiness?	Aknin et al. (2020)

avenues or aspects of kindness have been researched, driven or guided by research questions that direct the discovery of new scientific and applied information about kindness (see table 1.2).

The bulk of studies on kindness have been conducted with adult participants (e.g., Aknin et al. 2011; Chancellor et al. 2017; Trew and Alden 2015), leaving room for additional research on kindness in children and adolescents. Although emerging work has examined kindness in children (e.g., Blakey et al. 2019; Haslip et al. 2019; Layous et al. 2012) and adolescents (e.g., Cotney and Banerjee 2019; Datu and Park 2019), more research into the effects of kind acts on well-being within this population and how children and adolescents understand and demonstrate kindness is needed.

Last, the majority of studies published on kindness appear to use a standard research methodology that involves administering participants a battery of pre-test measures (typically on well-being outcomes), randomizing participants to treatment (i.e., an experience involving kindness) and a control condition (i.e., no kindness), and then administering post-test measures. As a result, there is room for research that uses qualitative designs and that tracks dimensions of kindness and the effects of kindness over time through longitudinal studies. There is a dearth of research identifying children's and adolescents' acts of kindness, and much of my research at the University of British Columbia has been devoted to uncovering just how students are kind, especially when in school (see appendix A for a list of the kindness-themed studies I have published).

Publication Frequency

I am not the only one with an interest in kindness, and the topic of kindness has experienced a surge in popularity and risen to the forefront in the thinking of educators, parents, and researchers. Focusing uniquely on this last group for a moment, the work that researchers undertake is important to examine, because it informs practice, especially within faculties of education, where instructors routinely incorporate the information gleaned from new research into teacher-training curricula. Looking at the number of kindness-themed publications in peer-reviewed journals reveals a robust upward trend (see figure 1.8 and appendix B for corresponding PRISMA flow chart). In a review of educational and psychological databases, which are outlets where we would expect research on kindness to be published, we see a recent surge in the number of peer-reviewed publications on kindness (as reflected by the appearance of kindness in the article title or abstract). Of course, it is important to recognize that research on kindness may be subsumed under publications examining constructs and emotions such as altruism, prosocial behaviour, sympathy, love, gratitude, and compassion (e.g., Algoe 2019; Batson et al. 1978; Leahy 1979; Oliner 2005; Smeets et al. 2014). As argued earlier, kindness is emerging more recently as its own field of study, and we now see studies explicitly addressing kindness as a distinct and principal topic of research (e.g., Clegg and Rowland 2010; Ko et al. 2019; Magnani and Zhu 2018). As figure 1.8 illustrates, there has been a marked increase in the number of studies on kindness published in peer-reviewed journals and interest from researchers curious to study kindness.

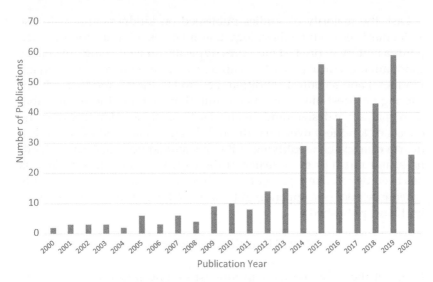

Figure 1.8. Frequency of kindness-themed publications across
databases, 2000–2020

Image credit: J.T. Binfet

This growth in the number of kindness-themed publications can
be explained partially by undergirding movements in the fields of
psychology and education. With the surge in popularity of Positive
Psychology (Seligman and Csikszentmihalyi 2000), Positive Education (Seligman et al. 2009; Suldo et al. 2015), and Social and Emotional
Learning (casel.org; Mahoney et al. 2018–2019), we see a corresponding increase in research conducted on kindness. Perhaps driving this
trend is the public's appetite to understand and read about the positive
dimensions of human behaviour, whether in a work, community, or
school context.

It might be easy to forget that we value kindness. Certainly, parents
value kindness in their children, and when asked what they wish for
their children, parents consistently rank "being kind" as a top character
trait (Diener and Lucas 2004; Seligman et al. 2009; Wang and Tamis-
Lemonda 2003). Psychologist Thomas Lickona (2018) offers advice to
parents seeking to raise kind children. He argues that strategies including routinely modelling kind acts for children and disengaging from
uncharitable talk about others to create a family culture that nurtures
kindness. Toward the end of this book, a range of strategies to cultivate
kindness are offered that educators can employ.

Educators value kindness as well, and the professional responsibilities of educators have moved past the promotion of academic achievement to fostering the development of students' social and emotional learning, of which being prosocial or kind to others is a part (Durlak et al. 2011a; Schonert-Reichl 2019; Taylor et al. 2017). Educators are increasingly asked to promote aspects of child development that were historically nurtured within the family context. For some students living with little parental support or community engagement, teachers are often the primary agents preparing children socially and emotionally for life's challenges (Downey 2010). With increased exposure to social and emotional learning in pre-service teacher-education programs and a proliferation of professional development opportunities focused on social and emotional learning for practising teachers, educators see the promotion of kindness within their classrooms as a vehicle through which student development may be fostered, a positive classroom and school culture may be nurtured, and academic success may be supported.

Present interest in kindness coincides with broader educational trends that have shifted from anti-bullying initiatives to a focus on the positive dimensions of child development and the school experience. Educators are increasingly interested in recognizing and encouraging positive aspects of their students' development and behaviour and perhaps less keen about policing and punishing student infractions. This shift in "celebrating the good" may be driven by educators seeking to establish positive rapport and relationships with children and recognizing that focusing on children's strengths (versus their misdeeds) fosters it. Support for this perspective has been fuelled by the field of Positive Psychology (Seligman and Csikszentmihalyi 2000) and the subsidiary field Positive Education (Morrish et al. 2018; Seligman et al. 2009; Vella-Broderick et al. 2019). Collectively, these fields emphasize the strengths and attributes, dispositions, and behaviours that educators want to cultivate in children rather than focus on identifying children's deficits and devising ways to fix them.

Research with Amy Gaertner took a first look at the ratio of published research on kindness versus bullying (Binfet and Gaertner 2015), and a more thorough analysis was done with student researcher Adam Lauze at the University of British Columbia. We examined the number of kindness- and bullying-themed publications across commonly used educational (e.g., ERIC), psychological (e.g., PsycINFO), and general databases (e.g., Web of Science) from 2000 to 2020 and identified a skewed publishing profile (see tables 1.3 and 1.4). For a detailed explanation of our search criteria and methods, see appendix C. Across

Table 1.3. Number of Kindness and Bullying Articles Published (2000–2019)

Database	Kindness	Bullying	Ratio
Education			
ERIC	157	2,743	1:17
Education Source	361	4,460	1:12
Australian Education Index	1,041	7,315	1:7
Psychology			
APA PsychINFO	772	6,389	1:8
General			
CINAHL	309	2,737	~1:9
Academic Search Complete	1,176	7,204	1:6
Web of Science*	1,246	7,567	1:6
Total	5,062	38,415	1:7.6

*Not all articles are peer-reviewed.

Table 1.4. Publishing Trend by Kindness versus Bullying (2000–2019)

	Kindness	Bullying	Ratio
Total search results	5,062	38,415	1:7.6
Total duplicates removed	2,232	23,090	
Total articles	2,740	15,325	1:5.6

Margin for error +/- 4%

databases, the number of peer-reviewed publications devoted to bullying is disproportionately high, compared to those addressing kindness. This disparity has ramifications for educators seeking to build knowledge on child and adolescent behaviour. This stark contrast in the availability of information influences practice and the implementation of programs and interventions as knowledge-seekers on student behaviour will find it easier to access information elucidating how students misbehave rather than dimensions of how they are kind. The articles I publish on kindness and this book are attempts to correct this imbalance.

Table 1.4 presents the findings of the overall literature search, after de-duplication and manual screening. Across databases, for every article published on kindness there are five articles published on bullying.

Moving beyond the living room, classroom, and publishing rates in academia, kindness is valued within a broader societal context. A study by McGrath (2015), which extended the initial work of Park, Peterson, and Seligman (2006), asked 1,063,921 participants across seventy-five countries to identify what dimensions of character are important. Ranked third only behind honesty and fairness, kindness is a treasured human trait. This finding is mirrored by similar research confirming the societal importance of being kind (e.g., Karris and Craighead 2012). Research has even explored the importance of kindness when we are selecting romantic partners! In a cross-cultural study of 2,477 participants in five countries, Thomas and colleagues (2019) found that only humour and creativity surpassed kindness as a valued trait in people seeking partners.

Evidence of the importance of kindness is also found outside the realm of research. The *Washington Post* (2016) found how one's previous acts of kindness are a barometer of potential and character – how, and the extent to which, an individual is kind reveals their suitability for acceptance into a target program. It is not yet a standard job interview question, but I am hopeful that employers might one day routinely ask applicants questions such as "Describe the last kind thing you did and why."

Illustration of a corporation integrating employee kindness into the workday is found in a *New Yorker* piece titled "In France, Elder Care Comes with the Mail" (Poll 2019). "Veiller surveiller mes parents" or "Watch over my parents" is a program that helps ease the burden of loneliness in France's senior citizens who live independently and alone. This innovative program allows letter carriers, as part of their routine work duties, to spend time with home-bound seniors. Visits last six to fifteen minutes, and senior citizens who spend time with letter carriers sign a tablet to confirm a visit has taken place. Such support from letter carriers, or kindness, occurred informally prior to the adoption of "Watch over my parents," but formalization of this *"institutional kindness"* accords importance to kindness in the workplace, and it encourages and gives permission to workers to incorporate kindness into their daily work routines.

What to Expect

Drawing from my own research and that of others, my aim in writing this book is to inform educators on how children and adolescents understand and express kindness and to offer strategies that educators can use to foster kindness in their classrooms and broader school and learning communities. My hope is to foster awareness of kindness among adults who shape the development of young people and as a way to help educators cultivate educational environments for children in which kindness propels optimal development and learning.

Here one can expect a research-informed approach to what it means to be kind from the perspectives of children and adolescents, an overview of the benefits of being kind, and a practical guide for educators wanting to foster kindness in students. Grounded in social and emotional learning and in positive education, this book will help educators reorient their thinking on the importance of kindness in fostering positive and healthy development in children and adolescents. Moreover, as this book draws from the science behind kindness, readers will be equipped to understand *why* kindness is important in the lives of children and adolescents and *how* kindness can be fostered by the adults responsible for shaping children's development.

As has been evident thus far, this chapter introduces the topic of kindness and defines and situates it within the broader psychological study of prosocial behaviour. Chapter 2 will situate and link kindness to the field of social and emotional learning (SEL). The next chapter explores how the practising of kindness allows children and adolescents to develop all five pillars of SEL (i.e., self-awareness, self-management, social awareness, relationship skills, and responsible decision-making).

Chapter 3 provides an overview of the methods and research done to study kindness and of the benefits of being kind. This chapter will review the findings of studies in which participants completed acts to boost their well-being. The benefits of being kind on a variety of dimensions of well-being will be presented, including an examination of the intra- and inter-personal benefits arising from enacting kindness.

Drawing from research on over three thousand Canadian students who were asked to describe kind acts they had done, the next few chapters will illustrate how children and adolescents are kind. Chapter 4 will provide an overview and examples of "responsive kindness" – which is done in reaction to a perceived physical, emotional, or social need. Chapter 5 will provide an overview of *intentional kindness* – when individuals plan and then deliver kindness to others. Chapter 6 provides an overview of *quiet kindness* – a subtle form of kindness that only the initiator knows about. Quiet kindness has been referred to as "kindness without an audience" and it is positioned within this book as a socially and emotionally sophisticated form of kindness. After this overview of the different ways that children and adolescents enact kindness, an examination of varied strategies for fostering kindness is offered in chapter 7. How can kindness be encouraged in young people and what is the role of educators in encouraging kindness and creating opportunities for children and adolescents to be kind?

As one author of the School Kindness Scale (Binfet et al. 2016), I would be remiss I did not include a chapter on measuring kindness. Thus, chapter 8 explores different indicators of kindness within the broader school context. This chapter will provide a framework for educators curious about determining the extent to which kindness is evident in a learning community.

The last chapter, chapter 9, will summarize key aspects from each of the previous chapters for readers. Future directions in which research on kindness is headed and the implementation of kindness within school and family contexts will be shared. For readers curious to learn more about kindness, an overview of key resources will be provided.

Grounded in science, supported with illustrations capturing the voice of students, and with a strong applied focus to enhance the understanding and skill set of educators, this book holds the potential to transform educators' thinking about kindness. In the next chapter, kindness will be contextualized within the framework of social and emotional learning. It will be argued that being kind is anchored in, and helps develop, several if not all, of the five pillars of SEL identified by the Collaborative for Social and Emotional Learning (CASEL 2022).

Chapter Two

The Interplay between Kindness and Social and Emotional Learning

Children's tendency to help, share, and spontaneously offer emotional support predicts a successful school career and counters aggression and depression.

Pastorelli et al.

The interplay between social and emotional learning and kindness has not yet been empirically well explored. More research examining whether the development of social and emotional skills fosters kindness in children and adolescents, whether completing a series of kind acts facilitates the development of social and emotional competencies, or if bidirectional influences are at play are questions meriting further attention from researchers. Do you need social and emotional skills to be kind? Can enacting kindness help you develop and hone your social and emotional competencies? I argue in this chapter that social and emotional learning lays a foundation for kindness, and the more socially and emotionally adept children and adolescents are, the easier it will be for them to perspective-take and identify the needs of others, and in turn plan and deliver acts of kindness. The twelve-year-old boy's definition of kindness (figure 2.1) illustrates his care and concern for others and his understanding that harm can occur both emotionally and physically. His definition reflects rich social and emotional content, and throughout this chapter, the interplay between kindness and social and emotional learning will be explored.

As will be evident in this chapter, the relation or interplay between social and emotional learning and kindness appears to be mutually informing – developing social and emotional competencies in children and adolescents likely equips them to be kind, but also practising kindness may help young people develop and hone their social

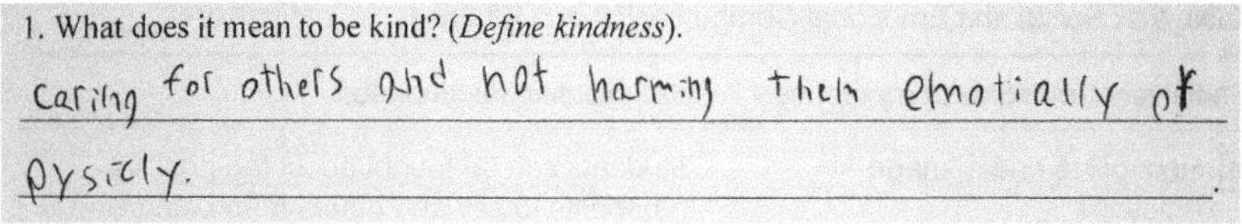

1. What does it mean to be kind? (*Define kindness*).

Caring for others and not harming them emotially of pysicly.

Figure 2.1. A twelve-year-old boy's definition of what it means to be kind.

Image credit: J.T. Binfet

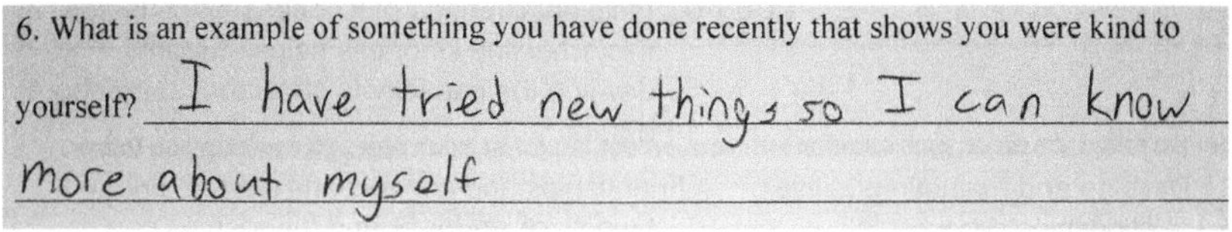

6. What is an example of something you have done recently that shows you were kind to yourself? I have tried new things so I can know more about myself

Figure 2.2. A twelve-year-old boy's example of kindness to self.

Image credit: J.T. Binfet

and emotional competencies. This chapter begins with an overview of social and emotional learning, a summary of educators' roles in fostering social and emotional learning, and an illustration of how social and emotional learning and kindness are interconnected. A curated list of resources for readers curious to learn more about social and emotional learning is provided in appendix D.

The Interplay between Social and Emotional Learning and Kindness

No published research on the relation between social and emotional learning and kindness could be found, but it is likely that both of the questions or explanations raised at the outset of this chapter are plausible. Coaching students through kind acts is likely to promote their social and emotional competencies, and bolstering students' social and emotional learning will probably equip students with the requisite skills to recognize the need for, and to enact, kindness toward others, including kindness directed toward themselves (see figure 2.2). As posited at the outset of this chapter, there may be a mutually informing interplay between social and emotional learning and kindness. Table 2.1 illustrates how the five social and emotional competencies comprising social and emotional learning might be brought to life when enacting kindness.

Table 2.1. Social and Emotional Competencies and Kindness

Social and emotional competency	Skill building for kindness
1. Recognize and manage emotions	Students can be taught about the positive benefits to self and others from being kind. Specifically, students can learn that positive emotions can arise from being kind and can replace negative emotions.
2. Show care and concern for others	Kindness requires perspective-taking. Encouraging students to generate a list of recipients in need of kindness helps foster this. Enacting kindness helps students develop the capacity to show they care about others.
3. Develop and maintain positive relationships	Friendships and connections may be bridged by acts of kindness and friendships can be fortified through kindness to one another.
4. Make responsible decisions	Students can be encouraged to reflect upon the quality of their kind acts and whether kind acts they have planned put themselves in harm's way (e.g., delivering kindness to strangers in a homeless camp).
5. Set and achieve positive goals	When kindness is random or responds to the immediate need of others, there may be little planning involved, but many acts of kindness require planning and a series of steps to execute. The frequent request that students plan and execute a series of kind acts falls into the category of setting and achieving a goal (i.e., "complete five acts within one week").

What Is Social and Emotional Learning?

There has been a surge in interest in recent years about social and emotional learning, and the sheer number of organizations, peer-reviewed publications, popular periodicals, and seminars and professional development workshops on social and emotional learning for parents and educators attests to the public's appetite to learn more about this set of skills. The Collaborative for Academic, Social, and Emotional Learning (CASEL; www.casel.org), an organization devoted to all things social and emotional learning, is considered by many as the seminal resource for those seeking information on this topic. Established in 2000 and adopting the CASEL name and acronym in 2001, CASEL has been a hub disseminating information about social and emotional learning to researchers, academics, and practitioners since the early days when social and emotional learning was far from its now familiar role in educational circles. Famous for its multi-coloured SEL Wheel of Competencies, CASEL has been instrumental in spreading science-informed information on social and emotional learning, sharing research findings on the effects of social and emotional learning, and rigorously assessing the programs that foster social and emotional learning.

CASEL defines social and emotional learning (SEL) as "the process through which children and adults understand and manage emotions, set and achieve positive goals, feel and show empathy for others, establish and maintain positive relationships, and make responsible decisions" (casel.org). Examining this definition closely we first see that social and emotional learning is acquired over time and that children and adolescents master social and emotional competencies to varying degrees. This variability might be evident in a second-grader who confidently shakes hands and introduces herself to a stranger, and the teen who avoids eye contact and is unable to maintain a conversation with others. Acquiring social and emotional competencies is a process in which individuals have low, medium, and high levels of proficiency. The implication is that this process can be nurtured and that social and emotional skills can be learned. Later in this chapter, the factors that foster or facilitate social and emotional competencies will be explored.

There is also an explicit reference to lifespan development in CASEL's definition. Social and emotional learning is developed across the developmental trajectory – from childhood through adulthood. The bulk of research (and information available) focuses on social and emotional learning in childhood, a time of rapid growth and development. But it is stated explicitly in the CASEL definition that social and emotional learning is not uniquely associated with childhood and that social and emotional learning plays a key role in development from childhood through to adulthood. Educators too are encouraged to reflect upon their own social and emotional development, and their "social and emotional competencies" (Jennings and Greenberg 2009, 491). How might your own social and emotional development affect your ability to foster social and emotional learning in students and more germane to the present discussion, your ability to teach kindness-related skills to students (see table 2.2)?

CASEL's definition shared at the outset of this chapter showcases cognitive, affective, and behavioural dimensions of social and emotional learning. The cognitive component requires individuals to learn about and understand emotions, recognize that there are steps involved in setting and achieving goals, and weighing the pros and cons of a decision they are considering. Social and emotional learning involves intellectual

Table 2.2. Reflecting on One's Own Social and Emotional Competencies

1. How socially and emotionally competent are you currently? In what area are you particularly strong? In what area might you need a stronger mastery of skills?

2. Who and what experiences most strongly affected your social and emotional growth and development?

3. Recognizing that social and emotional skills continue to develop across the lifespan, within your role as an educator, what do you do to foster your own social and emotional growth?

4. How does your social and emotional competence allow you to teach kindness skills to students, or prevent you from doing so?

Table 2.3. Illustration of Social and Emotional Skills within and between Individuals

Intrapersonal social and emotional skills (within the individual)	Interpersonal social and emotional skills (between individuals)
Recognize emotions	Show empathy for others
Manage emotions	Establish positive relationships
Set and achieve personal goals	Maintain positive relationships
Make responsible decisions	
Feel empathy for others	

work – it is not uniquely driven by emotion and about feelings! Understanding might manifest in students discovering the benefits of being kind to one's health, or conversely, learning how being angry affects one's ability to see another's point of view. The affective component of the definition draws attention to the importance of recognizing emotions and the indicators of how one might be feeling in response to events and interactions. The behavioural component of the definition is evident when students who, when developing their social and emotional competencies, are encouraged to see the link between how they feel and how they behave. Managing emotions is directly tied to behaviour because one's behaviour is typically a barometer for how one is feeling. Thus, examining the CASEL definition of social and emotional learning more closely reveals its cognitive, affective, and behavioural dimensions, especially in the recognition and management of emotions.

Last, within the CASEL definition, social and emotional learning is presented as comprising five pillars or competencies. It becomes evident that these competencies or skills comprise skills that are both intrapersonal (within oneself) and interpersonal (between oneself and others). (See table 2.3.) Thus, some of the skills require introspection (e.g., to

#5	Hold back insults	all my friends	Friday

Figure 2.3. A fourteen-year-old girl describes one of her acts of kindness in response to the prompt "What is an example of something kind you have done at school recently?"

Image credit: J.T. Binfet

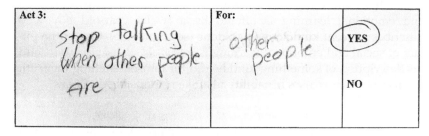

Act 3:	For:	
Stop talking when other people are	other people	YES
		NO

Figure 2.4. A twelve-year-old girl describes her act of kindness in response to the prompt "What is an example of something kind you have done at school recently?"

Image credit: J.T. Binfet

recognize how one is thinking and feeling) and others require more perspective-taking and outward engagement with others (e.g., establishing relationships with others).

It has been established that social and emotional learning is a process with individuals displaying varying proficiencies in their overall social and emotional competency and they may have variability in their mastery of the five social and emotional learning competencies. That is, someone may be strong in certain skills or competencies but struggle to master others. Optimally, educators want to see children and adolescents developing social and emotional competencies across all five domains. In the example of kindness in figure 2.3, a fourteen-year-old girl describes refraining from insulting others as an example of her kindness at school. This is a rich example of enacting kindness by self-regulating, and her restraint here is grounded in social and emotional competencies. A second example of self-regulation is found in the act of kindness described by a twelve-year-old girl who recognizes the importance of not talking over others (see figure 2.4).

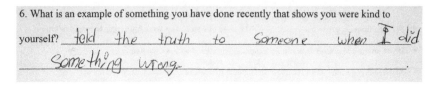

6. What is an example of something you have done recently that shows you were kind to yourself? told the truth to Someone when I did Something wrong.

Figure 2.5. A twelve-year-old boy describes his act of kindness.

Image credit: J.T. Binfet

Another rich example of the interplay between kindness and social and emotional learning is offered by a twelve-year-old boy who describes a recent kind act he had done (see figure 2.5). One of the pillars of social and emotional learning is *responsible decision-making*, and his description of something kind he did for himself – telling the truth in this case – showcases his ability to make responsible decisions.

THE BENEFITS OF SOCIAL AND EMOTIONAL LEARNING

Coinciding with the surge in interest and popularity of social and emotional learning is the proliferation of programs striving to boost children's and adolescents' social and emotional competencies. Often school-based curricula or programs are considered the only pathway through which social and emotional skills may be facilitated. In this section, both formal and informal strategies to fostering social and emotional learning are explored. To start, there is ample evidence that formally introduced social and emotional learning programs have positive effects on both student behaviour and academic achievement. In fact, several key studies validate the role that social and emotional learning plays in bolstering student development.

The first study by Joseph Durlak and colleagues in 2011 summarized the effects on students of participating in a school-based social and emotional learning intervention and examined findings from 213 studies involving an impressive combined sample of 270,034 students. Analyses of the findings across studies revealed not surprisingly that there were positive behavioural outcomes for children, including an increase or improvements in students' social and emotional learning, attitudes, and behaviours. A key finding from this study was that in addition to positive behavioural outcomes from participating in a social and emotional learning intervention, students also experienced an 11 per cent gain in academic achievement. This finding helped convince even the most reluctant school administrator that devoting school resources to social and emotional learning was in students' best interest.

Following up on this initial study, Taylor and colleagues (2017) conducted another meta-analysis to examine the extent to which school-based social and emotional learning programs had long-term effects on students. That is, did the benefits arising from participating in a social and emotional learning program persist? To do so, these authors examined eighty-two school-based social and emotional learning programs involving 92,406 kindergarten to high school students and assessed whether benefits were evident at six and eighteen months post-program. Across the eighty-two interventions examined as part of this study, students who participated in social and emotional learning programs experienced significant short- and long-term benefits. When compared to participants in control conditions (i.e., those students who did not participate in social and emotional learning interventions at school), students who participated in social and emotional learning programs had stronger overall social and emotional skills and improved attitudes, less emotional distress, and increased academic performance. In short, here is another review study amalgamating findings across a series of intervention studies attesting to the positive outcomes arising from participation in school-based social and emotional learning programming. These findings held regardless of the ethnic and socio-economic profile of the participants and were sustained – even years after the initial intervention (i.e., from 56 to 195 weeks). Readers curious to learn more about the short- and long-term outcomes arising from participation in school-based social and emotional learning programs are encouraged to read the update by Mahoney and colleagues (2018) on social and emotional research, along with recent overviews of the landscape of social and emotional learning by Schonert-Reichl (2019) and Weissberg (2019).

School-based programs offer distinct advantages for educators. There is continuity in lessons, the delivery of lessons to students is organized and structured (i.e., requires little preparation on the part of teachers), and there is a logical sequencing (with basic concepts introduced at the outset and more complex concepts introduced later within the program). CASEL offers a review of programs in its "CASEL Guide" on its website. Readers looking for rigorously evaluated programs and for a breakdown of the benefits or outcomes that arise from using a program will find this guide helpful in identifying an SEL program to meet their needs. As CASEL acknowledges, how programs are implemented is critical to the programs' success (see Binfet and Whitehead, 2019, for a discussion of the dimensions of program implementation that can affect success). Several variables merit consideration when implementing a program that can individually and collectively compromise the impact

Table 2.4. Things to Consider When Implementing a Social and Emotional Learning Program

---

1. Has the educator leading the program received sufficient training?

2. Did students participate in or attend all lessons?

3. Does the educator have the requisite social and emotional competencies needed to implement this program?

4. What was the completion rate for assignments or activities found within the program? To what extent did students do what was asked of them?

5. What dose intervention (the amount of the program required to be delivered) was attained?

6. Did students receive concurrent social and emotional curricula?

---

on students' mastery of social and emotional skills and their overall social and emotional competence (see table 2.4). A succinct summary of the impact of social and emotional learning on students is found in the work of Denham (2015, 285), who writes, "Children with SEL competencies participate more in the classroom, have more positive attitudes about and involvement with school, are more accepted by classmates, and are given more instruction and positive feedback by teachers." In short, findings from study after study attest to the positive impact on, and benefits to, students from participating in school-based social and emotional instruction.

The use of school-based social and emotional learning programs delivered to students through direct instruction is but one pathway through which the social and emotional competencies of children and adolescents might be bolstered. Other ways to foster social and emotional learning in students are found via teachers' instructional practices, the integration of social and emotional learning into existing curricula, and the learning climate in which students find themselves (Cohen 2006). Next, an examination is in order of the role that educators can play in fostering social and emotional competencies in children outside of an organized program. What can educators do to promote social and emotional learning?

The Educator's Role in Fostering Social and Emotional Learning

Educators play especially important roles in fostering the development of social and emotional skills, whether they be uniquely internal to the individual or more explicitly required for interactions with others. Although still an emerging topic within the field of social and emotional learning, with additional research needed, more has been written about the need for teacher preparation in social and emotional learning than has been written about parenting and social and emotional learning (see Schonert-Reichl et al. 2017 for a national scan of teacher preparation and social and emotional learning). As mentioned at the outset of this chapter, CASEL is well known for its SEL Wheel of Competencies, and the latest iteration of this wheel situates social and emotional learning within school, family, and community contexts, thereby asserting that social and emotional learning is not a set of skills needed uniquely for the school context. Rather, social and emotional learning is needed and useful across varied contexts and, as such, may be fostered within and across varied contexts.

An examination of how social and emotional learning might be fostered in children and adolescents, beyond their participation in structured, school-based social and emotional learning programs, reveals that educators can play key roles both formally and informally in fostering social and emotional competencies in students. Central to the promotion of social and emotional learning in students is that the learning context (above and beyond uniquely the curricula provided to students) created by educators must strive to foster optimal growth and development in children. An environment conducive to fostering social and emotional learning would be characterized by ample warmth and nurturing interactions between adults and children, clear behavioural and academic expectations, an organized structure that reduces unpredictability and uncertainty, plentiful opportunities for children and adolescents to have input as the authoritative or democratic leadership style of the adult welcomes and invites that, and regular opportunities to put into practice the newly learned and emerging social and emotional competencies.

What Does It Mean to Be a Socially and Emotionally Competent Educator?

Researcher Katherine Zinsser and colleagues (2015) inform our understanding of what it means to be an emotionally competent educator. Educators who are adept at fostering social and emotional growth are knowledgeable about emotions and able to regulate and express them. Situating the importance of that ability are Jennings and Greenberg (2009, 497), in their description of the teaching profession: "Unlike many other professions, teachers are constantly exposed to emotionally provocative situations and have limited options for self-regulation when a situation provides a strong emotional reaction." They further argue that educators who are socially and emotionally competent have

Table 2.5. Socially and Emotionally Informed Teaching Practices

Intrapersonal practices	Interpersonal practices
Uses breath to regulate emotion when teaching to avoid strong emotional reactions and to de-escalate reactions that might further distance students from teachers.	Teaching is informed and guided by an authoritative or democratic style that sees teachers consult and collaborate with students to capture and validate students' voices and perspectives.
Recognizes that stress can affect and impede interactions with students and regularly takes steps to monitor and reduce stress throughout the day when working with students to avoid emotional contagion or emotional spillover.	Recognizes the importance of teacher–student relationships and purposefully builds relationships with students as part of their daily routines (e.g., finds out the likes and interests of students, engages in discussions, shows care/concern for students).
Regularly practises perspective-taking to stand in the shoes of students as a way of understanding their experience in school.	Routinely infuses, embeds, or integrates social and emotional content into lessons to allow students to learn about, practise, and recognize social and emotional competencies.
Takes responsibility for misunderstandings and behaviour that failed to build trust in students or bridge relationships and bonds with students.	Recognizes and makes efforts to create a welcoming, non-threatening, and nurturing classroom climate within which students may prosper socially, emotionally, and academically.
Recognizes that educators serve as models for students and strives to be an exemplary model of social and emotional competencies at all times.	Considers and implements restorative discipline practices that elicit multiple perspectives around events, educate students about behaviour and its impact, and provide students with opportunities to restore relationships and make up for misdeeds.

high social- and self-awareness. Table 2.4 outlines the classroom-based practices of teachers who practise what they preach when fostering social and emotional development in students.

An Illustration of the Social and Emotional Skills Required to Enact Kindness to Others

Consider the kindness of a sixth-grade student that was done as part of a study I conducted in which students were asked to plan and describe

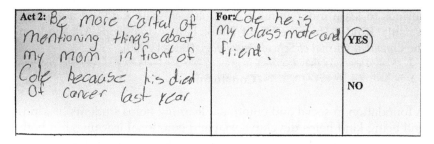

| Act 2: Be more carful of mentioning things about my mom in front of Cole because his died of cancer last year | For: Cole he is my class mate and frient. | YES |
| | | NO |

Figure 2.6. A twelve-year-old boy describes an act of kindness in response to the prompt "Plan and describe an act of kindness to be done over the course of the next week."

Image credit: J.T. Binfet

Table 2.6. Recognizing Social and Emotional Learning within a Kind Act

SEL competency	Evidence of SEL within kind act
1. Recognize and manage emotions	The classmate who initiated this kind act recognizes sadness or potential sadness in his classmate
2. Show care and concern for others	Ample consideration for the feelings of the classmate is evident in this kind act, and the initiator of kindness is able to perspective-take and imagine what it would be like to hear stories about a classmate's mother when someone has lost a parent.
3. Develop and maintain positive relationships	This act of kindness helps maintain a friendship, as the recipient of this kind act would feel safety and acceptance in the presence of the classmate who initiated this kind act.
4. Make responsible decisions	The initiator here is choosing how to behave in the presence of a friend who is grieving.
5. Set and achieve positive goals	The phrasing here of "be more careful of mentioning" indicates that the initiator is mindful of behaviour he would like to achieve. There is a certain goal-setting or direction to his behaviour.

kind acts at school. This example illustrates the interplay between social and emotional learning and kindness (see figure 2.6).

This sixth-grader's act of kindness toward a classmate is a socially and emotionally sophisticated example of kindness by a young person that challenges the stereotype of adolescents as egocentric and self-focused. Further, it demonstrates kindness steeped in social and emotional competencies (see table 2.6 for an illustration of the social and emotional content found within this act of kindness). Readers curious to learn more about how adolescents are kind are invited to consult "Kinder Than We Might Think: How Adolescents Are Kind" in the *Canadian Journal of School Psychology* (Binfet 2020).

Conclusion

A foundation in social and emotional learning helps students be kind, and being kind helps develop social and emotional learning, but both are less important than educators and parents who recognize the key role they play in creating learning conditions and opportunities that foster the growth of students' social and emotional competencies. That can be done through discussions about a character's intentions and behaviour as part of a novel study in a classroom setting or in discussions over dinner at the kitchen table. Students who are socially and emotionally proficient experience positive developmental outcomes that contribute to their resilience in the face of challenges and obstacles. Carrying the theme of development in school over to the next chapter, a review of key kindness research includes the methodologies of key studies that inform our understanding of what it means to be kind. As part of this chapter, kindness research in schools, including a review of research at the early and upper elementary, middle school, and high school grade levels, will be examined.

Chapter Three

Mechanisms Underpinning the Benefits of Kindness

Helping others remains among the most effective ways for the average individual to get happier, although this is hopefully more a by-product rather than a direct goal because the true motive should always be to benefit others.

Post (2017, 166)

It might strike you as odd that I have always thought of being kind to others as a bit of a selfish act. This is perhaps because I am a kindness researcher and I understand that kind acts not only benefit the recipient and also contribute to the initiator's well-being. That is, you might be motivated to be kind to others to do good for them, to show you care about others and your community; however, in the end, your act of kindness holds potential to do good for your recipient and for you. Drawing from peer-reviewed studies, I will do my best in this chapter to provide you with an overview of just how kindness is studied and the corresponding benefits that arise from being kind. This way, you will understand the positive outcomes that may be generated when you guide the children and adolescents around you in being kind. I will explore the outcomes of key kindness studies that have identified the mechanisms of kindness that contribute most to bolstering well-being – for the initiator and the recipient. I will argue in this chapter that enacting kindness can transform individuals, relationships, and communities (see figure 3.1).

A ninth-grader's insights into her experience participating in a kindness study at her school provides a window into her thinking about the role of kindness in her life and the effort it takes to be kind (see figure 3.2). Such is the potential of kindness research to explore previously unchartered research territory, to access the insights of students, and to help create knowledge of what it means to be kind within the school context.

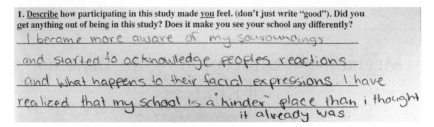

1. <u>Describe</u> how participating in this study made <u>you</u> feel. (don't just write "good"). Did you get anything out of being in this study? Does it make you see your school any differently?

I became more aware of my surroundings and started to acknowledge peoples reactions and what happens to their facial expressions. I have realized that my school is a "kinder" place than i thought it already was.

Figure 3.1. A fifteen-year-old girl reflects on participating in a middle school kindness study.

Image credit: J.T. Binfet

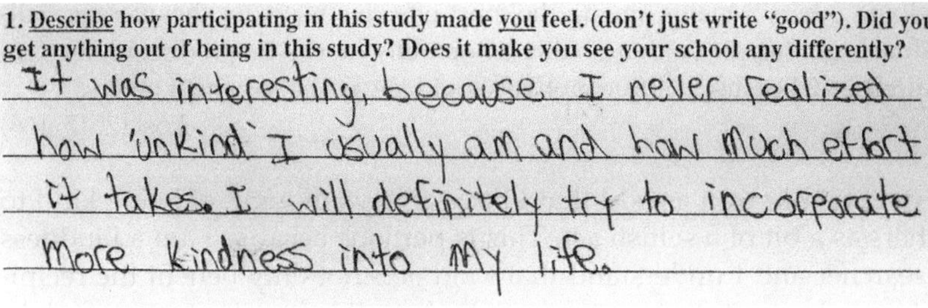

1. <u>Describe</u> how participating in this study made <u>you</u> feel. (don't just write "good"). Did you get anything out of being in this study? Does it make you see your school any differently?

It was interesting, because I never realized how 'unkind' I usually am and how much effort it takes. I will definitely try to incorporate more kindness into my life.

Figure 3.2. A fifteen-year-old girl reflects on participating in a kindness study.

Image credit: J.T. Binfet

In the review of kindness research that follows, I have founded my writing on peer-reviewed research (i.e., research that has undergone rigorous scrutiny to ascertain its merit) and not included unpublished research in the form of theses or dissertations – although many of them show strong promise to inform the field. The research cited here has limitations. First, there may be limitations to the studies themselves in their design or sample size, which the authors themselves have mentioned. Second, most studies reviewed here were conducted with participants from WEIRD (Western, educated, industrialized, rich, and democratic; Hendriks et al. 2019; Henrich et al. 2010) societies and therefore do not always fully represent diversified and cross-culturally informed perspectives of the human experience around kindness. I have attempted to include findings from studies that included non-Western participants (e.g., Datu and Park 2019; Kim et al. 2018; Shoshani and Slone 2013). Last, many of the studies on kindness have been done with convenience samples, often with university students who are within arm's reach of university researchers. There have been concerns about the extent to which this population represents the general public and the over-sampling of this population in social science research (Ferber 1977; Hanel and Vione 2016; Peterson and Merunka 2014). University students are certainly a well-studied population and concerns might be raised about whether there is sufficient cultural diversity within samples, whether self-selection might play a role in the study, whether self-reporting influencing outcomes, and whether incentives might affect participation in studies. With these concerns in mind, our discovery of what it means to be kind and of how kindness has been researched presses forward.

Theoretical Frameworks Guiding the Study of Kindness

Drawing upon theory helps provide frameworks that substantiate or build a case for the study of kindness. Next, I provide an overview of three theories that help explain why being kind might contribute to an individual experiencing enhanced well-being. First, the *positive activity model* posited by Lyubomirsky and Layous (2013) situates kindness within a well-being framework and argues that at the core of activities designed to boost well-being, there must be a "person-activity fit." This person-activity fit holds that there must be a certain synergy (or fit) between characteristics of the individual (e.g., he or she must believe that it is possible to complete the act, must be sufficiently motivated to complete the act, etc.) and characteristics of the activity itself (e.g., the number of acts completed or the dosage must be sufficient, the variety in acts performed, etc.). According to this model, optimal well-being benefits are achieved when there is strong alignment or fit between the individual and the acts to be undertaken. Thus, this model provides theoretical support for the idea that completing a series of kind acts should contribute to optimal well-being when characteristics of the individual align with characteristics of the kind acts.

A second theoretical framework lending support to the study of kindness is the *self-determination theory* proffered by Ryan and Deci (2000). Helping explain why individuals might be kind to others, the self-determination theory argues that people engage in activities because they find them interesting and satisfying and not because they are seeking an external goal (i.e., a reward). These authors argue that, over time, individuals internalize values and their corresponding behaviours. Ryan and Deci postulate that we all have a universal need to be *competent, autonomous*, and *connected* to others. Certainly, when educators think of encouraging children and adolescents to complete a series of kind acts, it can be argued that all three needs are brought into play – performing kind acts provides the child with a sense of accomplishment and competence, kind acts may be done independently and with little supervision, and being kind to others often acts as a social lubricant connecting individuals. As argued by Ryan and Deci (2000, 76), "If the social contexts in which such individuals are embedded are responsive to basic psychological needs, they provide the appropriate developmental lattice upon which an active, assimilative, and integrated nature can ascend." They further posit that "excessive control, nonoptimal challenges, and lack of connectedness" impede our engagement in activities aimed at boosting our well-being (76).

A third theoretical framework supporting the study of kindness is found in Bandura's (1977) *social learning theory* and in particular his notion of observational learning – that individuals learn behaviours from observing others within certain environments or contexts. Bandura's early work (i.e., Bandura et al. 1961) postulated that aggressive behaviour could be learned through the imitation of aggressive models. Similar to how emotional contagion can be both positive (e.g., joy) and negative (e.g., stress), the application of *social learning theory* to the topic of kindness lends support for the idea that prosocial behaviour such as kindness can be encouraged and learned by observing others performing kind acts.

Taken together, these three theories elucidate our understanding of the motivations, factors, and conditions explaining how educators might encourage optimal engagement in kind acts – that is, the factors that must be considered as educators strive to create opportunities for students to engage in and complete a series of kind acts to bolster their well-being.

How Kindness Is Studied

Reviewing studies on kindness reveals that although there are commonalities across researchers, there remain nuanced differences in how researchers approach the study of kindness. What follows next is a brief overview of the methodological approaches used to explore, measure, and assess the impact of kindness. Just as there are different theoretical frameworks helping explain why people might engage in kind acts, so too are there different methodological approaches to studying kindness. Recognizing that educators are often action researchers in their classrooms, what research questions do you have about kindness and what methodology might best respond to your question?

Box 3.1. Teachers as Action Researchers

1. What theory best aligns with your understanding of how to foster kindness in the classroom?

2. Teachers are often action researchers. What research questions do you have about kindness? What about teaching kindness or fostering kindness in students would you like to understand more fully?

3. Thinking about your research questions, what methodology might best address your question? Are you interested in assessing the effects of an intervention (thus a quantitative approach) or are you interested in delving into the lived experiences of students around some aspect of kindness (thus a qualitative approach)?

4. If you were to design a study on kindness in your classroom in which you played a central role, what might that look like?

QUALITATIVE STUDIES

There is certainly a lack of studies that employ qualitative methodologies to explore the topic of kindness. Qualitative research is driven by broader, more open-ended questions than the research done within a quantitative framework where researchers often strive to establish causality. For example, qualitative research questions might include overarching open-ended questions such as "How, when asked to be kind, do adolescents demonstrate kindness?" "What does it mean to be kind in the eyes of elementary students?" Or as researcher Nicholas Long (1997) asked, "Are acts of kindness remembered by troubled students?"

The methodology or approach to research required to explore answers to such questions might include the use of interviews, case studies, or open-ended surveys to capture participants' thoughts, views, and perspectives. Researchers Cotney and Banerjee (2019) employed a focus group (an approach that brings together a group of participants for discussion) to explore how adolescents understand kindness and what they perceive to be the links between being kind and their well-being. In a general sense, qualitative research strives to uncover and represent the *lived* experience of participants around an identified topic. Reviewing the published kindness research reveals that more qualitative research on kindness is needed, especially research that captures the perspective and experiences of children and adolescents on the topic of kindness.

QUANTITATIVE STUDIES

In contrast to the exploratory nature of qualitative research is research whose aim may be to establish causality through a quantitative approach. Differentiating these two approaches is the nature of the data they seek to capture – qualitative research strives to capture textual data (non-numerical that might take the form of interview transcripts, which are coded for their thematic content), whereas quantitative research seeks numerical data (e.g., frequencies of responses, changes in responses over time, etc.).

Intervention studies. The findings from intervention studies, an approach to research in which researchers assess participants on a variety of outcomes (or what researchers refer to as dependent variables) in response to the introduction of a kindness intervention (the independent variable), are commonly reported in the kindness-themed literature. Researchers typically use a pre-test, intervention, post-test design (and sometimes a follow-up assessment) to assess the effects of being kind. The most robust studies, called *randomized controlled trials*, see participants randomly assigned to treatment (i.e., doing a kindness intervention activity) or control (i.e., doing a neutral activity unrelated to kindness) conditions (Hendriks et al. 2019). This allows researchers to declare, with varying certainty, that engaging in a kindness intervention causes outcome variables to change in participants. That said, not all is perfect in the world of kindness research. In their systematic review and meta-analysis, researcher Oliver Curry and colleagues (2018) reported that the bulk of kindness intervention studies done are "under powered" – they have insufficient sample sizes to detect significant effects. In fact, arising from their initial screening of over 4,045 studies (of which only twenty-seven met inclusion criteria), the typical sample size of studies investigating the effects of being kind had but 79 participants. These authors argue that a sample size of 202 participants in each of treatment and control conditions is needed. Readers curious to learn more about kindness intervention research are encouraged to consult Curry et al. (2018).

In reviewing intervention studies on the effects of being kind, it is evident that researchers often ask participants to either recall or perform a series of kind acts as a way of determining if being kind produces benefits to well-being (e.g., Ko et al. 2019). Kindness interventions have been described differently within the context of different studies and this includes descriptions of kindness interventions as "happiness increasing strategies" (Lyubomirsky et al. 2005) or as "resource distribution strategies" (Blakey et al. 2019) – an intervention that might see participants spend money on themselves (i.e., kindness to self) versus on others (i.e., kindness to strangers). This subcategory of research has also been referred to as "pro-social spending" (Aknin 2013; Aknin et al. 2020; Dunn et al. 2008; Whillans et al. 2016).

Contexts in Which Kindness Has Been Researched

A review of the psychological, sociological, and educational research reveals that kindness has been studied across a variety of contexts, including not limited to kindness research within families (Pastorelli et al. 2016), the university campus (Binfet et al., in press; Clegg and Rowland 2010; Kosek 1995), the workplace (Chancellor et al. 2017; Gibb and Rahman 2019), and within the context of schools (Cotney and Banerjee 2019; Layous et al. 2012). For the purposes of our discussion here, I will restrict our focus in the section that follows to kindness research conducted within the school context and draw heavily on the research I have done to understand students' perspectives and experiences of kindness in school.

RESEARCH IN SCHOOLS

Early research on students' prosocial behaviour is found in the work of Katherine Wentzel (1993), who explored the link between students' social behaviours (e.g., sharing, cooperating, helping other students) and their academic achievement. Looking at the connection between classroom behaviours and achievement in school, Wentzel (362) explained the relation between behaviour and academic achievement: "Interventions designed to promote the development of socially responsible behavior at school often result in higher levels of academic performance. However interventions designed to promote academic achievement do not seem to lead to corresponding increases in socially appropriate forms of classroom behavior." This research helped establish the importance of prosocial behaviour on students' school achievement and served as pioneering research offering scientific evidence for educators that fostering kindness in students was positively linked to students experiencing success at school. What follows next is an examination of research findings across grade levels.

Kindness in grades K–3. When I began researching kindness in schools, very little research, if any, had been done with young children on the topic of kindness, especially the identification of how children are kind. In all fairness to researchers, conducting research with children whose ages range from five to eight years can be challenging. They can be distrusting of outsiders, slow to warm up to allow access to their thinking, and restricted in their ability to complete paper-and-pencil surveys. Thus, researchers must rely on interviews or innovative methods to capture the thinking of young participants.

To address this gap in the literature and to help answer questions on how young students understand what it means to be kind, I used a "drawing-telling" methodology (Einarsdottir et al. 2009). The drawing-telling approach involves giving students a prompt (e.g., "What does kindness look like to you?" Or "What is something kind you've done recently at school?") and having students draw or illustrate their ideas or examples related to the topic. This approach is effective in capturing the views of young participants who perhaps do not yet have the reading and writing skills to respond to survey-type questions or who might be intimidated by a sit-down interview with a researcher. Students are free to draw their interpretation of the concept at hand and, as some of the drawings can be very creative and difficult to interpret, the researcher asks, "Who is in this drawing?" and "What is happening?" and writes verbatim the description offered by the student underneath each drawing. This "in situ coding" also helps the researcher reduce biases when interpreting drawings, and asking these two questions assists with the coding used to make sense of each drawing and to determine collectively, across all children's drawings, what they have to say about being kind at school.

In a first study of 115 students in kindergarten to third grade (Binfet and Gaertner 2015), students were asked to draw pictures of what kindness looked like to them and an example of something kind they had done at school recently (see appendix E). Though it was a small pilot study, the findings revealed that young elementary students largely understood kindness as physically helping others (e.g., "My friend fell down and I helped her get up."), giving to others, acts that maintained friendships, and helping emotionally. This distinction that kindness, in the view of young students, can be physical or emotional is especially curious and was found in students' drawings of examples of kindness they had done at school. Such examples mirrored students' understanding of what it means to be kind and included physically helping others, including others, and kindness that helped maintain friendships (e.g., "We eat lunch together on Fridays and I said 'Thank you' for sitting with me").

Encouraged by these initial findings, I then conducted a larger study of 652 first-to third-grade students from thirty-nine elementary classrooms (Binfet 2016). For this study, I asked students to draw two pictures: an image of themselves doing an act of kindness, and a teacher doing something kind (see appendix F). The prevalent themes of kindness found in students examples included maintaining friendships (see figure 3.3), physically helping others (e.g., "I'm helping a student who is hurt. I am getting a supervisor"), and showing respect to others ("We're picking up trash because it's important to show respect to the school").

Step #1: In the box below, draw a picture of something you have done kind at school recently. What have you done to show kindness at school?

WHO? _Self · Friend._

WHAT? _I am asking my friend if he wants to be my partner because he was left out._

Figure 3.3. A nine-year-old boy describes his act of kindness at school.

Image credit: J.T. Binfet

These same students were also asked to draw a picture of a teacher being kind, and to my knowledge, this was the first study to explicitly ask students to illustrate teacher kindness. What was surprising in the findings was the overwhelming interpretation of teacher kindness as *teaching*: when asked for an example of a teacher being kind, students drew teachers in the classroom providing instruction to themselves or to another student in need (see figures 3.4 and 3.5). When asked to describe what was happening in their drawings, students said, "She's telling us to do our math. She helps us know stuff"; "My teacher helped me with my spelling. I messed up and she corrected me!"; and "Teacher is giving classmate ideas on what to write because they need help with their paper." To my surprise – and remember, I am a former classroom teacher and school counsellor – it was not the fancy field trips or extra recess time that students indicated were acts of teacher kindness but rather teachers *teaching*.

KINDNESS IN UPPER ELEMENTARY GRADES

The next study I will describe was the largest I have conducted in my career as a researcher. I had just arrived at the University of British Columbia and was eager and ambitious and, with my student research assistants, we surveyed 1,753 students in grades four through eight about how they understood what it meant to be kind and asked them to provide examples of kindness they had done at school (see Binfet and Passmore 2019). We visited seventy-eight classrooms and made 186 trips back and forth to various schools to collect data! It was a big undertaking and the findings from this study helped validate the School Kindness Scale (Binfet et al. 2016), which we will discuss in chapter 8. My aim in this study was to discover how elementary students defined kindness and to identify how they enacted kindness at school – to provide examples of things they had done that they themselves deemed as kind. In scanning the relevant literature, it was clear that, although people were talking about kindness in schools and in research communities, no one had yet identified, *how* students showed kindness.

The findings from this study helped elucidate just what it means to be kind – from the perspective of students themselves. In defining kindness, students overwhelmingly defined kindness in positive terms (e.g., "Kindness is helping others") versus negative terms (e.g., "Kindness means you don't bully"). Within students' definitions of kindness, the themes of helping others, showing respect to others, and encouraging or advocating for others were predominant. Students' examples of kindness in school revealed that students enact kindness largely by helping others. However, they do this in nuanced ways, and students'

Step #2: Draw a picture that shows a teacher doing something kind. What might a teacher do to show kindness at school?

WHO? Teacher + Classmates.

WHAT? Teacher is helping my friend with his work. She wants him to do his best.

Figure 3.4. A seven-year-old boy describes a teacher being kind.

Image credit: J.T. Binfet

Step #2: Draw a picture that shows a teacher doing something kind. What might a teacher do to show kindness at school?

WHO? _teacher + self_

WHAT? _My teacher says I can write squiggly words if I'm stuck on a word_

Figure 3.5. A six-year-old boy describes a teacher being kind to him.

Image credit: J.T. Binfet

examples of kindness indicated that being kind through helping others can take several different forms. Students *generically* helped others (e.g., "I helped a friend"), *physically* helped others (e.g., "A kid fell at recess and I helped him back up"), *emotionally* helped others (e.g., "He was crying so I asked him what was wrong"), and *academically* or instructionally helped others (e.g., "The teacher was busy so I helped him understand a math problem"). Thus, we see that children have differentiated ways of understanding and enacting kindness and that there is more than one way to be kind within the school context.

Kindness in middle school. At the outset of this chapter it was established that much of the research on kindness has been conducted with WEIRD participants within WEIRD contexts. A study examining kindness outside a WEIRD context by Shoshani and Slone (2013, 1174) explored "strengths of the heart" in 417 Israeli middle school students. These researchers wanted to understand how character strengths such as kindness were related to adjustment in middle school. Using a longitudinal survey design, they queried students throughout their seventh and eighth grades on a battery of measures including character strengths, life satisfaction, and positive and negative affect. In reporting their findings, they argue that interpersonal character strengths such as kindness likely contribute to adolescents forging social connections to others and feeling a sense of belonging. Moreover, and in support of what was argued in chapter 2 on social and emotional learning, Shoshani and Slone (1178) make a case for the integration of social and emotional learning opportunities into mainstream curricula. "Integrating the traditional school skills in the areas of mathematics, science, language, arts, and history with social-emotional skills, based on strengths building practices holds promise for producing a high quality education that helps adolescents to meet the varied demands of this developmental period." Two recent studies I conducted (Binfet 2020; and Binfet and Whitehead 2019) shed light on what it means to be kind in middle school and, moreover, challenge our thinking about just how kindness is manifested in adolescence. To uncover what adolescents think about and how they enact kindness, I asked 191 ninth-graders to rate the extent to which they thought they were kind (both in their face-to-face and online interactions) and to plan and do five kind acts over the course of one week. The pre- and post-intervention self-ratings of kindness revealed significant increases in both face-to-face and online reports of kindness. Not surprisingly, being kind to others boosts one's perception of oneself as a kind person. At the heart of this study, participants were asked to plan and do a series of kind acts and generated 943 acts of kindness within their school. Adolescents demonstrated kindness predominantly by helping (31.7 per cent), giving (21.4 per cent), and being respectful (16.6 per cent). Just as in the elementary study reviewed earlier, the adolescents in this study demonstrated kindness by helping in different ways. This included helping generally (e.g., "Sometimes I arrive early to class and I ask my teacher if she needs help"); helping physically (e.g., "A student tripped in the gym so I helped him up"); helping emotionally (e.g., "A girl in my class started crying so I led her to the bathroom"), and within the context of their home life, helping with chores (e.g., "I hate unloading the dishwasher but I'll do it when my mom needs cheering up") (Binfet 2020, 41). The last salient finding to emerge from this study was that, when asked to identify the recipient of their kind acts, the adolescents in this study enacted kindness largely to familiar others. In fact, 80 per cent of the time, the recipient of their kindness was someone known to them.

In the second study of kindness in middle school students, I randomly assigned 414 sixth- through eighth-graders to either a kindness intervention (i.e., plan and do three kind acts each week for four weeks) or a control (i.e., plan and visit three locations each week for four weeks) condition. For this study, I tracked the actual number of kind acts completed and was surprised to learn that, even when a study is integrated into the routine school day, the engagement in the task can vary considerably. Students in this study generated 2001 acts of kindness and, on average, each participant in the intervention condition completed roughly seven of their twelve acts. Much like other school-situated tasks, there can be variability in motivation, engagement, and follow through. Coding students' kind acts revealed that adolescents in this study demonstrated kindness by helping (39.5 per cent), giving (23 per cent), and being respectful (13.9 per cent). This mirrors the key themes identified in the study reported above and helps buoy our understanding of how, when asked to be kind, adolescents express their kindness. In this study, 61 per cent of the recipients of the kind acts were familiar or known others. An important finding arising from this study was that only students who did 60 per cent or more of their assigned kind acts reaped significant well-being benefits (i.e., reductions in negative affect and increases in their self-ratings of face-to-face and online kindness). Thus, it appears one must hit a certain threshold of kind acts before experiencing any corresponding well-being benefits.

Kindness in high school. There has been relatively little research exploring kindness with high school students. In a recent study by Datu and Park (2019), 116 students (average age of seventeen years) were asked to complete a battery of measures to examine the relation between perceptions of school kindness and academic engagement.

As the authors summarize the key finding from their survey research, "These results indicate that students' perceived level of school kindness was associated with higher levels of motivation to master the content of learning material and to outperform other students" (68). As you know in your role as an educator, how kind students perceive their school to be influences how they engage with curriculum, with their classmates, and with their teachers.

A second study of high school students by Gillham and colleagues (2011) merits mention here as it informs our understanding of the role of kindness in relation to negative affect. They employed a longitudinal survey design to explore how "other directed character strengths," including being kind to others, were linked to well-being in adolescence. In their study of 149 ninth- and tenth-graders, they describe their salient finding as: "Adolescents' character strengths predicted their subjective well-being. Other-directed strengths (e.g., forgiveness, kindness, teamwork) and temperance (e.g., self-regulation, perseverance) at the start of high school predicted fewer symptoms of depression through the end of 10th grade" (40).

Taken together, findings from the two studies above reinforce the notion that, in order for adolescents to do well in school, attention must be paid and effort must be made to create a nurturing and caring learning ethos within schools and that opportunities for students to engage in kindness is related to favourable outcomes, including motivation to learn and overall well-being.

Kindness Bolsters Well-Being

Across studies, including studies from meta-analyses (studies that summarize findings across other studies), the consensus is that being kind is an effective way of increasing the subjective well-being of the initiator (see figure 3.6). That is, generally speaking, being kind contributes to the individual who performs the kind acts feeling better (Curry et al. 2018; Lyubomirsky and Layous 2013; Magnani and Zhu 2018; Rowland and Curry 2018). When researchers report that participants' well-being was increased after being kind, they are often referring to the extent to which individuals report feeling happy, being satisfied with life, and experiencing positive affect or emotions (Dolan and Metcalfe 2012). In a student's example (figure 3.7) we see how her insights support the science behind kindness that argues being kind to others is one way through which our well-being can be enhanced.

As an educator interested in the topic of kindness, you have perhaps previously heard of the term "helper's high" – first introduced by Alan

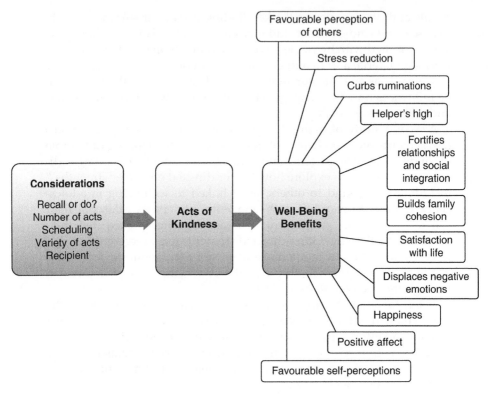

Figure 3.6. Conceptualization of well-being benefits.

Image credit: J.T. Binfet

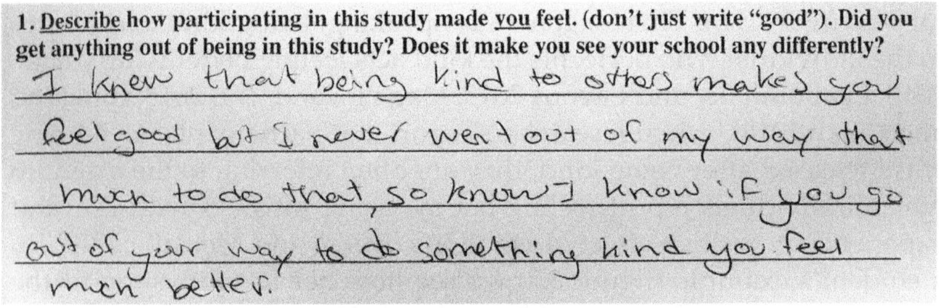

1. <u>Describe</u> how participating in this study made <u>you</u> feel. (don't just write "good"). Did you get anything out of being in this study? Does it make you see your school any differently?

I knew that being kind to others makes you feel good but I never went out of my way that much to do that, so know I know if you go out of your way to do something kind you feel much better.

Figure 3.7. A fifteen-year-old girl shares insights after participating in a kindness study.

Image credit: J.T. Binfet

Luks in 1988. Luks described it as being akin to the "runner's calm" and as a euphoria that arises from engaging in behaviours that help others. This concept was popularized by Stephen Post (2005). In short and simply put, we feel better when we are kind to others.

Relevant to our discussion here is the early work by Midlarsky (1991), who described a series of outcomes experienced by people who help others. Although the participants in this study were older adults, her findings nevertheless inform our understanding of children and adolescents. Midlarsky argued that people who help others, who are altruistic, experience:

• Enhanced social integration
• Greater distraction from their own problems
• Increased meaningfulness
• Increased self-efficacy and competence
• Improved mood
• Increased active lifestyle

These findings are echoed in work of Lyubomirsky, Sheldon, and Schkade (2005), who paint a favourable portrait of individuals who complete acts of kindness. In summarizing the benefits of being kind, they argue that several outcomes arise: increased self-ratings of happiness; the fostering of a "charitable perception of others and one's community" (125); changes in the way people see themselves, including seeing themselves as cooperative and interdependent (i.e., connected to others); and increased liking by others. Certainly, this last outcome contributes to individuals building social capital, which, in turn, helps foster resilience.

Combined, the findings above are certainly desirable outcomes educators want for young people. Underlying these benefits that arise from being kind to others and possibly explaining how it is that people reap all of these benefits when considering and acting on behalf of others is the work of researchers Raposa and colleagues (2016), who suggest that a key benefit to being kind is stress reduction. In their study of seventy-seven adults, they used smart phones to send daily surveys to participants and asked them to track their prosocial behaviour (e.g., holding doors open for others, helping with school work, etc.) and to complete surveys on their stress and mental health. As the authors explain, "Results suggest that engaging in higher than usual rates of prosocial behavior on a given day might buffer the negative impact of stress on positive affect and ratings of overall mental health on that day" (692). Undergirding the kindness intervention used in this research was ample structure and support – participants were reminded of, and encouraged to complete, kind acts each day and this structure appears important in eliciting well-being benefits. Offered next is an examination of what is known about the dimensions or components of kind acts that optimally contribute to well-being.

Understanding the Mechanisms Underlying Kind Acts

Do you actually have to do kind acts, or is recalling them enough? As illustrated earlier in this chapter, there are two distinct approaches undertaken in kindness intervention research: (1) researchers ask participants to recall kind acts they have done; and (2) researchers ask participants to plan (and subsequently sometimes do) a series of kind acts. Which approach yields the best well-being outcomes for participants? Researchers from the University of California, Riverside, a hub of kindness research, designed an experiment to assess just this (see Ko et al. 2019). When compared to control participants (who did nothing connected to completing kind acts), well-being benefits were the same for both participants, whether they simply reflected upon and recalled previous kind acts they had done or planned and performed a series of kind acts. It might be easy to conclude from this study that simply reflecting on our previous prosocial behaviour is sufficient to boost our well-being. However, and as was seen in chapter 2 on social and emotional learning, much can be learned throughout the process of planning and delivering kindness to others and experiencing first-hand the reaction of the recipient to one's kindness. Our understanding of the importance of whether one recalls or plans and enacts kindness will be further informed by the chapters that follow as they illustrate the nuanced ways in which kindness might be enacted. Not all kind acts are the same, and there is room for those who are already kind to refine, enhance, and deliver varied acts of kindness to a variety of recipients.

How many kind acts must be done to reap well-being benefits? Does the number of kind acts one does matter? Kerr, O'Donovan, and Pepping (2015) explored the "dosage," or the number of kind acts done, and the effect of being kind to elicit positive well-being in clinically depressed adults. Using a daily diary format, participants were provided the following prompt: "Kind acts are behaviors that benefit other people, or make others happy. They usually involve some effort on our part. On the lines below describe as many as five acts that you did for someone else today. Be sure to include at least one act that you did intentionally" (24). Although they failed to demonstrate a strong link between being kind and a corresponding boost to one's well-being, their study of sixteen participants who documented their daily kind acts over two weeks revealed that, on average, participants performed 2.5 acts each day. Considering the mental health challenges facing this subsample of participants, the finding that participants completed over two kind acts each day and sustained that number over the course of two weeks is encouraging. This discovery of the number of kind acts completed by these participants holds potential to help determine the number of kind acts we might encourage young people to do.

How many kind acts might we ask and expect young people to do? In innovative yet methodologically simple research done by Otake and colleagues (2006), a kindness intervention asked students to track the kind acts they completed. In a study of 119 female undergraduate students, Otake and colleagues (2006) asked them to simply count their kind acts over the course of one week. As the authors themselves acknowledge, there were limitations to this study (e.g., no random assignment to treatment or control conditions), so the results are interpreted here with caution. However, the findings suggest that (1) merely counting one's kind acts can contribute to increased self-perceptions of happiness, and (2) the more kind acts that an individual performs appears to significantly increase one's self-ratings of happiness, and gratefulness in response to kindness from others. This last finding is in concert with the work of Raposa et al. (2016) reviewed earlier in this chapter – it appears that the more kind acts done, the better. That is, it appears one must do more kind acts than one would typically do to experience boosts to one's well-being.

Next, I set out to uncover just how much kindness should be done – what "kindness dosage" helps us feel better? Our understanding of how much kindness is required to boost well-being can be informed by returning to the work of Stephen Post (2017), who explores the link between altruism and physical health. Post advocates *prescribing* volunteering to boost patients' mental and physical health and recommends two hours of volunteering per week for adults and one hour per week for adolescents. As he explains, "There is no particular dose of volunteering to be prescribed for every individual, other than to state a couple of hours per week seems to make an impact on well-being. Going far beyond this threshold does not necessarily increase benefits" (166). Here we find a guideline that informs our approach to mentoring children and adolescents on incorporating kindness into their weekly well-being regime. Considering too that being kind may be incorporated into the curriculum and thus supported within schools and, by extension, within the family context, we might ask that a dose of thirty to sixty minutes each week of kind behaviour to others is reasonable for young people.

Does the scheduling of kind acts matter? The previous section explored just how much kindness might be done to boost the well-being of children and adolescents. What remains important to understand is how best to schedule the completion of one's kind acts. Does it matter when kind acts are done? Although this is an under-researched area of kindness, the description of a study done by Lyubomirsky, Tkach, and Sheldon (as cited in Lyubomirsky et al. 2005) informs our thinking, as it draws attention to the effects of scheduling or timing of kind acts as a factor in producing positive well-being. In a study asking participants to perform random acts of kindness and to count their blessings over the course of six weeks, these researchers found that the well-being (i.e., the happiness) of participants increased only for those who performed their kind acts all on the same day (versus spreading the delivery of the kind acts out over the course of one week). They suggest that kind acts, especially if they are small, might have a diminished effect on well-being and not be powerful enough when done individually throughout the week. Perhaps several small acts of kindness must be clustered or delivered together in order for well-being benefits to arise – sort of a "kindness blitz."

In studies done at the University of British Columbia described earlier in this chapter, I asked middle school students to complete a series of kind acts, and their completion rates across two studies inform our thinking about how adolescents respond to requests to plan and complete acts of kindness. In the first study (Binfet and Whitehead 2019), students were asked to do three kind acts each week for four weeks. Examining the completion rates of 193 participants, it was found that, on average, only 7.45 of the 12 total possible acts were completed. Findings from another study (Binfet 2020) in which 191 ninth-graders were asked to do five kind acts over the course of one week corroborate this result. Although there was strong overall engagement in completing the kindness tasks, 29 per cent of the students completed all five acts and 47 per cent completed four of their five acts. Like many school-situated tasks, there is variability in the extent to which students invest in and complete kindness assignments. Findings like these attest to the importance of educators mentoring, monitoring, and supporting children and adolescents in their completion of kind acts. Just asking them to be kind is not enough. As researchers Magen and Aharoni argued (1991, 140) in their study of adolescent prosocial behaviour and its ability to expand the awareness of adolescents to others and society, "The effect of guidance, feedback, follow-up, and support during such involvement should also be considered, in terms of their impact on continued involvement and increased desire for transpersonal commitment."

Does it matter to whom you are kind? This is an especially important question when discussing kindness in schools, as there is a tendency for students to enact kindness to those whom they already know – familiar others. To be clear, when, for example, a teacher spearheads a kindness initiative in a classroom for which students are asked to perform a series of kind acts, children and adolescents will be kind primarily to those with whom they have friendships or connections. In studies I have undertaken in which thousands of students were asked to describe and deconstruct their kind acts at school, there was some variability in the rates of known versus unknown recipients. Recall the findings reported previously in this chapter from two middle school studies I conducted on kindness in adolescents. When asked who received their kindness, 61 per cent of participants enacted kindness to individuals familiar to them (Binfet and Whitehead 2019). In a separate study of 191 ninth-grade students who planned and performed five kind acts over the course of one week, 80 per cent of the students chose familiar others as the recipients of their kindness (Binfet 2020).

As argued above, this inclination to be kind to those already known by the initiator likely helps to maintain and fortify relationships. Educators certainly want students to be well connected to those around them, and such an emphasis is important for all students. However, a potentially troublesome ramification arises when students are largely kind to only those they already know, so students who are not well integrated into social spheres – social isolates – are unlikely to be on the receiving end of other students' kind acts. This experience may, in turn, further isolate them. But there is potential for these students to bridge connections to others by being kind, and in chapter 7 a review of strategies is offered to help these students forge connections to other students by completing a series of kind acts.

Outside of school, the importance of being kind to others has been researched by Dunn and colleagues (2008), who explored the effects of "prosocial spending" – spending money on others rather than oneself. Their methodology was simple: take a baseline measure of happiness, have people spend money (five or twenty dollars) on themselves or on others over the course of one day, and then measure happiness again. Participants who spent money prosocially – on strangers – reported the greatest gains in happiness.

Benefits beyond Well-Being

Acts of kindness can build trust and acceptance between people, encourage social bonds, provide givers and receivers with the benefits of positive social interaction, and enable helpers to use and develop personal skills and thus themselves.

Kerr et al. (2015, 20)

Being kind fortifies relationships and helps builds social capital. In an innovative randomized controlled study by Layous and colleagues (2012), nine- to twelve-year-old public school students were asked to do three kind acts each week for four weeks (treatment condition) or visit three locations (control condition). The findings are curious, as students in both conditions experienced corresponding increases in their well-being at the end of the study, but students who performed acts of kindness were found to have significantly greater ratings of "sociometric popularity" – the extent to which they were accepted by their peers. This finding holds relevance for our understanding of the dosage of kind acts required to boost well-being (i.e., twelve acts were done by students in this study over the course of one month), and for our understanding of what being kind to others does for pre-adolescents – it boosts their chances of being accepted by their peers. This is a particularly important and salient finding for educators seeking strategies to bolster the social situation or profile of children and adolescents who struggle to fit in at school. The findings of this study hold hope for helping students build social capital.

Kindness may build family cohesion. It is not only within the school context that acts of kindness bring people together. In an example from a recent study of kindness in middle school, generated by an ninth-grade boy, is a planned kind act that bridges his connection to a parent (see figure 3.8). Here students were asked to plan and do five kind acts over the course of one week, after which they were asked to rank order their kind acts – from least to most kind.

There may be opportunities for kindness in family life, and when children and adolescents are asked to provide an example of recent kindness, they will often describe an act directed toward a family member (see figure 3.9). Being kind to family members reflects perspective-taking (i.e., "What must it be like for my mom to work full-time and come home to have to make dinner?") and can help to unite or fortify relationships. Being kind within one's family may be a safe and nurturing space in which young people can practise being kind and enacting kindness to others more broadly. It is worth noting that not all families

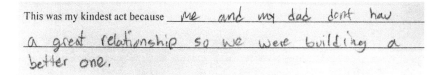

This was my kindest act because *me and my dad dont haw a great relationship so we were building a better one.*

Figure 3.8. A fifteen-year-old boy reflects on the quality of his kind acts.

Image credit: J.T. Binfet

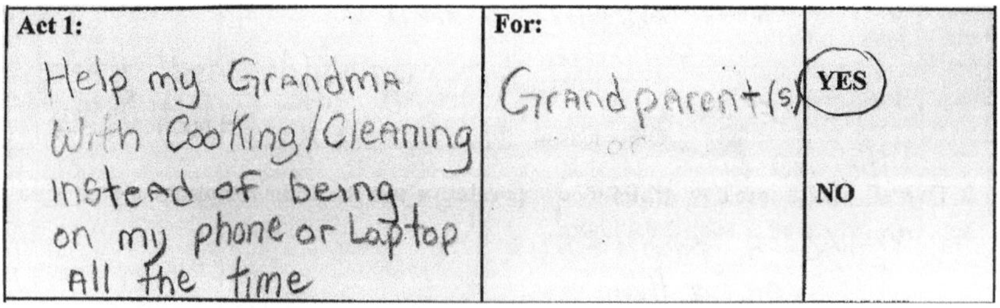

Act 1:	For:	
Help my Grandma With Cooking/Cleaning Instead of being on my phone or Laptop All the time	Grandparent(s) or	**YES**
		NO

Figure 3.9. A fourteen-year-old girl reflects on her kindness toward a grandparent in response to the prompt: "Plan an act of kindness to be done over the course of the next week."

Image credit: J.T. Binfet

may provide a "safe and nurturing space" within which kindness can be practised and thrive. We know, for example, that LGBTQ+ adolescents are particularly vulnerable to family strife (Mehus et al. 2017), and for children and adolescents whose family environment is unstable, transitory, or rife with conflict, educators and their classrooms may be the only available "safe and nurturing space." What follow are examples of kindness done by children and adolescents within their families (see figures 3.10–3.12).

In one example, a middle school student was asked to plan and do five acts of kindness over the course of one week (see figure 3.10). Her two acts of kindness for her family reflect perspective-taking (i.e., understanding that her mother is stressed and would appreciate help) and introspection (i.e., recognizing her own role in being kind without complaining).

The topic of kindness within the family is discussed further in chapter 7 when strategies to foster kindness in children and adolescents are explored. Having young people first practise kindness to family members may be a safe context in which to develop children's *prosocial*

#1	help my mom unstress by helping her with dinner	mom	after school/ tonight or wednesday
#2	compliment a random stranger as im walking	a random person who looks like they are sad	when ever i get a chance
#3	offer help to my family out with something big without complaining	mom or dad	thursday
#4	bring someone a little no cost gift to make them smile	friend, someone close to me	by friday
#5	make a friend smile by singing them a song & laugh	" "	" "

Figure 3.10. A sixteen-year-old girl lists her planned acts of kindness.

Image credit: J.T. Binfet

confidence. Here children can perspective-take and devise kind acts that align with the needs of immediate and extended family members.

Kindness helps displace negative emotions and curb rumination. It has been argued that being kind to others helps reorient from a preoccupation with the self to a focus on others (Anderson 2003; Post 2005). Because performing acts of kindness requires perspective-taking – putting oneself in the shoes of others – being kind to others can shift negative affect, or, as Post (2005, 72) described it, "Positive emotions (kindness, other-regarding love, compassion, etc.) enhance health by virtue of pushing aside negative emotions." Thus, individuals who are ruminating on negative events or experiencing negative emotions might be encouraged to plan and enact kind acts as a way to recalibrate their thinking from a focus on the self to a focus on others. Even for individuals who are low on the trait of "agreeableness" (i.e., "unpleasant, offensive, and contentious in their relationships"; Mongrain et al. 2018, 324), being kind to oneself and engaging in acts of kindness has proven to reduce self-reports of depression. Even two months post-intervention, participants reported significant boosts to their well-being arising from participation in a kindness intervention.

Step #1: In the box below, draw a picture of something you have done kind at school recently. What have you done to show kindness at school?

WHO? ___Self · Brother___

WHAT? ___I'm holding my brother's hand while___
___we walk to school.___

Figure 3.11. An eight-year-old boy illustrates how he is kind to his brother.

Image credit: J.T. Binfet

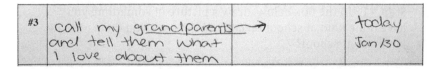

| #3 | call my grandparents ⟶ and tell them what I love about them | | today Jan /30 |

Figure 3.12. A fifteen-year-old girl describes her act of kindness
for her grandparents.

Image credit: J.T. Binfet

Conclusion

Looking back over this chapter, several key findings inform our understanding of kindness. Recall that the aims of this chapter were to provide an overview of kindness research and to review the benefits that arise from being kind. It was noted that much of the research employs a standard pre-test, intervention, post-test design to assess whether being kind positively affects outcome variables. Also noted was that there is a distinct lack of qualitative research exploring how young people experience and understand kindness. Next, attention is turned to understanding the findings from peer-reviewed studies that attest to the benefits of being kind. Several studies in which participants had their well-being measured at the outset and then participated in a kindness intervention in which they generated a series of kind acts, reported boosts to their happiness, life satisfaction, and positive emotions and a reduction in negative emotions. Also discussed in this chapter were the benefits that arise beyond boosts to one's immediate well-being. They included kind acts helping build social capital, and the extent to which we feel connected to others and situated within a community of support. Examples throughout this chapter of young people's kindness illustrated that, when asked to do an act of kindness, they often do something kind for a family member, thus fortifying family relations. Having established that being kind elicits a host of positive well-being outcomes, it remains important to explore the different approaches to crafting acts of kindness. In the chapter that follows, an introduction to the first of three different ways in which children and adolescents might structure their kindness is offered, beginning with an examination of *responsive kindness*.

Chapter Four

Responsive Kindness

Why Fostering Kindness in Children Is Important

The three chapters that follow will provide overviews of three different approaches to having children and adolescents enact kindness – a how-to-guide for being kind to others. You might think of these chapters as different ways to structure or deliver kindness. Leading kindness researcher Lee Rowland, from Oxford University, reflects on what is needed to advance our understanding of kindness and, in doing so, makes a case for understanding how kindness may be structured differently: "I think that the effects of kindness could be more compellingly explored if the different types of kindness, by different types of givers, and different types of receivers, were systematically varied. Investigating kindness in this way would, I predict, have a dramatic influence on wellbeing (and other measures) and give us greater insight into the effects of kindness on psychological flourishing" (Rowland 2018, 32). Complementing Rowland's calling for the need to understand different types of kindness, Lyubomirsky and Layous offer further support for the notion that being kind in varied ways is important. They argue that "participants who performed varied kind acts every week increased their levels of well-being more than did participants who performed the same kind acts" (Lyubomirsky and Layous 2013, 59). It remains important to understand why encouraging young people to be kind is important and how kindness is situated vis-à-vis its counterpart – aggressive or externalizing behaviour. What follow in this and the next two chapters are suggestions for how children and adolescents might structure their kind acts – a guide to three different approaches to delivering kindness.

Consider the Developmental Implications of Low Prosociality. Recall from chapter 1 that prosocial behaviour was initially defined as

Step #2: In the box below, draw a picture of something you have done kind at school recently. What have you done to show kindness at school?

WHO? my friend in Kindergarten, self
WHAT? I'm helping him up b/c he fell off a slide.

Figure 4.1. An eight-year-old boy shares his example of kindness at school.

Image credit: J.T. Binfet

"voluntary behavior intended to benefit another" (Eisenberg et al. 1999, 1360). Building on Eisenberg's definition, Mesurado and colleagues (2019, 259) recently described it as "voluntary actions aimed at sharing, comforting, and helping others." In our previous chapter we reviewed the well-being benefits that arise from being kind. Developmental benefits also occur when children and adolescents are prosocial. Consider for a moment the developmental implications (the factors that affect, influence, or propel development in children and adolescents) that arise when children and adolescents engage with the world by sharing, comforting, and helping (see figure 4.1). There are both intrapersonal and interpersonal developmental implications that arise when children "share, comfort, and help" others.

Intrapersonally, we see children engage in perspective-taking and develop empathy as they imagine what it might feel like to be in someone else's situation. In sharing, comforting, and helping others children learn about themselves and they build *prosocial confidence* that they carry forward from one prosocial act to the next. Interpersonally, we see rich social exchanges that occur when children are kind. They draw upon and hone their observation, communication, and listening skills as they deliver their acts of sharing, comforting, and helping to those around them. In short, when children enact kindness, they are immersed in rich learning opportunities – to learn about themselves, to build skills, and to interact with and learn from others. When children and adolescents are not encouraged to be kind or have few opportunities to be kind they miss out on these opportunities to learn, practise, and grow.

Does Prosociality Counter Aggression? The relation between prosociality and aggression is complex and, much like many fields of research, there are disparate views, each with its supporting studies attesting to different interpretations of the link between these two variables. One camp sees prosocial and aggressive behaviour as uncorrelated and independent. As Padilla-Walker and colleagues (2018, 962) point out in their review of the link between prosociality and aggression in adolescence, "Children may strategically use both prosocial and aggressive behaviors in social settings with peers to gain social capital and acceptance." Much like feeling both happy and sad are not mutually exclusive, the thinking here is that individuals can be both kind and unkind. In contrast, a substantial body of literature attests to the relation between prosociality and aggression as being "inversely proportional" – as one increases, the other decreases (see research by Laible et al. 2014; and Nantel-Vivier et al. 2014). The discrepancies across findings might be explained by variations in the scales or instruments used to measure prosociality and aggression, the methodologies undertaken to study the relation between these two behavioural profiles in children and adolescents, or even how these terms are conceptualized and operationalized (see Padilla-Walker et al. 2018, for a review).

Tipping the scales in this discussion in favour of the interpretation that prosocial and aggressive behaviours are inversely related is the longitudinal study by Padilla-Walker and colleagues of 500 US adolescents from age twelve to eighteen: "The findings also suggested that prosocial behavior and aggression were bidirectionally negatively associated at every time point from age 12 to 18, and that prosocial behavior was negatively associated with delinquency from age 12 to 18" (Padilla-Walker et al. 2018, 973).

Plasticity. Children's development has been described as having "plasticity" or malleability (Cantor et al. 2019; Mesurado et al. 2019). As children develop they are "in formation" and are especially receptive to input and interventions designed to enhance their growth. In fact, some have argued that this receptivity to enrichment (and deprivation, for that matter) is heightened during childhood and adolescence and then later fossilizes or becomes increasingly resistant to change. As Cantor and colleagues (2019, 307) describe it, "Contextual factors nourish or hinder their development," especially during childhood, a time of rapid growth and development. In a low-stimulus environment, growth can be thwarted, whereas a rich and stimulating environment can facilitate growth. As we think about encouraging children and adolescents to be increasingly prosocial and adopt a routine kindness practice, educators play especially important roles in creating rich learning environments characterized by ample modelling of kindness, discussions of perspective-taking and empathy for others, and support for young people to plan and design, deliver, and reflect upon how to be kind to others. Having established that there are multiple developmental benefits arising from having children and adolescents engage in kindness, let me introduce you to the first of three ways in which young people might enact kindness – by being *responsively kind*. We begin by first exploring the topic of random kindness.

Random Acts of Kindness

Popularized by placemats and bumper stickers, the origins of today's commonly used phrase "random acts of kindness" was derived from Anne Herbert's (1985) slogan "Practice random kindness and senseless acts of beauty." The term *random acts of kindness* was further popularized by Herbert and Pavel's (1993) book of the same name. Those of us who research and work in the area of kindness owe a debt of gratitude to Herbert's coining of this phrase, as it has propelled interest in, and the actualization of, kindness in countless schools and communities all over the world.

As research has emerged exploring the topic of kindness, our understanding of how kindness is brought to life has advanced, and we are no longer beholden to sweeping terms such as "random kindness." Random kindness implies that kindness is haphazard and unpredictably enacted. Such is not the case, however, and deconstructing just how kindness comes about is a topic worthy of research and of exploring here in this book. Admittedly, my own understanding of how to define it and how it is enacted or delivered has evolved. My understanding of what it means to be kind and how kindness occurs in schools has been informed and shaped by the thousands of students I have asked to draw or describe what it means to be kind and how they are kind. In this chapter, I will lean on these examples to inform, shape, and refine your thinking about how young people are kind.

We now understand that there are nuanced and distinct ways in which people are kind, and the aim of this chapter is to describe the first of three approaches to being kind – *responsive kindness*. Responsive kindness can be physical (e.g., a student dropped his books in the hall and a classmate stops to help pick them up), emotional (e.g., a student stumbles upon someone crying and asks if he is okay), social (e.g., a student sees a new student looking for somewhere to sit in the school cafeteria and invites her to sit at the table where her friends are gathered), and environmental (e.g., picking up trash outside the school to show respect) and arises in response to our perception of a need. Responsive kindness offers a form of support to someone or something in a moment of need – it is reactionary.

Prerequisites to Being Kind

Both the understanding of others' inner status (i.e., perspective-taking) and the experience of feelings of concerns for others (i.e., empathic concern) are believed to facilitate prosocial behavior.

Van der Graaff et al.

Undergirding our ability to recognize this need to enact kindness on behalf of others is our ability to perspective-take and empathize with others. These foundational skills are worthy of discussion here, given the important role they play in helping students recognize the need for kindness as a response to the situations and individuals they encounter.

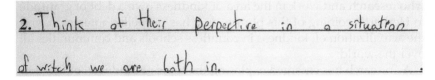

2. Think of their perspective in a situation
of witch we are both in.

Figure 4.2. An elementary student describes his act of kindness at school in response to the prompt "What is an example of something kind you have done at school recently?"

Image credit: J.T. Binfet

Perspective-Taking

"Perspective taking is the cognitive skill of understanding the situation of others" (Davis et al. 2019, 209). In order for children and adolescents to be responsively kind – to react with kindness to those around them, they must first imagine what it is like to be the person in need. This is a foundational step for students, as it allows them to figure out the appropriate response to help meet the needs of others (see figure 4.2). It is through perspective-taking that the child or adolescent is able to recognize a need in the other and can then begin to reflect upon and craft a response or act of kindness.

Empathy

Empathy has been described as a social phenomenon that is "the capacity to be affected by and share the emotional state of another" (de Waal 2008, 281). The link between empathy and behaviour is directional – empathy is a necessary but not sufficient condition for individuals to be kind. "Individuals who feel emotions congruent with others may be motivated to engage in prosocial behaviors aimed at helping others" (Davis et al. 2019, 207). Remember that students' abilities to put themselves "in the shoes of the other" (i.e., to perspective-take) and to *feel* what it might be like "to be the other" are foundational skills that increase the likelihood that students can generate responsively kind reactions to those around them. Certainly, there is individual variability in how empathic each of us is, and it is hoped, especially through school-situated programs grounded in social and emotional learning, that students have regular opportunities to practise recognizing and showing empathy to others as part of their routine school experience.

Box 4.1. Encouraging Perspective-Taking and Empathy

1. Use stories/literature to allow students to practise taking the perspective of others to identify their thoughts and feelings.

2. To familiarize students with the process, co-create empathic responses with them to the plight of characters in stories shared in class.

3. Incorporate perspective-taking into your classroom management approach or plan to addressing disagreements between students or student misbehaviour/misconduct.

4. Use roleplaying that requires students to take the viewpoint of others, which can be done by having students describe an event from where they are sitting and then sitting in a different location in the room (e.g., at the teacher's desk) to describe the event from a different viewpoint.

5. Use prompts to help guide students' thinking (e.g., "How might this character be feeling right now?"; "If you were this character, what might you be thinking?"

6. Create a wall display and have students brainstorm in response to the prompt: "Who in our community needs our empathy and compassion?"

7. For younger students, trace or create large paper shoe prints that students can step onto, to remind them to "put themselves in the shoes of the other." This can be linked to an art activity in which students "design their own pair of perspective-taking shoes."

8. Model thinking out loud for students as you encourage them to perspective-take and generate empathic responses.

Questions
- Which character in this story is facing a challenge? What is the challenge that character is facing?
- What are three words that describe how this person might be feeling?
- Who has ever felt this way? Does anybody know what it might feel like to have these feelings?
- Now, who can help me figure out a way we might support, encourage, or help this character? What could we do? If you were a character in this story, how might you act?

As with the development of perspective-taking skills, educators are encouraged to help children and adolescents practise and hone their ability to recognize the emotions of others and feel empathy for them. This is one of the mandates of social and emotional learning that we discussed back in chapter 2. We want young people to pause before acting to help others, to reflect on the experience of others and to imagine what it would feel like to be in their situation, facing the challenges

PHYSICALLY HELPING

Step #2: In the box below, draw a picture of something you have done kind at school recently. What have you done to show kindness at school?

WHO? _teacher and self_

WHAT? _teacher carrying box so students helps her open the door_

Figure 4.3. An eight-year-old student describes physically helping a teacher.

Image Credit: J.T. Binfet

before them. This, in turn, helps align the act of responsive kindness to the needs of the other.

Being Responsively Kind

Examples of Responsive Kindness

Next, you will find a series of examples in which students were responsively kind (see figures 4.3 through to 4.6). They illustrate the breadth of kind acts of children and adolescents in response to a perceived need: they physically helped others, emotionally supported others, socially included others, and environmentally helped their surroundings. As you review these examples, ask yourself what perspective-taking skills were required by the student to recognize the need for kindness in others and the role that empathy for others might have played in willing these students to do these acts of kindness to their fellow students, teachers, or school community.

EMOTIONALLY HELPING

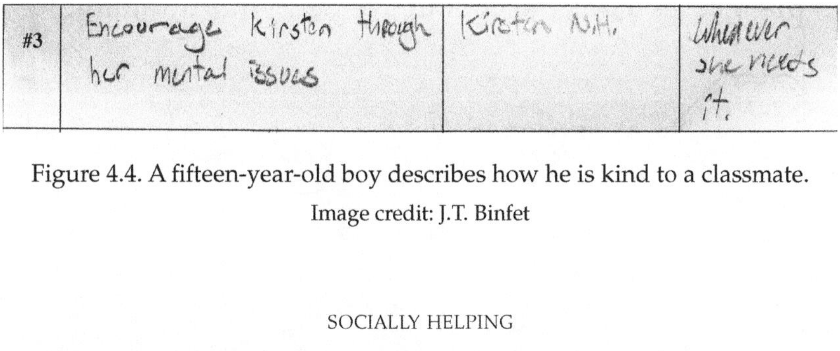

| #3 | Encourage Kirsten through her mental issues | Kirsten N.H. | Whatever she needs it. |

Figure 4.4. A fifteen-year-old boy describes how he is kind to a classmate.

Image credit: J.T. Binfet

SOCIALLY HELPING

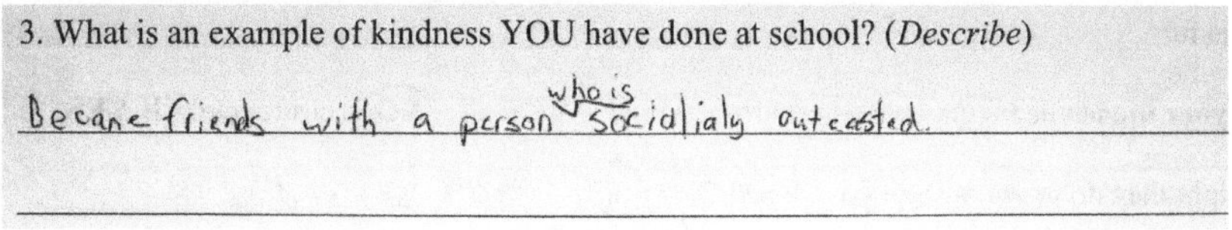

3. What is an example of kindness YOU have done at school? (*Describe*)

Became friends with a person who is socidially outcasted.

Figure 4.5. A fourteen-year-old boy describes how he is kind to a socially outcast student.

Image Credit: J.T. Binfet

ENVIRONMENTALLY HELPING

Step #1: In the box below, draw a picture of something you have done kind at school recently. What have you done to show kindness at school?

WHO? _____Self_____

WHAT? _____I'm picking up garbage. I'm helping my school and the students._____

Figure 4.6. A nine-year-old girl draws herself helping the school and her fellow students.

Image Credit: J.T. Binfet

These examples illustrate that children are able to put themselves in the shoes of others and to respond with kindness that is tailored to a perceived need. Children and adolescents are able to see situations from the viewpoint of those around them and empathize with others struggling to carry a heavy box (see figure 4.3), grappling with mental health challenges (see figure 4.4), feeling socially outcast (see figure 4.5), or a school environment disrespected by discarded trash (see figure 4.6). Next, it warrants examining just how perspective-taking and empathy might be fostered in children and adolescents – with a little practice and guidance from adult mentors, these foundational underpinnings for kindness can be honed.

Practising Perspective-Taking and Developing Empathy for Others

Sharing examples of scenarios in which *responsive kindness* is the appropriate reaction can reorient students' thinking and help them practise being responsively kind. It is important that educators do not simply tell or ask children and adolescents to be kind, as they might not have the requisite skills to be kind, especially when a kind response is warranted in their interactions with others. If students do not recognize the need for kindness in others, it is tough to convince them to be kind. Share the scenarios that follow with the children and adolescents around you who struggle to see the perspective or situation of others and encourage them to reflect upon and to discuss: (1) how might the person in the scenario feel?; and (2) what would a kind response to the situation look like? (see appendix G for additional examples).

CREATING KIND RESPONSES: ELEMENTARY STUDENTS

1. Second-grade student Juanita stood overtop her dropped lunch. Her apple had rolled across the room and her drink had spilled, forming a puddle at her feet. How might Juanita be feeling? What could one of her nearby classmates do to show kindness to Juanita?
2. This new game was exciting but Billy didn't understand all the rules. He wanted to play but things were moving too fast and he was lost. He could feel tears forming and worried he'd cry in front of his classmates. Looking up, Jeff sees that Billy is struggling. How might Billy be feeling? What might Jeff do to show kindness to Billy?
3. "Grab a toy and let's go!" shouted the teacher. By the time Sandra arrived to the toy bin, nothing was left. Her teacher's favourite line was "You get what you get and you don't get upset" so she just stood watching her classmates run outside for recess. Looking over her shoulder as she was heading outside, Rachel sees Sandra back

in the classroom. How might Sandra be feeling? What might Rachel do to show kindness to Sandra?

4. With a new cast on her arm from a skateboarding accident, Katie struggled to carry her backpack as she got off the bus in front of the school. Rachel didn't know Katie but could see her struggling. How might it feel to be Katie? What might Rachel do?

CREATING KIND RESPONSES: MIDDLE SCHOOL/HIGH SCHOOL EXAMPLES

1. After the teacher handed out field-trip forms for students to take home to their guardians, Billy watched Curtis tear his form up and toss it in the recycling bin. He overheard Curtis say his family can't afford stuff like this so why bother taking the form home. How might it feel to be Curtis? What might Billy do?
2. "Get a partner!" the teacher shouted as students in gym class got ready for conditioning drills. As Sarah was on the swim team and worked out regularly, she was immediately surrounded by class-mates wanting to be her partner. Over her shoulder she saw Janice slump and sit down on a bench as if she'd given up before even try-ing. How might Janice be feeling? What might Sarah do?
3. Jim was self-conscious about his weight and when a classmate cracked a joke about their teacher being heavy enough to cause a small earthquake, he immediately felt uneasy. Jim wanted desperately to fit in with his classmates but knew what it felt like to be teased for being heavy. How might Jim be feeling? How might Jim respond?
4. Frustrated with his mom, fifteen-year-old Frank yells, "You're always telling me to consider other people. Who considers me? Does anyone care about how I feel?" How might Frank be feeling? How might Frank's mom respond?
5. "This helps keep the janitor employed!" said Becky as she drew with a permanent marker on the wall of the bathroom stall. "I'll use black and you use red" she said as she passed Sarah a marker. How might the janitor feel upon seeing graffiti in the bathroom? How might Sarah respond?

Guidelines for Being Responsively Kind

Offering a structure to students to support them responding kindly to those around them helps ensure that students are thoughtful about their approach and mindful of their intention when enacting kindness. The following is intended as a rough guide to help students reflect upon the kindness they are about to enact.

When presented with an individual or situation in which you think responsive kindness is called for:

1. How might it feel to be in this person's shoes?
2. What is the challenge that person is facing?
3. What actions on my part could make the situation better?
4. How might this individual react to my kindness?
5. Does being kind put anyone in harm's way, myself included? (i.e., could I get hurt trying to help?)

Apply the above guide to the following scenarios to assess whether or how responsive kindness might be enacted.

1. Driving with his mom to soccer practice, Will sees a dog trotting on the inside lane of the freeway and yells at his mom to stop so he can jump out and help him.
2. "But they need socks" pleaded Rebecca who argued with her mother. "If I'm old enough to take the bus by myself I'm old enough to pass out socks to homeless people on skid road."
3. "I know he's hungry, he's always watching us eat in the cafeteria but never eats himself," Jackson told his mom. "What's the harm in bringing him some food?"
4. "Everyone knows smoking is bad for you. I just want to tell that mom she shouldn't smoke around her children. You're always telling me to be kind and those kids need kindness."
5. In a heated discussion with her mother, fourteen-year-old Lisa justified her behaviour. "Listen, it's not the first time she's asked me to help her steal. Don't act so surprised. If she doesn't have any money, how is she supposed to get stuff? You're always telling me to be kind to others. Well, this is me being kind!"

Conclusion

In this chapter the first of three types of kindness was introduced – *responsive kindness*. Recall that when being responsively kind, one responds physically or emotionally to the needs of someone else. Reviewed in this chapter was the importance of perspective-taking and demonstrating empathy as foundational skills that underlie recognition of the need for kindness. Guidelines to encourage children and adolescents to take the perspective of those around them were offered, as were scenarios to help young people build this skill. In the chapter that follows, the second type of kindness, *intentional kindness*, is introduced, thereby equipping educators to build upon and expand the approaches to fostering kindness in the children and adolescents under their care.

Chapter Five

Intentional Kindness

An act of kindness from a sixth-grade girl illustrates her intention to respond kindly to a unique scenario she faces within her school (see figure 5.1). As a one-time interaction it might be considered responsive kindness (i.e., how might she react to initially being mistaken as this young girl's best friend?) but the ongoing nature of this relationship allows this young student to practise *intentional kindness*. That is, she makes a decision, a priori, to play along with another student's perception of her and to demonstrate kindness in her reaction. Her decision is thoughtful and intentional.

Remember that children and adolescents enact kindness is a variety of ways – that is, not only do their individual acts of kindness vary but their approach to being kind can also differ. This chapter provides an overview of the second type of kindness done by children and adolescents – *intentional kindness*. Using the same format as was found in chapter 4, you will be guided through examples of *intentional kindness* and the chapter will outline how educators might facilitate *intentional kindness* in young people. The information shared in this chapter is inspired by Binfet (2015).

The previous chapter provided an overview of *responsive kindness* – in which individuals respond to a perceived need for physical or emotional help. In contrast, *intentional kindness* requires reflection, perspective-taking, and planning. In another example (see figure 5.2), a fourteen-year-old girl describes how she will intentionally respond with kindness to assist her technologically challenged grandparent. Here we see intentional kindness as kindness that is planned, organized, and goal directed. Next, each step of the planning of an act of intentional kindness is outlined (see appendix H for sample planning sheets).

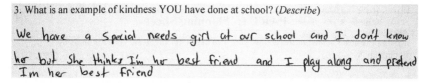

3. What is an example of kindness YOU have done at school? (*Describe*)

We have a special needs girl at our school and I don't know her but she thinks I'm her best friend and I play along and pretend I'm her best friend

Figure 5.1. A twelve-year-old girl describes her act of kindness toward a student with special needs.

Image credit: J.T. Binfet

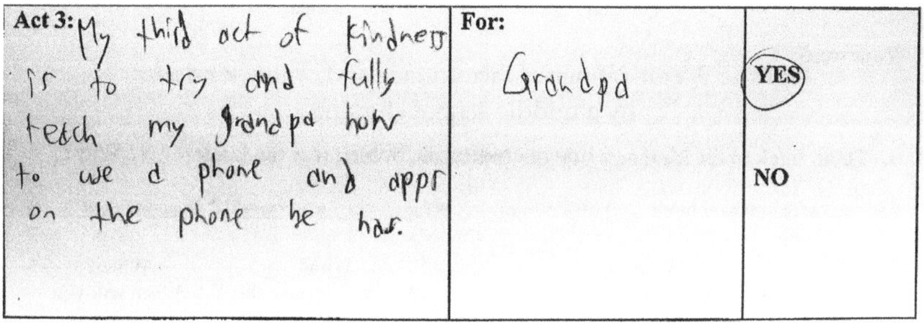

Act 3: My third act of kindness is to try and fully teach my grandpa how to use a phone and apps on the phone he has.

For: Grandpa   YES   NO

Figure 5.2. A fourteen-year-old girl shares her act of kindness toward her grandfather in response to the prompt "Plan an act of kindness that you could do over the course of the next week."

Image credit: J.T. Binfet

Step One: How Full Is Your Kindness Tank?

As a starting point, it is important to ask children and adolescents to reflect upon their current level of kindness – that is, just how kind they are. This is a frequently overlooked question that often flies under educators' radar. Educators tend to talk a great deal about kindness with children in their classes but do not always ask them about their kindness as a dimension of who they are or to self-evaluate how kind they are. Doing so allows educators to compare their perception of a child's kindness profile with the child's self-perception. In the study of 191 ninth-graders described in chapter 3 (Binfet 2020), I asked students to rate both their face-to-face and online kindness using a five-point, Likert-type scale that ranged from 1 = *not at all kind* to 5 = *very kind* (see figure 5.2). Two curious findings emerged. First, when asked to assess their own kindness, on average they saw themselves as "somewhat

---

PART 1: Planning Sheet

1. Using the scale below, indicate how kind you are generally. Rate your kindness by placing an X.

a. In your *face-to-face interactions* (place an X)

☐	☐	☐	☐	☒
Not at all kind	Somewhat unkind	Average	Somewhat kind	Very kind

b. When *online* (e.g., when using social media) (place an X)

☐	☐	☐	☒	☐
Not at all kind	Somewhat unkind	Average	Somewhat kind	Very kind

Figure 5.3. Self-ratings of face-to-face and online kindness by a middle school student.

Image credit: J.T. Binfet

Act	**What?** Describe what you will do for each kind act (**be specific/give details**).	**Who?** Who will receive this kind act from you?	**When?** When will you do this kind act this week?
#1	Offer My brother My Pizza. (Two Slices)	Dryden (my brother)	January 31
#2	I held a door to Pedestrians at Wal-mart	Strangers	Feb 3rd
#3	Unpack groceries from my Mom's Car	My Mom	Feb 3rd
#4	Give Change to a homeless individual	A Homeless Person	Feb 4th
#5	Buy Something for a close friend	Close friend	Feb 5th

Figure 5.4. A middle school student plans his acts of kindness for the week.

Image credit: J.T. Binfet

How kind are you currently? Indicate on the gas tank your current level of kindness.

Is there room for improvement?

Figure 5.5. Kindness gas tank.

Image credit: J.T. Binfet

kind" (a 4 out of 5). It is encouraging that even ninth-grade adolescents, a group often stereotypically perceived as selfish and mired in conflict, see themselves as largely kind. This positive self-rating also holds ramifications for educators working with this age group who are trying to foster kindness whose attempts to encourage the completion of a series of kind acts can be met with "But I'm already kind. Why do I have to do this?"

And when these self-ratings (see figure 5.3) were administered before and after students completed five kind acts over the course of one week (see figure 5.4), students' self-ratings of kindness showed significant gains (i.e., from 4.10 to 4.25 and 4.24 for face-to-face and online kindness respectively).

This introspection is important, as it often leads to children realizing that there is room for them to do additional kindness or to be increasingly kind. One way that educators can encourage introspection around kindness is to ask students to indicate on a gas tank indicator how much kindness they practise (see figure 5.5 below). Doing so invites discussion, and a student who indicates his kindness tank is "Full" could be asked questions to unpack the type of kind acts done, the recipients, and the quality of kindness enacted. Conversely and a more commonly found profile, students who indicate that there is room to practise additional kindness can be led through the steps below to identify the recipients in need of kindness around them and to brainstorm recipients (see figure 5.6) and ways to be kind (see figure 5.7).

Step Two: Identifying a Recipient Bank

When fostering kindness in children and adolescents, one important job of educators is to help create conditions that increase the likelihood that kindness can occur. The second step in helping children

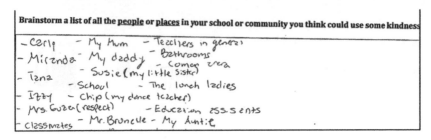

Figure 5.6. A brainstormed list of possible recipients of kindness.

Image credit: J.T. Binfet

	What? Describe what you will do for each kind act (be specific/give details).	Who? Who will receive this kind act from you?	When? When will you do this kind act this week?
#2	I will try to get this kid on my hockey to score cause He sucks	My Friend on my hockey tram cause He is bad at Hockey and never scores	Sunday

Figure 5.7. A middle school student's act of intentional kindness for a friend.

Image credit: J.T. Binfet

and adolescents be intentionally kind is to help them brainstorm and identify a recipient bank or a repository of individuals, places, or agencies that they see as needing kindness. Asking children to simply "be kind" is too vague. Their thinking about kindness needs to be concretely anchored in people, materials, and actions (see table 5.1). As such, educators might ask, "Who around you needs kindness?" This step is not to be rushed and educators are encouraged to challenge students to perspective-take and identify those around them who deserve a kind act.

Having asked thousands of public school students this very question, a few patterns in their responses can be anticipated. First, they can be stumped by this question, leaving educators with a "I dunno" or "Ahhhh, everyone" response. Gentle guiding can help students dig more deeply to identify those around them who could use kindness. Second, they are likely to initially and uniquely include their friends as individuals in need of kindness, perhaps because they are more acutely aware of, or have insights into, their friends' lives and who among their peers

Table 5.1. Suggestions for Developmentally Appropriate Kindness

	Early elementary	Upper elementary	Middle school	High school
Act	Consider kind acts that involve sharing toys or food (i.e., something concrete or tangible)	Kind acts may be anchored in materials but may also involve kind acts of communication (e.g., showing appreciation, giving compliments)	Kindness may reflect increased perspective-taking	Kindness should reflect increased perspective-taking
	Limited in their ability to take others' perspective		Can vary their approach to delivering kindness (e.g., can respond to a perceived need for help, can plan and be intentionally kind to a deserving recipient, etc.)	Can vary their approach to delivering kindness (e.g., can respond to a perceived need for help, can plan and be intentionally kind to a deserving recipient, etc.)
	Kindness may be co-constructed with an adult		Kindness may involve helping by instructing/ tutoring others	Kindness may involve helping by instructing/ tutoring others
			May co-create kind acts with peers	May co-create kind acts with peers
Recipients	Kind acts to one recipient (versus a large group)	Kind acts to individuals or small groups	Kindness to peers may be especially appealing (i.e., helps fortify relationships)	May consider extending kindness to school community or broader community (e.g., an organization in need)

(Continued)

Table 5.1. (*Continued*)

Early elementary	Upper elementary	Middle school	High school
Kindness to known or familiar others	Kindness to known or familiar others	May consider extending kindness to school community or broader community beyond school	May be challenged to show leadership in kindness (e.g., implement a kindness initiative in the school)
		Can be challenged to be kind to unfamiliar others	Can be challenged to be kind to unfamiliar others

might need cheering up by receiving kindness. And third, students may identify their friends as the recipients of their kind acts because doing so may be self-serving. Being kind to those around us helps to reinforce the social bonds that maintain friendships and keep friends close, letting these friends know they are important and cherished.

In this initial brainstorming phase, it is simply important to have students identify as many recipients as possible. This might include people they know, people unfamiliar to them but within their community, people further afield they have read about in the news who have suffered a hardship, or agencies (e.g., the Humane Society or animal shelter in their community), or even unfamiliar others within their community.

Once the brainstormed bank of recipients has been generated, educators can guide students in reflecting on their list of recipients and use further questions to help them reflect upon and evaluate their list. Prompts that might help guide this process could include:

1. Looking at your list, how can we group these people? Let's start by circling the names of all the people you already know.
2. Let's then draw a rectangle around all the people you don't know but who you think could use some kindness.
3. Next, let's look at your list and see who might need kindness the *most*. Are there people or places on your list that *really* need kindness – more than other people? Let's put a star beside their names.

4. Last, let's identify two people you know already and two whom you don't know. We can then use these recipients to figure out the kind of kindness you'd like to do.

Having students reflect upon the needs of others and sift through their bank of recipients helps them perspective-take – a key element in the development of empathy (Davis et al. 2019).

Tendency to Be Kind to Familiar Others

In study after study, when children and adolescents are asked to be kind, they have a strong tendency to enact kindness to familiar others. As we discussed in chapter 3, upwards of 80 per cent of the time, when given the option to be kind to any recipient, children and adolescents will be kind to those they already know (Binfet and Whitehead 2019). Certainly, this helps strengthen existing bonds and relationships but fails to forge new friendships and connections.

The implications of this tendency have far-reaching consequences for students who are socially isolated or maladjusted – who struggle to establish social connections with others. Take the example of a classroom in which the teacher, an advocate of having students be kind and of promoting kindness, assigns students to complete a series of kind acts. This activity might be an extension of a language arts lesson based on a book read in class. As science informs practice, a teacher who is aware of the propensity for students to be kind to those they already know would ensure that as students plan their kind acts, varied recipients within the class are chosen. To not do so contributes to socially disconnected students experiencing further social isolation, and acts of kindness being received only by those who have established relationships with the initiator of kindness.

Step Three: Planning a Kind Act

Once a recipient or group of recipients has been identified, the planning begins! Remember that there are different ways to be kind, and students can be guided in tailoring their kindness to the needs of their recipient(s). Guiding questions such as "Tell me again why you put _____ on your list of recipients of people needing kindness." Identifying the need of a recipient or the motivation behind enacting kindness can help shape the *kind of kindness* to be done. One means of guiding students in the planning of their acts of kindness is to have

Step #1: In the box below, draw a picture of something you have done kind at school recently. What have you done to show kindness at school?

WHO? _Self + New kid at School_

WHAT? _I am introducing myself to a new student to make her feel welcome._

Figure 5.8. A seven-year-old girl introduces herself to a new student.

Image credit: J.T. Binfet

them determine if they would like to do an act that involves materials, time/energy, or both. An examination of each of these options follows.

It Takes Guts to Be Kind

Children and adolescents, and admittedly many adults, can be shy about being kind. It takes a certain bravery to step up and offer assistance or take action, especially in contexts where this might not be the norm (see figure 5.7). In light of this, children and adolescents must not be thrown too quickly into the deep end of the kindness pool. Rather, it is best that students practise small acts of kindness that are met positively by the recipient, thereby bolstering students' "*kindness confidence.*" The subsequent acts they perform can become incrementally complex (recall table 5.1 outlining developmentally aligned suggestions for kindness). Remember, the job of educators is to instil and nurture a prosocial behavioural pattern of responding in students. Having them experience positive feedback as they practise being kind is key to helping ensure this behavioural pattern is reinforced and sustained.

Consider for a moment, a child whose act of kindness is rebuked. This might take the form of a recipient who misunderstands the intention behind the act and abruptly tells the child to "get lost." A former dean of my faculty went for a coffee with her husband early one Sunday morning. His order was straightforward, just black coffee; her order was complicated, involving precisely heated coconut milk, chocolate shavings, and extra foam topping. Not a morning person and having just rolled out of bed, the husband patiently waited for his wife to get her order. As he was waiting outside the coffee shop, holding his coffee cup, people dropped coins into his cup, thinking he was homeless and begging for change. Here, this act of kindness was met with laughter but that does not always happen when the intention behind a kind act is misunderstood.

Kindness through Materials

Planning an act of kindness that focuses on giving an object can help reduce anxiety that children might feel about being kind. Remember, and especially for students who are unaccustomed to doing kind acts, it takes confidence to step up and be kind to others. Grounding a kind act in an object can help redirect the focus or attention away from the individual initiating kindness. Consider the child who decides to welcome a new student to his fifth-grade class by drawing a map of the school, highlighting the best place to spend recess and where the coldest water fountain can be found. Introducing oneself and explaining all of this information could be intimidating and a task beyond the social capacity of the student. Having a map to share with the new student helps ease discomfort around the delivery of this act of kindness and moreover, giving a school map in this situation is a concrete reminder to the new student of the welcoming climate characterizing his new school.

Examples of kind acts that might involve materials could include:

- Making a homemade birthday card
- Putting a gift basket together to cheer someone up
- Sharing a snack or meal, buying someone a coffee
- Donating food to the local food bank

Kindness through Time or Energy

- Explaining an assignment to a student who has been absent
- Shovelling snow off a neighbour's driveway
- Babysitting with no expectation of payment
- Inviting someone to join an existing friendship group
- Giving directions to someone who is lost
- Unpacking groceries for a parent

Examples of kindness that combine both materials and time/energy might include:

- Baking a homemade treat for someone
- Fixing the flat tire on a friend's bike
- Collecting raffle items and selling raffle tickets as a fundraiser
- Making dinner for your family, including doing the dishes
- Tutoring a classmate in the design of a science experiment
- Making someone breakfast in bed

Step Four: Gathering Materials and Scheduling

It remains important that the materials required for an act of kindness are accessible to the child and are not cost prohibitive. It is also important that children's kind acts be developmentally appropriate. Sometimes they will need guidance to ensure their kind act is in alignment with what is expected for their age and in accord with the expectations their adult mentors have for their interactions with others. Consider the following exchange between a fifth-grade boy and his teacher:

TEACHER: "You've identified your dad as the person most needing kindness around you. What is something you could do for your dad?"

STUDENT: "Well, I could get him some beer. He drinks a lot of beer. That makes him happy. I can ask my older brother to buy him some. He's in high school."

A supportive teacher might respond: "I get that, but let's think about something that you don't need to buy. Is there something you can *do* for your dad to show him kindness?"

Scheduling the delivery of a student's kind act is important, as educators want to help create conditions that help ensure that the act done by the student is well received and the student, in turn, receives feedback about the behaviour. Ensuring the recipient is at home or available and that an interaction can take place between the child and the recipient during which the child delivers a kind act and the recipient can express gratitude for this act, are key elements to building kindness confidence and to reinforcing kind behaviour in the child. Consider for a moment, a child who gathers materials, is excited to deliver a homemade gift basket to a deserving recipient, only to find no one home. It amounts to a missed opportunity to experience what Post (2005) and others have called "the helper's high" that we discussed in chapter 3 – the rush of positive feelings arising from having been kind.

Step Five: Verification of Kind Acts

It is always important, especially when kind acts are planned for delivery within the community, that children and adolescents run their ideas for their kind acts by an adult caregiver. This helps ensure that the act is within the child's capability, that the act is likely to be well received by the recipient, and that doing the kind act does not put the child in harm's way. Recall our discussion of the guidelines for being responsively kind in the previous chapter, which included scenarios to foster discussion about the safe delivery of kindness to ensure child safety and welfare when doing kind acts. Imagine, for a moment, the child who, unbeknownst to his or her caregiver, decides to hand out homemade care kits (e.g., toothbrushes, toothpaste, new socks, etc.) to homeless people on skid row. Taking the bus and independently delivering these care kits without supervision could put the child in harm's way and run counter to his or her caregiver's expectations around being kind.

Step Six: Delivering the Kind Act

The sixth step in enacting intentional kindness involves the child enacting a kindness – delivering a kind act. Some children might need some mentorship here, which could take the form of practice sessions where the child practises delivery of his or her kind act. When, for example, the act of kindness is to give a compliment, this might be an act of kindness that could be practised before it's given. Roleplaying with a teacher or a peer can help clarify the intention, refine the language to be used, and decrease anxiety by practising.

Step Seven: Reflection

It is not enough that children and adolescents identify the recipients to receive their kindness, plan their acts of kindness, gather materials if needed, schedule the delivery of their kind acts, and bring their kind acts to life by being kind. It remains important that children are encouraged to reflect upon what they have done (see figure 5.9). First, it encourages children to continue perspective-taking. Identifying the recipient bank and planning kind acts required perspective-taking, that children considered and imagined the needs of others. Reflecting on the kind acts they have done encourages children to take part in additional perspective-taking. Second, reflecting on one's kindness invites a certain critical evaluation of one's behaviour. Was I kind enough? Am I kind in just one way? Am I kind only to people I already know? These questions encourage the initiators of kindness to self-assess or evaluate. This is important in order to identify areas of growth – ways that the planning and delivery of kindness can be improved. Last, reflecting on one's kindness reminds the initiator that he or she is a kind person and helps reorient a definition of the self in positive terms. This has implications for children's self-efficacy and self-esteem.

Educators can encourage children to reflect on their kindness by asking the following probing questions:

1. We know that not all kindness is the same. Of the kind acts you did this week, which was the kindest. Why?
2. Think back to when you did your kind acts this week. What words describe how the recipients of your kindness felt? What was it like for them to receive kindness from you?
3. We often think that it's just the people who receive our kindness who benefit. I want you to think about how *you* felt after being kind. How did being kind make you feel?

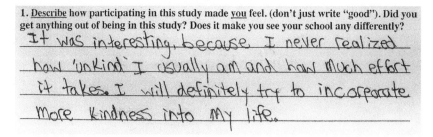

Figure 5.9. A fifteen-year-old girl reflects on the extent to which she is kind.

Image credit: J.T. Binfet

4. You're getting pretty good at being kind. If someone joined our group who was new to doing the kind acts we've been working on (say someone who didn't have a lot of practice being kind), what advice would you give them about how to be kind?
5. Now that you've had some practice being kind, who are your next recipients and how might you be kind to them? What are you thinking?

Conclusion

This chapter provided an overview of the second type of kindness: *intentional kindness*. Reviewed here were a series of steps that educators might use to guide children and adolescents in being intentionally kind to others. They included identifying a recipient bank, planning, organizing, delivering a kind act, and post-delivery refection. Being intentionally kind is an accessible way for young people to kickstart their kindness action plan, as there is ample structure to guide the crafting of their kind acts. Having introduced *responsive kindness* in the previous chapter and *intentional kindness* in this chapter, the last of the three types of kind acts children and adolescents might do is presented next – *quiet kindness*.

Chapter Six

Quiet Kindness

The example of kindness described by a seven-year-old boy is an act of kindness illustrating strong social and emotional skills (see figure 6.1), especially for such a young student. That he recognizes the importance of self-regulating his reaction to others and recognizes his doing so as an act of kindness provides a rich example of kindness that is socially and emotionally advanced. Recall the next example of kindness from our discussion in chapter 2 of the interplay between kindness and social and emotional learning (see figure 6.2). In that chapter I argued that this was an example of socially and emotionally sophisticated kindness as it required ample perspective-taking and empathy – key foundational skills that help predispose children and adolescents to being kind to others.

This example of kindness is shared again here as it illustrates an example of a third type of kindness – *quiet kindness*. Done by an sixth-grade boy, this is a sophisticated example of kindness in middle school, as it is grounded in ample perspective-taking (i.e., what would it be like to be Cole and hear others talking about their moms?) and empathy (i.e., how might this classmate feel when hearing other students talk of their mothers?).

Quiet kindness is defined as "kind acts that do not draw attention to the initiator and in which the initiator is anonymous, where recipients remain potentially unaware of the act, and acts that are not likely acknowledged by external agents whose role within the school might be to reinforce students' prosocial behaviour" (Binfet and Enns 2018, 31).

In my role as a researcher I spend a lot of time with students and with data – analysing findings and looking for trends across datasets. In scouring and reviewing the thousands of examples of kindness done by the students in my studies I was able to see patterns or similarities in

Step #1: In the box below, draw a picture of something you have done kind at school recently. What have you done to show kindness at school?

WHO? _____ self _____

WHAT? __ I don't laugh at people. _____

Figure 6.1. A seven-year-old boy shares his act of kindness.

Image credit: J.T. Binfet

| Act 2: Be more careful of mentioning things about my mom in front of Cole because his died of cancer last year | For: Cole he is my class mate and friend. | (YES) |
| | | NO |

Figure 6.2. A twelve-year-old boy describes his quiet act of kindness for a classmate in response to the prompt "Describe and act of kindness that you can do over the course of the next week."

Image credit: J.T. Binfet

Describe each kind act below (be detailed!).	Describe who this kind act is for and how you know this person (e.g., classmate, friend, teacher, stranger)	Do you know this person or group? Circle one.
Act 1: Leave money in the vending machine for someone	For: Stranger	YES (NO)

Figure 6.3. A middle school student leaves change for a stranger.

Image credit: J.T. Binfet

how young people demonstrated kindness. In effect, this is how I identified the three categories of kindness that are at the core of this book. It was during my analysis of these examples of kindness that I was struck by the kind acts done by students that were not big Broadway productions – publicly enacted and drawing the attention of all those around the initiator or recipient. Hidden among the many examples of *responsive* and *intentional* kind acts were kind acts that flew beneath the radar of all those around them – except the initiator and possibly the recipient. Take, for example, the example in which a fourteen-year-old boy describes his act of kindness of leaving leftover change in the vending machine for the next person to arrive (see figure 6.3). This example of kindness fits our criteria for an act of *quiet kindness,* as it is anonymously delivered and there is no acknowledgment of the act or appreciation of the act expressed by the recipient to the initiator. What follows is a review of acts that are quiet on all levels – in their planning, in their delivery, and in how the recipient experiences the kind act.

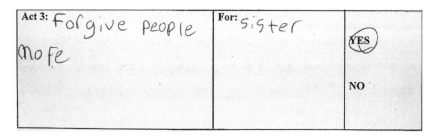

Figure 6.4. A fourteen-year-old boy's act of quiet kindness toward his sister in response to the prompt "Describe an act of kindness that you can do over the course of the next week."

Image credit: J.T. Binfet

Kindness without an Audience

Quiet kindness is an act of kindness for which there is no immediate audience. As quiet acts of kindness are done without the recipient being aware of who initiated the kind act, the initiator does not receive immediate feedback to reinforce his or her behaviour. Further, there is no external agent standing nearby to praise and celebrate a child being kind to others. It can be considered, then, an advanced form of kindness that might be delivered by children and adolescents who are socially and emotionally advanced in their development.

Pedagogical implications arise when children and adolescents are quietly kind. As these acts typically go unnoticed by adult caregivers and educators, they do not contribute to the perception and understanding of the child as prosocial. That is, educators will expect the children around them to be prosocial, and when children are quietly kind, they furnish no evidence to the adults around them that they are, in fact, kind (see figure 6.4). So adults must have a sensitivity to recognize that kindness comes in multiple forms and that not all children demonstrate their prosociality in overt, easily recognizable ways (see table 5.8 in the previous chapter as a reminder of the developmental differences in kindness). Imagine the child who, when told she needs to be kind to others, responds with "But I'm already kind!" because she engages in regular *quiet kindness* to others.

Educators are also encouraged to consider that children and adolescents may have rich prosocial online lives. Even, for example, within the often violent world of online gaming where battles with others are common, children and adolescents will report being kind to others (e.g., "I could have taken him out but I let him live").

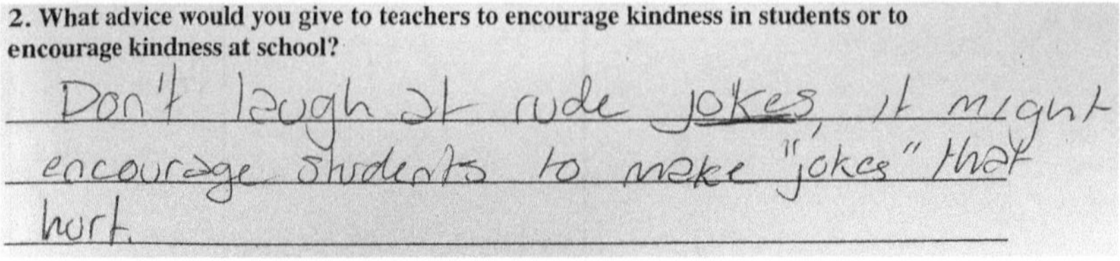

2. What advice would you give to teachers to encourage kindness in students or to encourage kindness at school?

Don't laugh at rude jokes, it might encourage students to make "jokes" that hurt.

Figure 6.5. A fifteen-year-old girl gives advice to teachers about how to encourage kindness.

Image credit: J.T. Binfet

The Role of Reinforcement in Shaping Prosocial Behaviour

Not surprisingly, prosocial behaviour throughout childhood may be shaped through socialization from parents, educators, peers, and media, which all reinforce children's behaviour and their understanding of what is expected of them in their interactions with others (see figure 6.5). This reinforcement might take the form of a child receiving praise or even a reward for being kind, engaging in a pleasant interaction with someone as a result of a kind act, experiencing positive emotions after being kind, and a certain satisfaction from adhering to social norms (Davidov et al. 2016).

Educators are encouraged to reflect on their approach to, and beliefs about, reinforcing the kind acts they see the young people around them complete. As with many topics situated within the realm of education, not everyone agrees on the reinforcing of prosocial behaviour (Biglan 2003; Dahl 2015). In fact, there is evidence to suggest that reinforcing children for being kind can thwart their motivation to continue engaging in kind acts. In a study by Warneken and Tomasello (2014), toddlers in three reinforcement conditions (social praise, material reinforcement, no reinforcement) were assessed to determine the effect of reinforcement on their prosocial behaviour. Findings from their study revealed that the use of material reinforcement (i.e., a reward) did not encourage prosocial behaviour in young children. Certainly, the liberal overuse of rewards is likely to be ineffective, but as Dahl (2015) argues, reinforcements can be especially potent when the motivation of children is low. Educators might begin by using material reinforcements to engage and motivate a child to engage in desired behaviours and then reduce the frequency of rewards or wean the child off reinforcements.

In light of the complex social and emotional environments in which children find themselves, there is ample variability in the extent to which children's kindness is encouraged and reinforced, especially within their home environment. This variability is consistent with broader parenting practices that see children receive varying levels of reinforcement, depending on the social environment within which they are raised (Bower and Casas 2016). As a general trend noted by educators across contexts, educators are increasingly seeing children arrive to school underequipped socially and emotionally to face the challenges of public school education (Jennings and Greenberg 2009). The social and emotional skills that were historically taught within the home environment are now being taught as part of the routine educational experience for children. This shift puts particular onus on educators to help shape the social and emotional lives of the young people under their tutelage.

High- versus Low-Cost Prosocial Behaviour

Not all kind acts are the same. Whereas some kind acts require time or energy of the initiator (e.g., shovelling snow from a neighbour's sidewalk), other kind acts can involve coordination of elaborate materials (e.g., creating a gift basket for a friend who is ill). Little has been written on how kind acts are differentiated. But we find a framework for understanding just how kind acts differ or vary by complexity in the work of Padilla-Walker and colleagues (2018), who argue there are *low-* versus *high-*cost prosocial behaviours. As they posit, "High-cost prosocial behaviors are those that require some sort of expenditure from the individual (e.g., money, time, emotional capital) such as moral courage or personal burden" (1855). They further argue that high-cost prosocial behaviours comprise two types of actions predominantly: defending behaviours ("e.g., defending a sibling against a bully," 1854); and including behaviours ("e.g., helping an ostracized peer feel part of the group," 1854). Prosocial behaviours such as defending and including others help to build relationships and contribute to one's community. In adolescence certainly, these acts reflect young people's increasing engagement and concern about community, civic responsibility, and politics.

This discussion of *low- versus high-cost* prosocial acts helps advance and contextualize our understanding of acts of *quiet kindness*, as *quiet kindness* may be considered a *low-cost* act of kindness in light of the low expectations around interacting with others to deliver the act and the extent to which the individual doing the quiet kind act is socially engaged with recipients. Certainly, in contrast to *high-cost* prosocial acts such as defending and including, quiet acts of kindness do not offer initiators the opportunity to receive feedback from their recipient, and initiators of *quiet kindness* might be considered to be kind within a low stimulus or low feedback context. These individuals are not typically thanked for their kindness, nor do they typically witness the gratitude of their recipients. Our discussion above helps us understand that there are a range of kind acts done by children and adolescents and that they vary considerably. Future research would be wise to disentangle the complexities of the kind acts done by children and adolescents to ascertain if young people themselves are aware of the differences inherent in the kind acts they perform and if performing *low-* versus *high-cost* acts has a differential impact on well-being.

Which Kind Act First?

Thus far in our discussion and differentiation of kind acts, we have reviewed *responsive* kindness (i.e., physically or emotionally responding to someone in need), *intentional* kindness (i.e., planning a kind act), and *quiet* kindness. Reflecting on these three and in light of the sophisticated nature of *quiet* kindness with its requisite social and emotional skills, educators might have children and adolescents practise *quiet* kindness after they have practised *responsive* and *intentional* kindness. There is one exception to this recommendation, however: might *quiet* acts of kindness appeal to shy or introverted students?

Quiet Kindness for Introverted Students?

When we think about what is involved in children and adolescents engaging in *responsive* or *intentional* kindness, there are social expectations of the delivery of these kind acts. That is, the initiator is required to interact and engage with others. This might prove a barrier for some students and may thwart their engagement in any kindness planning and discussions educators might want to undertake with them. For socially shy or introverted students, enacting kindness to others can be overwhelming and outside their comfort zone. In this regard, we see *quiet* kindness – which requires little social interaction – an appealing entry point into the world of kindness for particularly shy students. Planning and enacting *quiet* acts of kindness can be less threatening than performing other forms of kindness and may be an entry point for some students to get them engaged in being kind to others (see figures 6.6, 6.7, and 6.8).

Step #1: In the box below, draw a picture of something you have done kind at school recently. What have you done to show kindness at school?

WHO? <u>Self + teacher</u>

WHAT? <u>She is doing her homework and behaving for her teacher.</u>

Figure 6.6. A seven-year-old's illustration of her kind act for her teacher.

Image credit: J.T. Binfet

Step #2: In the box below, draw a picture of something you have done kind at school recently. What have you done to show kindness at school?

WHO? _Self + teacher_

WHAT? _I'm helping the teacher by listening_

Figure 6.7. A six-year-old boy illustrates listening as his kind act.

Image credit: J.T. Binfet

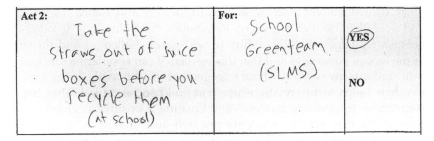

| Act 2: Take the straws out of juice boxes before you recycle them (at school) | For: School Greenteam. (SLMS) | YES NO |

Figure 6.8. A fourteen-year-old boy describes his kindness to his school's recycling club in response to the prompt "Describe an act of kindness that you can do over the course of the next week."

Image credit: J.T. Binfet

Kindness for Organizations

Related to our discussion situating *quiet* acts of kindness as perhaps appealing to introverted students, they might also find performing kind acts for organizations rather than individuals, appealing. Organizations or agencies might consist of the student's local food bank, homeless shelter, or humane society/animal shelter. In doing acts of kindness for an organization, the child is able to sidestep many of the social interactions associated with delivering an act of kindness to any one individual. In this regard, having children and adolescents plan, design, and deliver acts of kindness to organizations might be a first step to building children's *kindness confidence*. In turn, as their confidence builds around being kind, these children can expand their recipient bank to include both organizations and individuals.

How Can I Ask My Students to Help Others When They Themselves Need Help?

Is it reasonable for a teacher working in an under-resourced school within an underserved community, where students may struggle with food insecurity, transient housing, and a host of challenges related to poverty (e.g., high rates of parental unemployment, community violence), to encourage and ask students to be kind, especially to an organization in need? We might find partial answers to this question by drawing on what is known about the benefits of being kind for individual well-being discussed in chapter 3. As a starting point, it is important to recognize that in schools in underserved communities, many factors work against student motivation to learn, student attendance at school, and overall student engagement. Remember that being kind to others bolsters resiliency (i.e., the ability to withstand challenges and thrive in the face of adversity) and that this resiliency can counter factors that pull students away from school engagement. Additionally, being kind to others helps fortify relationships and build social capital. This, too, contributes to unifying students and creating a positive peer subculture or alliance. Having students research and identify a non-profit organization within their community that needs support provides an opportunity for students to perspective-take, to identify needs "in the other," and to strategize ways that kindness might be delivered to offer support. Engaging students in this exercise, whether they manifest a donation or an action item for the organization, might be of secondary importance to the process.

Conclusion

Quiet acts of kindness can reflect advanced social and emotional development of the children and adolescents who do them. They require strong perspective-taking and empathic skills – to imagine what it is like to "be the other." Given their relative sophistication, educators might have students first practise *responsive* and *intentional* acts of kindness and then graduate to planning and enacting *quiet* acts of kindness. That said, for shy or especially introverted students, being *quietly* kind can be appealing and inviting, especially when the other forms of kindness are socially intimidating. The aim of these last three chapters has been to illustrate that not all kindness is the same and that children and adolescents can and do engage in differentiated ways to demonstrate they are kind. Many educators strive to create conditions in which kindness can flourish for the young people under their care, where expectations for being kind are established and communicated, and where guidance is provided, as needed, to support young people being kind to others. In the chapter that follows, an applied look at just how educators might foster kindness in children and adolescents is offered.

Chapter Seven

Fostering Kindness in Students and in Schools

Perhaps you have picked up this book because you are keen to help the young people around you or because you would like to see your environment characterized by increased kindness. Whatever the reason, recognize that, as an educator, you play a key role in creating and shaping the extent to which kindness is evident around you. I refer to teachers as the *custodians of classroom kindness* and encourage them to be thoughtful about how they cultivate kindness – let the science-informed ways and the benefits that arise from being kind discussed in chapter 3 inform your approach to fostering kindness (revisit figure 3.6 for an overview of the benefits arising from being kind). The aim of this chapter is to take an applied focus and explore strategies that educators might use to create the conditions in which kindness might thrive within their classrooms and beyond and to mentor and educate young people about how they might enact kindness to those around them (see figure 7.1). While you read this chapter, keep the students you are concerned about at the forefront of your thinking as you determine which strategies will best support their kindness journey. Remember, being kind to others has transformative power – it can change the way students think about themselves, about those around them, and about their communities.

Although this book was written primarily as a guide for educators, it will inform how parents interact with and nurture the development of their children. It also stands to teach children and adolescents themselves. I will be thrilled to receive correspondence from students writing to tell me this book affected their thinking about kindness and how they interact in the world, especially within school. The decision to be kind to others and complete a series of kind acts can be made by students themselves – and often is. That is, children and adolescents do not have to wait for the guidance and direction of adults but can initiate

Step #2: Draw a picture that shows a teacher doing something kind. What might a teacher do to show kindness at school?

WHO? _Teacher + Classmates._

WHAT? _Teacher is helping my friend with his work. She wants him to do his best._

Figure 7.1. A seven-year-old boy's observation of his teacher being kind.

Image credit: J.T. Binfet

kind acts themselves, recognizing that kindness has been described as a "happiness-increasing strategy" (Lyubomirsky et al. 2005).

Related to the idea of students participating in a *kindness regime* – thoughtfully and purposefully being kind to others to boost their well-being – is the broader philosophical question that educators might consider as they reflect on how best to support children: Should children in need of social and emotional support uniquely be the recipients of resources, or should they also generate support for others as way to bolster their well-being? The typical approach to supporting young people, especially those who struggle, is to pour resources into them – to have adult caregivers offer strategies or service. Although this approach is warranted, it might be done in conjunction with students themselves participating in their own search for solutions. By completing kind acts, the child or adolescent is positioned as the recipient of resources, but also as the generator of service to others – it is through giving of themselves that young people activate a solution to their situation or challenge. As argued by Magen and Aharoni (1991, 140), "Academic and social settings should be planned to provide adolescents with opportunities for committing themselves to giving to others."

Take, for example, a high school student who notices he is losing interest in previously enjoyed activities and in spending time with others. Wanting to share with the school counsellor how he is feeling, he puts his name on a waitlist and, in the meantime, as he has been taught in his high school introductory psychology class about the benefits of being kind, he initiates a kindness well-being plan to dig himself out of his rut. As his homeroom teacher always told his class, "The last thing you want to do is the first thing you should do," so he started small by saying hello to three people in the hall and holding the door open for one person each day. The immediate feedback made him feel more hopeful and positively shifted his outlook – ever so slightly.

Once children and adolescents have a foundation in "how to be kind" and understand the benefits of being kind, they can self-administer kindness as a strategy to bolster their well-being. Kerr and colleagues (2015) refer to this as "pre-treatment activities" – a way of taking care of oneself while awaiting outside help. At the very least, children and adolescents should participate in maintaining and safeguarding their well-being. And as Lyubomirsky and Layous (2013) argue in their description of the *positive activity model* covered in chapter 3, there must be alignment between the interests of the individual and the acts of kindness being performed. In this regard, educators might consider guiding or coaching children and adolescents in customizing their kind acts to reflect who they are and their interests.

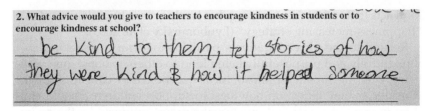

Figure 7.2. A sixteen-year-old girl gives advice on how teachers
can encourage kindness.

Image credit: J.T. Binfet

What follows is a review of strategies for educators to help create optimal conditions in which kindness can flourish in the lives of children and adolescents (see figure 7.2).

Considerations for Educators

Fostering Kindness Can Be a Low-Cost and Low-Resource Undertaking

In addition to the intra- and interpersonal benefits of having children and adolescents complete kind acts, benefits that can positively influence well-being and classroom climate, having students perform kind acts can be a low-cost and low-resource-intensive undertaking. Educators working in under-resourced schools where, for example, the purchasing of, or access to, resources or professional development opportunities are restricted, can find comfort in knowing that enacting kindness to others need not be expensive or require a variety of materials (see box 7.1). After asking thousands of students about how they are kind in school, it is evident that students show kindness to others by designing acts of kindness reflecting a commitment of only time or energy.

Stress Counters Kindness

As educators strive to create optimal conditions for children and adolescents in which kindness can thrive, keep in mind that stress can thwart and hinder prosocial behaviour. Kindness in children and adolescents is best showcased when stress is low. Davis, Martin-Cuellar, and Luce (2019, 205) argue that prosocial behaviour is inversely related to stress experienced: "Stressful experiences can contribute to negative behavioral outcomes, particularly when the stress is overwhelming, because young adults may have become depleted of emotional and cognitive resources and become increasingly withdrawn from social interactions as a result of exposure to stressful events."

Box 7.1. Low-Cost/Low-Resource Acts of Kindness Students Can Do at School

1. Show respect for the school community by picking up trash around the school.

2. Identify five people to say hello to in your school and mention their name as part of your greeting.

3. Hold the door open for the people behind you.

4. Make sure you smile at three people as you make your way from the gym to your classroom.

5. Tutor someone in a subject that you're strong in.

6. Offer to be the technology resource person in your class to help your teacher.

7. When asked to work in cooperative groups by your teacher, be the first to invite a student who might struggle to find a group to join your group.

8. When in an online learning classroom, use the "thumbs-up" or "applause" icons to let classmates know you appreciate what they've shared.

9. Show appreciation to your teacher at the end of class (e.g., by saying "Thanks for a good class today").

10. Not laugh at a joke made to embarrass a classmate.

But not all stress is the same. Readers curious to learn more about stress and the impact of stress are encouraged to consult Cantor and colleagues (2019). They provide an overview of the science behind stress, illustrating that it may take one of three forms: positive, tolerable, and toxic. Each is accompanied by corresponding physiological indicators that have varying developmental implications for children and adolescents. Of particular concern to educators is when young people experience toxic stress, which is described as "frequent, prolonged, and unbuffered by adequate adult support" (Cantor et al. 2019, 323). The developmental repercussions of prolonged toxic stress are alarming. "The resulting chronic elevation of stress hormones can disrupt the maturation of children's developing brain architecture and physiological systems, with major implications for later life health, learning, and well-being" (323).

Joy and stress contagions. Did you know that we engage in "emotional state matching" (Huber et al. 2017, 703)? This is a fancy term for our tendency to align our emotions with the emotions of those around us. This sharing or passing of emotions can work positively and negatively. Popular terms to capture this process are "joy contagion" (i.e., when an individual with heightened positive emotions passes them to those around him or her) and "stress contagion" (i.e., when the

Step #2: Draw a picture that shows a teacher doing something kind. What might a teacher do to show kindness at school?

WHO? _teacher_

WHAT? _My teacher smiles to the class to show she is happy._

Figure 7.3. A six-year-old boy's illustration of his teacher being kind.

Image credit: J.T. Binfet

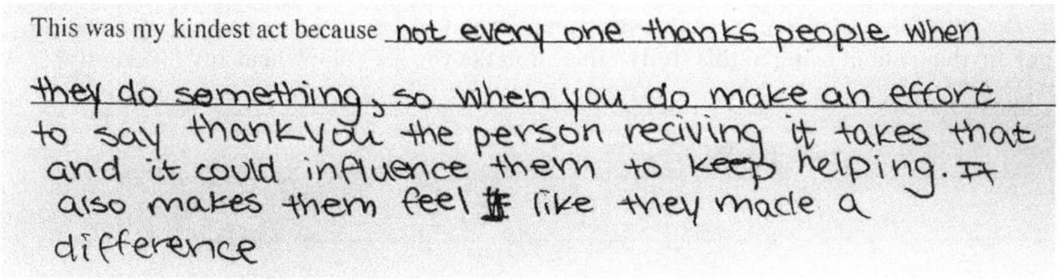

This was my kindest act because _not every one thanks people when they do something, so when you do make an effort to say thankyou the person reciving it takes that and it could influence them to keep helping. It also makes them feel like they made a difference_

Figure 7.4. A fifteen-year-old girl describes her thoughts on her kindest act.

Image credit: J.T. Binfet

stress of an individual with elevated stress is passed to an individual who is not experiencing it). Other terms that capture the transmission of emotions from one individual to another include emotional contagion, *emotional crossover, emotional spillover,* and *emotional transmission,* among others, and research has examined affective constructs that include stress and strain, depression, burnout, anger, joy, flow, and well-being (Frenzel et al. 2018).

There has been more research done on stress contagions than on joy contagions, though the latter field is gaining ground, thanks to the early work of Fowler and Chistakis (2008), who examined the spread of happiness in large social networks. In their longitudinal study of 4,739 participants spanning twenty years, they explored how positive emotions are transferred among individuals in social networks (see figures 7.3, 7.4, and 7.5). A key finding of their research was that happiness was indeed spread through social connections and that "happy people tend to be located in the centre of their local social networks and in large clusters of other happy people" (7).

WHEN KINDNESS IS CONTAGIOUS.

The benefits of prosociality do multiply, favoring not only those who give but also those who receive and observe.

Chancellor et al.

Research by Sparks, Fessler, and Holbrook has brought attention to the notion of "prosocial contagion," which they describe as the "process whereby witnessing a prosocial act leads to acting prosocially" (Sparks et al. 2019, 1). This is akin to the "ripple effect," whereby one act of kindness inspires and propels subsequent acts of kindness (see figure 7.4). This notion of kindness cultivating additional kindness has been popular on web-based kindness platforms and is linked

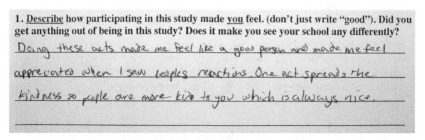

1. <u>Describe</u> how participating in this study made <u>you</u> feel. (don't just write "good"). Did you get anything out of being in this study? Does it make you see your school any differently?

Doing these acts made me feel like a good person and made me feel appreciated when I saw peoples reactions. One act spreads the kindness so people are more kind to you which is always nice.

Figure 7.5. A fifteen-year-old girl reflects on her participation
in a middle school kindness study.

Image credit: J.T. Binfet

to the social media phenomenon known as "pay it forward." Often within the context of fast food drive-through outlets, pay it forward sees a patron buy the beverage of the customer behind her who, in turn, buys the beverage of the next patron in line.

On the flip side of joy contagion or prosocial contagion is stress contagion, and innovative research done by Eva Oberle and Kimberly Schonert-Reichl (2016) explored the link between a teacher's stress level and the stress levels of his/her students. Using biomarker indicators of stress (i.e., collecting cortisol samples) from teachers and students, these researchers found that classroom teachers' burnout levels predicted higher morning cortisol levels in children. As these researchers describe, "Occupational stress affects the health and well-being of educators ... and it can also have an impact on the students they interact with on a daily basis" (Oberle and Schonert-Reichl 2016, 35).

Remember that the aim of this chapter is to guide educators on fostering kindness in students. We know that heightened stress works against kindness – we are less kind when we are stressed. We also know that emotions, whether passed from parent to child or from teacher to student, and whether the emotions are positive or negative, can spread from one individual to another (see figure 7.6). As we strive to create optimal conditions in which kindness can flourish in the lives of young people, we are reminded that the adult caregivers must be mindful of their own stress and happiness levels and the influence of their emotional state on the emotions of those under their charge.

Innovative research by Krane and colleagues (2017), in which they used semi-structured interviews and focus groups to ask high school

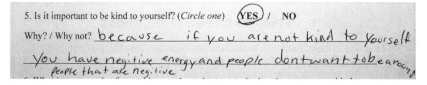

5. Is it important to be kind to yourself? (*Circle one*)   YES / NO

Why? / Why not? because   if you are not kind to yourself
You have negitive energy and people dont want to be around
people that are negitive

Figure 7.6. An eleven-year-old girl shares her thoughts on why
it is important to be kind to oneself.

Image credit: J.T. Binfet

students about kindness in teachers, informs our understanding of joy contagions within the school context. As one participant in their study summarized his expectations for teacher kindness, "I think it is important that the teacher smiles when he enters the classroom. He must greet the students and ask us how we are doing, and then the class can begin" (Krane et al. 2017, 383). The advice here from this student in the study is in concert with the early work of Rogers and Renard (1999), who wrote of the importance of "relationship-driven teaching" as a way to bolster motivation for learning in students. The link between joy contagion and relationship-driven teaching is captured in the voice of one other participant in the study of Krane et al. (2017, 383), who described the effect her teacher had on her disposition: "I get in a good mood when others are ... so that teacher makes schooling easier by smiling and being happy in class."

Educators, especially those working in under-resourced settings, can use several strategies to help understand the role of stress and its influence on student behaviour (see box 7.2).

Fostering a Positive Peer Culture

Related to the idea of joy contagion, the notion that happiness and positivity might be spread by those around us and through one's social networks is the idea of helping create positive peer cultures or positive peer micro-climates of social support for children and adolescents. The thinking here is that a child's peers help positively shape behaviour and can influence the extent to which kindness is evident within friendship or social microcultures (see figures 7.7 and 7.8). This might include peer modelling and encouraging kindness, co-opting help in being kind to others, and on the flipside, discouraging unkind behaviour, as the examples from middle school students indicate.

Box 7.2. Low-Cost Stress-Reduction Strategies for the Classroom

1. As a way to foster kindness in students, incorporate "mindful moments" into lessons. This might include leading students in a deep-breathing exercise or by having students reflect upon and express gratitude to others. Teachers can provide structure to a gratitude activity by having students use a template such as "I know I'll feel better if I let _____ know how grateful I am for _____."

2. At the start of a lesson, have students indicate their stress level with a sticky note on a large thermometer posted in the classroom. This helps the teacher track stress trends in the classroom and provides a starting point for discussion on the importance of lowering stress when it rises.

3. Have students reflect upon and identify a "resource bank" – people, places, or activities students can access to reduce their stress. Titled "Where Can You Turn?," it helps reduce feelings of isolation and having to cope alone.

4. Consider collaborating with students to create a social and emotional recalibration station! This SEL recharging station can consist of a collection of resources (e.g., a stress ball to squeeze, a mirror to monitor breath, an hourglass to watch, etc.), and students can access it within their learning environment to reduce their stress.

5. Related to the resource bank and the SEL recharging station, guide students in creating an individualized resource titled "Things that make me smile." Personalized for each student, it comprises images of people, places, or things that make the student happy. Older students can include inspirational quotations combined with images.

6. Lead a discussion with students on stress and behaviour, showcasing that we become impatient, less tolerant of others' ideas, and more easily angered when we are stressed. Redirect the conversation to the notion of joy contagion and a discussion of our behaviour when we are feeling joyful (e.g., we are open to the ideas of others, we readily share materials, we collaborate).

7. Routinely lead the class in classroom climate-building to unite students and foster a sense of belonging. Activities could include (1) leading a discussion of how students received their name; (2) leading a discussion of crazy pizza toppings, with each group member adding an ingredient and collectively the group naming their pizza; or (3) leading the group in a collective counting where students close their eyes and, without two people calling out the same number at the same time, try to count to ten. Calling out two numbers at the same time requires students to start back at zero.

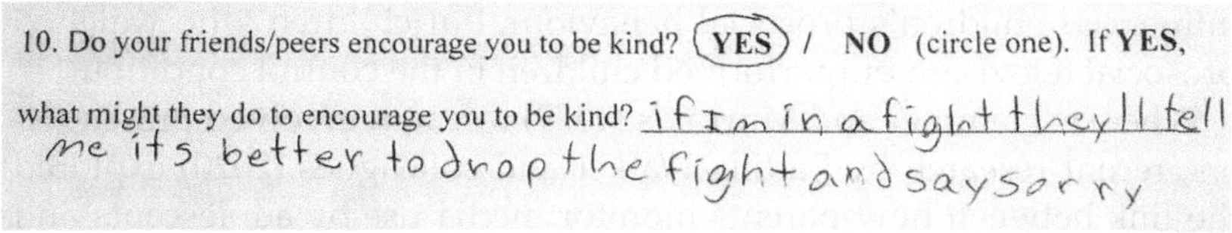

10. Do your friends/peers encourage you to be kind? (YES) / NO (circle one). If YES,

what might they do to encourage you to be kind? if I'm in a fight they'll tell me its better to drop the fight and say sorry

Figure 7.7. A twelve-year-old boy shares how his friends influence his behaviour.

Image credit: J.T. Binfet

10. Do your friends/peers encourage you to be kind? (YES) / NO (circle one). If YES,

what might they do to encourage you to be kind? if I say something mean they say that wasn't very nice.

Figure 7.8. An eleven-year-old girl describes how her friends influence her kind behaviour.

Image credit: J.T. Binfet

Ensuring There's a "Prosocial Media Diet"

Adolescent exposure to aggressive content in the media has consistently been related to increased aggressive behavior and decreased prosocial behavior with peers and strangers.

Padilla-Walker et al.

Hammer and Murray's (1979) pioneering study of the effects of prosocial television is a reminder of the importance of encouraging children and adolescents to consume "prosocial media" – at least to the extent that it counters media replete with aggression and violence toward others. In their early study of the effects of a "prosocial television diet" on ninety-seven preschool children, they assessed the effects on the prosocial behaviour of children who role-played altruistic scenarios, watched thirty minutes of prosocial television programs (i.e., where altruistic behaviour and low aggression was showcased), or watched neutral television programs (i.e., the control condition). The prosocial themes or content used in this study included examples that showcased "delay of gratification, task persistence, sympathy, resistance to temptation, control of aggressive impulses, and explaining feels of self or others" (139). Participating in altruistic role-playing most strongly influenced children's prosocial behaviour, but children who watched prosocial television outperformed children in the control condition.

Whereas Hammer and Murray's (1979) research involved preschoolers, recent research by Padilla-Walker and colleagues (2020) explored the link between how parents monitor media use by adolescents and the impact on adolescents' aggressive and prosocial behaviours. In their study of 945 ten- to eighteen-year-olds, they surveyed adolescents on variables such as their parents' monitoring of their media use, their secrecy and disclosure around their media use, and their engagement in aggressive and prosocial behaviour. Their findings revealed that the monitoring style parents employ on their children's media use influences several outcomes. As these authors summarize, "Parental media monitoring that encourages adolescent autonomy while still placing time and content limits ... or actively discussing the real-world implications of content seen in the media ... is related to decreased negative outcomes associated with media use" (192).

Extrapolating the early findings of Hammer and Murray (1979) and the more recent work of Padilla-Walker et al. (2020) on today's media-saturated environment suggests that, at the very least, educators remain mindful of the "prosocial media diet" available to children and adolescents. Whether it is being mindful of overall media consumption, balancing prosocial media and typical (i.e., uncensored) media, or engaging children and adolescents in generation of their own prosocial media content, it is important that educators remain cognizant of media access and exposure. Educators who incorporate media studies and technology into their teaching are encouraged to have students identify and generate examples of prosocial media as a way to help create a micro-climate that conveys the message to children and adolescents that prosocial behaviour can be normative, can be encouraged, and should be showcased.

Connections between social media use and our discussion earlier in this chapter on joy and stress contagions is established by the timely work of de Vries and colleagues (2018), who remind us of how social media may undermine well-being. They argue that "evidence ... suggests that individuals detect emotions in social media posts and adopt the emotions displayed in the posts themselves" (228). In their study of 130 university students, they found that participants who were high in social comparison (students who placed importance on how they measure up compared to others) were particularly susceptible to experiencing decreased positive affect after viewing other people's positive Instagram posts. For them, viewing others' positive social media posts failed to boost their own positive affect and had the opposite effect. The

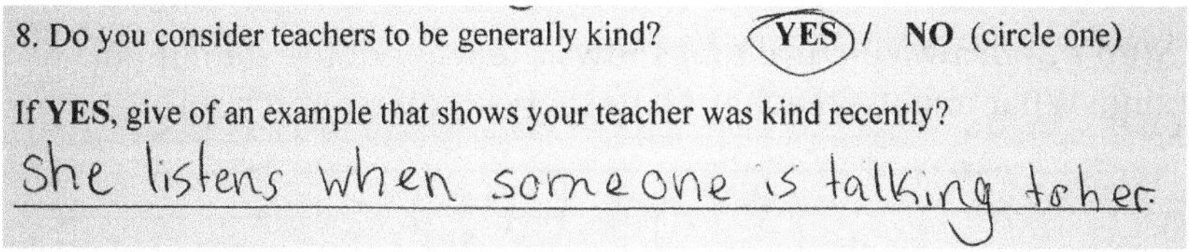

8. Do you consider teachers to be generally kind?   YES / NO (circle one)

If **YES**, give of an example that shows your teacher was kind recently?

She listens when someone is talking to her.

Figure 7.9. An elementary student describes teacher kindness as listening.

Image credit: J.T. Binfet

findings of this research help substantiate the idea that emotional contagion may occur via social media and support the notion of equipping children and adolescents with strong "media literacy skills" to help them navigate their use of social media.

The Power of Modelling

All eyes are on the teacher. The power and importance of a teacher modelling prosocial behaviour in the classroom cannot be overstated (see figures 7.9 and 7.10). In chapter 3 during our discussion of kindness research, I presented the findings of a study on teacher kindness that uncovered surprising findings about just how attentive or attuned children were to teacher kindness. In a study of 652 public school students in kindergarten to grade three, I asked students to draw an example of a teacher being kind. Findings revealed that students are highly observant of nuanced acts of kindness done by educators. Student observations could be categorized into (1) general behaviour directed toward the entire class; (2) interactions between the students themselves and the teacher; and (3) interactions of classmates and teachers. To illustrate students' understanding of examples of educators' kindness, a series of examples are offered.

Pedagogical Kindness

The term "pedagogical kindness" was coined in an article I published with Holli-Anne Passmore (2017) after reviewing student and teacher examples of kindness at school (see figures 7.11, 7.12, and 7.13). Initially described rather broadly as "an approach to instruction that integrates academic and social-emotional support" (47), I now see *pedagogical kindness* as an approach to teaching in which educators embed kindness within their pedagogical approach to supporting students' physical, emotional, or academic needs. Being

Step #2: Draw a picture that shows a teacher doing something kind. What might a teacher do to show kindness at school?

WHO?   Teacher + Teacher

WHAT?   Teacher is giving another teacher a coffee

Figure 7.10. A nine-year-old boy draws and describes his teacher being kind.

Image credit: J.T. Binfet

Step #2: Draw a picture that shows a teacher doing something kind. What might a teacher do to show kindness at school?

WHO? _____Teacher + Student._____

WHAT? _____Teacher is explaining something to someone
who doesn't understand._____

Figure 7.11. A seven-year-old girl draws how she perceives her teacher being kind.

Image credit: J.T. Binfet

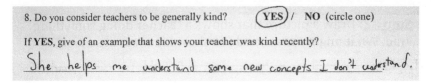

Figure 7.12. An elementary student describes a teacher teaching
as kindness.

Image credit: J.T. Binfet

"pedagogically kind" may be considered a part of educators' routine
professional duties.

The notion of teachers teaching through pedagogical kindness is
reflected in the work of Hyson and Taylor (2011, 76–9), who offer suggestions for adults seeking to foster children's prosocial behaviour.
They recommend that teachers strive to:

○ Build secure relationships
○ Create classroom community
○ Model prosocial behaviour
○ Establish prosocial expectations
○ Support families

Hamre and Pianta (2006) also inform our understanding of the role
of teachers in fostering students' prosocial behaviour. Their recommendations for facilitating close student-teacher bonds also help us
understand how to create conditions in which kindness can flourish.
Strategies that parents and educators might incorporate into their practice could be to:

○ Increase availability and reduce the barriers to accessing adults
   within the school
○ Explicitly teach students about social and emotional learning
   and development (i.e., increase and build students' "emotional
   vocabulary")
○ Engage children and adolescents in regular discussions and social
   conversations about life outside of the classroom (or living room)
○ Value the perspectives and ideas of children and adolescents by
   acknowledging their contributions
○ Employ behaviour management strategies anchored in clear
   expectations

Step #2: Draw a picture that shows a teacher doing something kind. What might a teacher do to show kindness at school?

WHO? _teacher_

WHAT? _My teacher shows us how to do work instead of just saying "Do it!"_

Figure 7.13. A seven-year-old boy draws his teacher being kind.

Image credit: J.T. Binfet

Box 7.3. Professional Development on Kindness: Workshop Ideas

The benefits of being kind: An overview of how kindness boosts well-being

Coaching kindness: How educators can guide students in being kind at school

Custodians of classroom kindness: Creating optimal learning conditions in which kindness can thrive

Catching kindness: Understanding emotional transmission within the school context

Modelling kindness: Understanding how educators can model kindness for students

Kindness in the community: Strategies for extending kindness to the broader school and community contexts

Collectively, addressing these different dimensions of the school experience helps children and adolescents understand that being kind to others is valued, expected, and nurtured.

Devote Professional Development Time to
Understanding Kindness

Though professional development opportunities vary from one school district to the next, teachers can advance their knowledge and skills via professional development training and information sessions. Educators must advocate for professional development on the topic of kindness as a way of helping create educational communities that value prosocial interactions among all the stakeholders within a school. Possible topics for kindness-themed professional development workshops might include any or all of the topics found in box 7.3.

In a pioneering article titled "Can Kindness Be Taught?" Schachter (1999) raised the importance of educators using prosocial literature to help students develop empathy – a necessary condition for students to recognize the need to be kind to others (see appendix I for a curated list of kindness-themed books for children and adolescents). Certainly educators can teach "stand-alone" lessons on kindness but kindness-themed information can also be integrated into existing curricula. Educators across disciplines can integrate kindness-themed content into their lessons by including mathematical word problems with prosocial themes, selecting a kindness-themed novel to read aloud in class, or having students identify examples of prosocial YouTube videos as part of a media studies class.

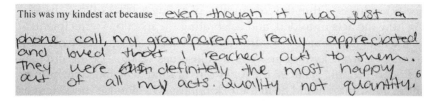

This was my kindest act because _even though it was just a phone call, my grandparents really appreciated and loved that I reached out to them. They were definitely the most happy out of all my acts. Quality not quantity._ [6]

Figure 7.14. A fifteen-year-old girl reflects on the quality of her kind acts.

Image credit: J.T. Binfet

The Importance of Reflecting on One's Kindness

It is not enough to encourage young people to be kind, as there can be rich growth in understanding kindness when we ask them to reflect on kindness and on their acts of kindness (see figure 7.14). In my research, I often include a question on the post-test survey that asks students to rank their kind acts from least to most kind. This helps me understand the qualities or mechanisms of kind acts that young people consider to be especially kind (note: this research is still underway and I have no definitive response on this just yet). Reflecting on one's kind acts evokes ample perspective-taking – how might the recipient have felt upon receiving this kindness?

Help Develop a Kindness Action Plan

One gift that educators can give to children and adolescents above and beyond helping to create conditions that encourage them to be kind is to mentor them in developing a *kindness action plan* or what I referred to earlier in this chapter as a *kindness regime*. The thinking here is that children and adolescents start by participating in a structured routine of being kind to others and then, over time, it becomes integrated into who they are as young people in their communities. Remember too, depending on the developmental level of the child, educators might be co-conspirators or collaborators and perform acts of kindness along-side children to get the ball rolling. Keep in mind that you will have to help initially, but once they are underway, the acts themselves will help sustain children being prosocial, given the well-being benefits that arise from being kind. Just like a parent who asks her children over breakfast, "Have you done your chores this week?," educators might ask, "Have you done your kind acts this week?" Extending kindness to the family context, discussions at the dinner table can include identifying who needs kindness within the community, planning acts for others, dissecting how the acts unfolded, and celebrating the reactions of recipients.

The kind acts done by children and adolescents, as guided by adults, should be what Lyubomirsky and colleagues (2005, 119) describe as "self-concordant." That is, the repertoire of kind acts done by children and adolescents should be in their "kindness wheelhouse" and align or fit with their interests, as advocated in the *positive activity model* (Lyubomirsky and Layous 2013) presented in chapter 3. A child who, for example, is an avid animal advocate, would derive joy from doing kind acts geared toward helping animals in his community. Likewise, a child with a strong interest in cooking or baking might do kind acts directed toward a local food bank. Aligning a child's repertoire of kind acts with the child's interests helps ensure there is sufficient motivation to complete the acts and also allows for innovation in the design and delivery of kind acts on a topic of keen interest.

Delving further into the development of a kindness action plan and building on the different types of kindness discussed in the preceding chapters, educators can assist children in creating action plans that comprise *responsive, intentional,* and *quiet* kind acts. As discussed previously, children might first practise *responsive* and *intentional* kindness to build their prosocial behavioural skill set and then graduate to doing *quiet* acts of kindness that require more advanced social and emotional competencies. Encouraging and mentoring children and adolescents in being kind in a variety of ways and to a variety of recipients is the goal.

Kind Acts and Students with Special Needs

I feel strongly, as do many parents and educators, that kindness initiatives that are undertaken, certainly those done within school contexts, must include all children, especially children and adolescents with exceptional or special needs. In an extensive search of peer-reviewed publications on kindness and children with special needs, no studies were identified. There has been limited scholarship on this topic, and what has been written is situated within the context of early childhood education. Here, authors recommend using social skills training programs that emphasize "kindness, empathy, and play skills" (Watson and McCathren 2009, 23). Watson and McCathren recommend that kindness, empathy, and cooperative play skills are best taught using four techniques: (1) modelling, (2) prompting, (3) puppetry, and (4) storytelling. This last strategy, the use of storytelling, enhances social skills in children with disabilities (see Lynch and Simpson 2010). Recall that

Box 7.4. Strategies to Make Classroom Kindness Activities Accessible for All Students

1. Recognize the power of modelling kindness as a teaching strategy. Reduce outside distractions for students to allow them to focus upon, and to draw their attention to, acts of kindness modelled as a part of lessons.

2. Identify each student's individual strengths and help students tailor their kind acts to reflect their skill set. For example, a student who is technologically proficient can do an act of kindness grounded in technology.

3. Calibrate the number of kind acts to be done by students to their developmental needs and capabilities.

4. In lieu of having students deliver acts of kindness to varied members of their class, consider pairing students and having students practise being kind within a small and supportive context.

5. As students with special needs develop their "kindness confidence," have them initially participate in kind acts grounded in materials (e.g., passing out sticky notes to classmates containing inspiring quotations) or definable actions (e.g., holding the door open until three people have passed through the doorway). Also consider scripting for students on how to deliver kindness to others or presenting information in a step-wise format. This might take the form of something like:"My name is _____ and I would like to do an act of kindness for you."My kind act today is to _____."Thank you for being my kindness buddy."

6. Be sure to pre-teach vocabulary and concepts needed as part of activities. Making use of visual and organizational prompts helps render the content of lessons accessible for students.

7. As perspective-taking can present a challenge for some students with special needs, use concrete reminders such as paper cut-outs of large shoes to remind students to "step into someone else's shoes" to understand how they might be feeling. Keep prompts short and to the point (e.g., "Who else around us has feelings?").

8. Encourage students with special needs to recognize how they feel when they are kind as a way of having them see and experience the stress-reduction and well-being benefits that arise from doing kind acts.

9. Consider co-constructing and co-delivering kindness alongside students, offering support where needed and stepping back when appropriate to allow students to flourish independently.

> Box 7.5. Strategies for Incorporating Kindness into the Classroom
>
> 1. Create a kindness corner where, using sticky notes, students can document and share the kind things they've done or received.
>
> 2. Host a calling out kindness discussion with students in which they can showcase and share kind things that happened to them during the week. This discussion can be linked to the kindness corner.
>
> 3. Give students a kindness media challenge that requires them to find the kindest video on YouTube to share with the class, including an analysis of the prosocial content found in the video and a justification of their choice.
>
> 4. Have students create a bank of ideas on how to be kind in response to the question, "If someone wanted to do an act of kindness in our school, describe what he or she could do." This repository of ideas inspire classmates seeking inspiration on how to be kind.
>
> 5. Guide students in identifying prosocial behaviour in course content and integrate kindness-themed literature (where aligned) into curricular expectations for students.
>
> 6. Give students a kindness ripple effect challenge in which they try to make kindness contagious.
>
> 7. Spearhead a kindness collection that requires the class to identify a nonprofit organization in need of support and to devise a campaign to raise awareness and funds to support the organization and its cause.
>
> 8. Give students a kindness on the downlow challenge and guide them in designing a series of quietly kind acts they could deliver within their school community. Afterwards, lead a discussion on what they know about how their kindness was received.

appendix I provides a curated list of kindness-themed books that might be used as part of a storytelling program to initiate discussions with children and adolescents about kindness.

Once the topic of kindness has been introduced, children, to the extent they are developmentally able, should be involved in the identification of recipients, the planning, designing, and organization of kind acts, the delivery of the acts, and the post-delivery reflection on what it was like to be kind to others (see boxes 7.4 and 7.5 for strategies). Materials may need to be adapted, acts modified to reflect the talents and interests of students, and timelines adjusted, but being kind to others should be an expectation for all students, and all students should receive the encouragement and support they need to help them enact kindness. Students with special needs stand to reap the well-being rewards that come from being kind – boosts to well-being and fortified social connections, among others. If there is one thing evident throughout this book, it is that kindness comes in many shapes, sizes, and forms, and it can be delivered via multiple pathways (e.g., *responsively, intentionally,* or *quietly*). In this regard, kindness is a flexible concept and topic for children and adolescents to tackle – there is ample freedom in how kindness may be crafted and expressed. There is no single right way to be kind. Educators working with children and adolescents with special needs are encouraged to engage the young people under their tutelage in exploring developmentally aligned ways to be kind. A list of resources to assist with supporting the learning of students with special needs can be found in appendix J.

TEACHERS AS CUSTODIANS OF CLASSROOM KINDNESS

Thus far in our journey, a great deal of material and terrain related to kindness has been covered. How this information is put into action is determined by you – an educator curious to implement kindness initiatives into your teaching. Educators must recognize that they are at the helm of their classrooms – creating the tone or climate, helping establish expectations, and nurturing or guiding students as they learn about themselves, the curriculum, and the broader world at large. The phrase *"custodians of classroom kindness"* is important to me, as I see the role of educators as nurturing a space in which students can be exposed to, experiment with, and develop proficiency in the concept of kindness and in how to be kind. Much like a custodian within a school ensures the school is safe and free of hazards, and that all moving parts are in working order, the teacher ensures that the mechanics of kindness are in place in a classroom – that kindness is modelled, expected, encouraged, and celebrated.

Conclusion

My hope in writing this book – and in particular, in including this chapter – is that it will provide ideas, strategies, and structure to educators seeking to create conditions in which kindness might thrive in the lives of the children and adolescents under their care. At the outset of this chapter, the role that stress plays in undermining the likelihood of kindness was explored. A discussion followed on how best to situate young people in a positive peer culture, and an environment with a strong prosocial media diet that encouraged young people to be kind was offered. Next came an examination of the importance of educators, recognizing the powerful role they play as prosocial models in the lives of young people, arguing that "all eyes are on them" in their role as mentors. The chapter ended with a look at the importance of professional development and its role in fostering professional competencies in the promotion of kindness. The strategies shared here lay the foundation for the next chapter on school kindness, where the key indicators of kindness in a learning community are explored.

Chapter Eight

Measuring Kindness: How Kind Is Your School?

This chapter provides an overview of the key indicators of school kindness and review measures that might be used to assess the perceptions of school kindness among the very stakeholders who want to create a school context characterized by kindness – educators, parents, and students themselves (see figure 8.1). What follow are descriptions of individual components of schools that, when combined, collectively indicate or provide a barometer for school kindness. Informed by current and seminal research, this chapter offers applied strategies for assessing the extent to which kindness is evident within a school context. We begin with an exploration of why the measurement of kindness might be important.

Is Measuring Kindness in School Important?

As a kindness researcher and a professor who regularly gives workshops, lectures, and public talks on kindness, I am clearly biased in my view that kindness should be situated front and centre in schools and that teachers should accord it ample importance as they navigate and negotiate life in the classroom with their students. As we have discussed throughout this book, a host of well-being benefits can arise from being kind. And teachers who want to foster kindness in their schools, knowing the extent to which kindness is already enacted and the perceptions of their school as a kind context, inform the delivery and implementation of any subsequent kindness initiatives.

As a scientist who studies kindness, I would argue that it is important for schools and for teachers at the helm of classrooms to have a sense of their starting point – the *kindness temperature* of their classroom (or larger school community). Doing so allows teachers to recognize how much is known about what it means to be kind and what students

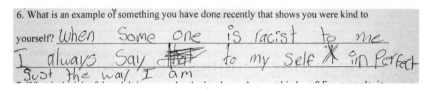

6. What is an example of something you have done recently that shows you were kind to yourself? *When Some one is racist to me I always Say to my self X in Perfect Just the way I am*

Figure 8.1. An eleven-year-old boy shares his strategy for dealing with racism at school.

Image credit: J.T. Binfet

understand about being kind at school and their responsibility to be kind at school. Taking the kindness temperature of a classroom or school can be done informally through observations and through discussions with students but can also be done more formally by using a scale to assess perceptions of school climate. Initiating discussion about kindness and the perceptions of kindness can also help identify barriers to kindness (e.g., elevated levels of stress experienced by students or staff) that might undermine the implementation of a kindness initiative. In short, measuring kindness informally or formally is an important step in understanding the context in which teachers might be trying to cultivate kindness.

Teacher-Student Rapport and Relationships

Healthy interpersonal relationships are facilitated, in part, by students' prosocial behavior, in which kindness can play a key role.

Binfet et al.

How students perceive their relationships with teachers in the school is of primary importance. Introduced in the previous chapter was the notion of "relationship-driven teaching" – a phrase coined by Rogers and Renard. They posit that "students are motivated when they believe that teachers treat them like people and care about them personally and educationally" (Rogers and Renard 1999, 34). Definitely progressive at the time of publication over twenty years ago, the suggestions from these authors to foster positive student-teacher relationships still ring true. Rogers and Renard advocated that educators adhere to six standards:

1. Create a learning context that is *safe*.
2. Ensure there is *value* in the work students undertake.

What is an example of the kindness this person might do?

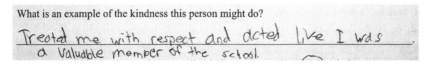

Figure 8.2. A fourteen-year-old boy describes a teacher's respect for
him as an act of kindness.

Image credit: J.T. Binfet

3. Ensure students experience *success*.
4. Implicate or involve students by creating opportunities for students to participate.
5. Show care and concern for students.
6. Enable learning by incorporating progressive teaching strategies and methods.

In concert with the idea that student-teacher rapport must be nurtured are arguments and findings in the field of social and emotional learning. The Collaborative for Academic and Social and Emotional Learning, or CASEL, which we reviewed back in chapter 2, shares information that echoes the early work of Rogers and Renard (1999) outlined above. In their blog featured on the CASEL website, Pekel and Scales (2018) argue that student–teacher relationships are the "missing link" in social and emotional measurement. They recommend that educators let the following characterize their interactions with students:

1. Expressing care
2. Challenging growth
3. Providing support
4. Sharing power
5. Expanding possibility

School Culture, Class Climate, and Sense of Belonging

School climate is informed by the accepted and endorsed norms, values, and expectations that together reflect the quality of school life.

Binfet et al.

Across suggestions for building positive student-teacher rapport are the recommendations that teachers take an interest in students outside a uniquely academic realm and that students are actively implicated in their learning (see figure 8.2). The importance of students' connections to teachers cannot be overstated, and Allen and colleagues (2018) go so far as to argue it is the most important determinant affecting students' sense of belonging. Goodenow and Grady (1993, 80) define school belonging as "the extent to which students feel personally accepted, respected, included, and supported by others in the school social environment." Their sense of school belonging affects the extent to which students engage in and demonstrate prosocial behaviour (Demanet and Van Houtte 2012). Having students engage in regular acts of kindness informs and shapes student–teacher relationships and students' sense of belonging as members of the school community. When teachers mentor and guide students in planning and delivering acts of kindness – intrapersonal, interpersonal, and contextual –benefits can arise.

Across the many studies I have conducted on kindness with public school students in which I asked students to plan and then do a series of kind acts, a recurring finding is that students are kind to those with whom they already have a relationship or connection (see figure 8.3). This was discussed in chapter 5 when we explored the ramifications: there will be socially isolated students who are overlooked and are not the recipients of their classmates' kindness. When given free rein to be kind to anyone within their social sphere, students largely choose to be kind to students they already know. As educators reflect on strategies to increase student-to-student cohesion, having students reinforce their bonds with their fellow students through acts of kindness is obviously a good thing. Of course, the flip side is that students who are not well connected to their peers are unlikely to receive their fellow students' kindness. In fact, when classroom or school-wide kindness initiatives are spearheaded, they run the risk of encouraging a flurry of kind acts within the school while further reminding isolated students that they are not on the radar of their peers. One indicator of a school's kindness would be how wide a net students cast when enacting kindness within the school context.

Having students participate in a series of school-situated kind acts builds their sense of belonging. As Riley (2019, 92) describes it, "Young people's sense of belonging in school is shaped by what they bring to it – their histories, their day-to-day lived realities – as well as schools' practices and expectations."

Returning to the work of Rogers and Renard (1999, 35) raised at the outset of this chapter, we see they argue for an approach to teaching that "involves managing the learning context, not the learners." As classroom climate is determined, in part, by the behaviour of students and teachers and a reflection of their interactions, class climate may be heavily influenced by the extent to which these interactions embrace kindness (see figure 8.4).

Step #1: In the box below, draw a picture of what kindness looks like. What does kindness look like to you?

WHO? _Self + classmate_

WHAT? _We're going to hug each other_

Figure 8.3. A six-year-old boy describes his act of kindness for a classmate.

Image credit: J.T. Binfet

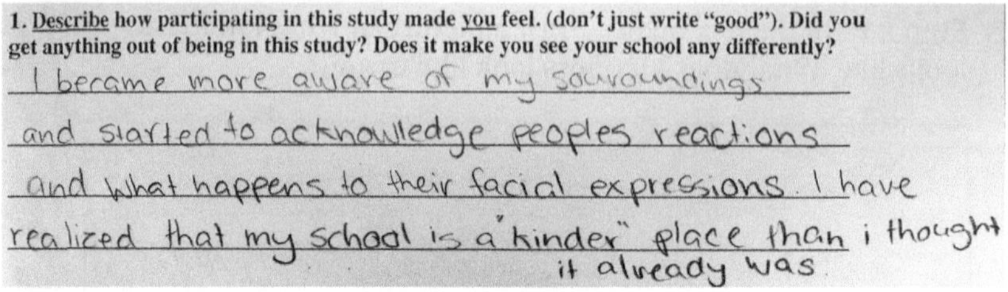

1. <u>Describe</u> how participating in this study made <u>you</u> feel. (don't just write "good"). Did you get anything out of being in this study? Does it make you see your school any differently?

I became more aware of my surroundings
and started to acknowledge peoples reactions
and what happens to their facial expressions. I have
realized that my school is a "kinder" place than i thought
it already was.

Figure 8.4. A fifteen-year-old girl reflects on participating in a middle school kindness study.

Image credit: J.T. Binfet

Teachers' Perceptions of Kindness at School

The bulk of our focus thus far in this book has been devoted to understanding students' perceptions of what it means to be kind and their examples of how kindness is enacted. It also remains important to examine educators' perceptions of kindness. In a study done with colleague Holli-Anne Passmore (Binfet and Passmore, 2017), we asked 257 public school elementary, middle, and high school teachers (with a mean age of forty-five and who had, on average, seventeen years' teaching experience) to share with us what kindness meant to them and how kindness was evident within their school, including what they did to demonstrate it. To our knowledge, this was the first study exploring kindness from the perspective of teachers. That, in and of itself, is surprising, given the key role teachers play in fostering kindness in students. It struck us that it might be important to explore just how kindness was understood and demonstrated by the very agents responsible for encouraging it in students.

Sampling across three school districts, we asked teachers to complete a teacher kindness survey (see appendix K). Teachers' definitions of kindness reflected three dominant themes: (1) caring (e.g., "Kindness is caring for the people around you and wanting good things for them" [Binfet and Passmore 2017, 42]); (2) perspective-taking/showing empathy (e.g., "Striving to understand the feelings and emotional states of others, and doing whatever they need" [42]); and (3) being respectful (e.g., "Kindness is showing respect to self and others through actions that reveal acceptance of individual differences" [42]). Teachers' acts of kindness within the school context revealed that the recipients of teachers' kindness are students (61 per cent) and fellow teachers (31 per cent) and that their acts reflected three themes: (1) helping (e.g., "Stay after school to sit and help students on course work one-on-one"); (2) giving (e.g., "Bought shoes for a student of mine in need"); and (3) caring (e.g., "Pull students aside to chat with them if I get the feeling they need to talk to someone" ([42]). Supporting teachers' kind behaviour in schools can be encouraged and supported by a school's mission statement. What follows is the examination of the important role a mission statement plays in declaring the importance of kindness for a school community.

The Importance of a School's Mission Statement

One indicator of the importance that a school places on kindness or prosocial behaviour can be found in the school's mission (or perhaps vision) statement. Designed to capture the key elements that represent the educational philosophy and commitment of the collective school body, the mission statement is an opportunity to declare publicly that kindness is valued, important, and nurtured. Coinciding with the shift more broadly from emphasis on uniquely academic dimensions of the school experience (e.g., "academic excellence"), we now see mission statements reflect dimensions of social and emotional learning (e.g., self-regulation, social responsibility). A school's code of conduct can also reveal the school's emphasis on kindness and reflect the importance accorded to negative (i.e., sanctions for misdeeds) versus positive (i.e., encouragement of desired behaviour) approaches to governing students. The code of conduct for an elementary school near my office contains a subsection titled "Be Respectful to Others" and encourages students to be "considerate of and caring for others' feelings and property." Underneath this subheading, students are provided with examples of ways to demonstrate how to be considerate of others, of which "Be kind and helpful" is listed. Posted on their website, this declaration of the importance of kindness for this school community can be seen by staff, parents, students, and the broader community.

When a school explicitly identifies kindness or the promotion of kindness as part of its mission, vision, or conduct code, it gives permission to school personnel to undertake initiatives within classrooms, hallways, playgrounds, and cafeterias that foster kindness. Not all schools (or administrators) will recognize the importance of kindness in fostering student development, peer relations, and overall school climate. But teachers working in such contexts are still able to undertake initiatives within their classrooms to foster kind behaviour in students (see box 8.1).

Box 8.1. When Enthusiasm Lags: Strategies for Teaching Kindness in Contexts
Lacking Broader School or Administrative Support

1. Let the decor of your classroom reflect the importance you place on
   kindness. Let your students be reminded visually of examples of kindness
   and inspirational quotations about kindness to encourage them to be kind.

2. Where content aligns with curriculum, integrate literature/stories containing
   prosocial themes. Use guided prompts to showcase the prosocial behaviour
   of characters within stories (e.g., "What is an example of the protagonist
   showing care and concern for others?")

3. Offer to start a kindness club within your school. As the faculty mentor, you
   can guide and mentor students in school-wide kindness initiatives.

4. Where content aligns with curriculum, invite community members or guest
   speakers to share inspirational stories of the kindness they've done or received.

5. Model kindness at every opportunity for students by walking the talk (e.g.,
   holding doors open for students and colleagues).

6. Let your classroom management plan be influenced and guided by the
   notion of kind discipline (Winkler et al. 2017).

7. When communicating with parents/guardians about student progress, be
   sure to comment and share with examples of students being kind.

8. Recognizing the potential of prosocial contagion, showcase and share
   examples of kindness you witness at school, especially those done in your
   classroom.

9. Create opportunities for students to be kind by asking for help with your
   in-school kindness initiatives (e.g., "I'm seeking three volunteers to help me
   create a kindness bulletin board in the front entrance to the school. Who can
   help?")

10. Place a jar or fishbowl on your desk and ask students to help you fill it with
    ideas on how to be kind. Incorporate it into your classroom management
    plan, encourage students to add ideas and select from the jar to do kind acts
    within the school.

The Hidden Curriculum

There is the school climate and culture that adults strive to create, and
then there is what Jackson (1968) coined "the hidden curriculum." "It is
the unspoken and unofficial norms and expectations that students learn
as part of their experiences at school (e.g., what is valued in a school)"
(Binfet et al. 2016, 114). Thus, there may be a discrepancy between the
climate and culture as seen through the eyes of the adult stakeholders in a school and the lived climate and culture experienced daily by
students, faculty, and staff (see figure 8.5). Jerald (2006, 3) describes the

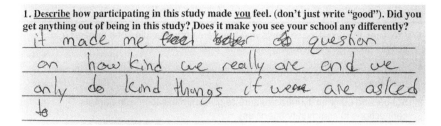

1. <u>Describe</u> how participating in this study made <u>you</u> feel. (don't just write "good"). Did you get anything out of being in this study? Does it make you see your school any differently?

it made me feel better to question on how kind we really are and we only do kind things if were are asked to

Figure 8.5. A fifteen-year-old boy shares his insights after participating in a kindness study.

Image credit: J.T. Binfet

hidden curriculum as comprising the overt lessons (e.g., curriculum emphasized) and the subtle messages (e.g., one trophy case in the foyer of the school celebrating athletic achievements) that are conveyed to students and the broader school community.

To address this discrepancy and own their hidden curriculum, some schools will attempt to demystify and render their hidden curriculum explicit. Capturing the voice of a middle school principal's efforts to do just this, Jerald (2006, 3) wrote, "In addition to [a] close emphasis on classroom instruction, we have what we call our 'hidden curriculum,' which develops personal relationships between faculty and students and deliberately works at developing character." Such attempts to minimize the discrepancies between adults' understanding of school climate and culture and the lived hidden curriculum as experienced by students can incorporate and be grounded in kindness. Our previous discussion of *responsive, intentional*, and *quiet* kindness can inform a school's mission statement and its hidden curriculum. It is by addressing, valuing, and supporting the desired behaviour and interactions within a school that all school stakeholders can be informed of, and work toward, these goals.

Kind Discipline

In scouring the kindness-themed literature, the work of Winkler and colleagues (2017) stands out as innovative and progressive. They encourage us to re-evaluate common practices on how school personnel support students who misbehave. They build a case for suspensions being ineffective and contributing to a host of negative outcomes for students. They argue for the need for "an alternate approach for school discipline that is grounded in neither individual punitive exclusionary nor reward-based systems, but rather supports students in thriving" (16).

Table 8.1. Characteristics of Kind Discipline (Adapted from Winkler et al. 2017)

1. Practices that facilitate students and teachers understanding one another (e.g., social and emotional learning principles, peer mediation)

2. Adult education (e.g., mentorship, faculty who seek to understand why students misbehave)

3. School and community infrastructure (e.g., communication with parents, connections to community agencies)

4. Student-centred accountability and connections (e.g., develop a "kind code" of conduct, student buy-in)

5. Collaborative and cooperative school climate (e.g., common language, non-judgmental support from adults)

6. Accountability with dignity (e.g., transparency, timely responses)

7. Honouring the kindness potential of every child (e.g., being proactive, avoiding embarrassing students)

8. Cultivation of positive character (e.g., fostering trust, practising patience, using humour)

9. Compassionate boundaries and empathetic reinforcement (e.g., forgiveness, clear expectations)

10. Collaborative expectations that empower growth (e.g., goal setting, opportunities for self-reflection)

11. Developing prosocial and conflict-management skills (e.g., understanding context, discussing possible choices)

Aligned with the concept of restorative justice, this study invited key school personnel to brainstorm, sort and rank, and interpret data on the characteristics or components of kind discipline as envisioned by teachers, administrators, and support staff attending a kindness-themed conference. Arising from this process were eleven qualities characterizing and defining kind discipline (Winkler et al. 2017, 17; see table 8.1). The characteristics here dovetail nicely with the qualities listed at the outset of this chapter of strategies to foster strong student-teacher rapport. The qualities we hope to see in the day-to-day school-situated behaviours of students are the same as those that educators are encouraged to embrace when addressing student infractions – humility, respect, trust, and forgiveness to name but a few.

Measuring Kindness

As argued in chapter 3, the chapter that provided an overview of research on kindness, overall, it was established that research on the topic of kindness is still emerging and finding a foothold in the psychological and educational literature. That is, there is a dearth of research on kindness, and of the published work done on this topic, only a small sub-component of the research is applicable to children and adolescents or is relevant for the school context. There are only a few scales available for researchers or practitioners to measure kindness and even fewer that are appropriate for use with young people.

Canter and colleagues (2017) published a forty-item kindness scale, normed on adults eighteen to seventy years, and Pommier et al. (2020) developed a *compassion scale* that includes a four-item kindness subscale, normed on 465 undergraduate students. Stiff et al. (2019) developed the *student prosociality scale,* designed to assess prosocial behaviour among university students. Normed on 428 students ranging in age from eighteen to sixty-four years, the scale required students to rate items such as "Provide emotional support to peers," "Help new students," and "Pick up other people's rubbish." One last kindness scale that merits mention is the *kindness frequency questionnaire* developed by Gherghel and colleagues (2019). Normed on American, Japanese, and Romanian adults, it asks participants to rate the frequency (*never* to *very often*) of nine items such as "I have actively listened to someone's worries and tried to cheer them up" and "I have helped someone by holding or carrying their things."

Historically, kindness researchers are indebted to the early work of Anna Comunian (1998) who, over twenty years ago, saw the need for a scale to measure kindness. Called the *"kindness scale,"* this twenty-five-item measure was normed on a sample of 407 participants aged thirteen to sixty years. Items found in the scale include "I am kind because people need kindness" and "I also know how to be kind to others" and were designed to measure kindness as a personality trait. It was not designed to measure kindness within any given context per se, nor to assess school-situated kindness. In my early academic work, after I reviewed the published kindness scales, it was clear that there was still a need for a measure to assess kindness within the school context. With the help of Ann Gadermann and Kimberly Schonert-Reichl of the University of British Columbia, I set out to develop such a measure.

The School Kindness Scale

The *school kindness scale* (SKS) is designed for research but with strong practical application (Binfet et al. 2016). Comprising five statements, this survey is an efficient (and psychometrically sound) way to measure students' perceptions of school kindness. Readers curious to learn more about the *school kindness scale* can easily find information about it online. Translated into several languages, the SKS is freely available to researchers and practitioners wanting to use it to assess kindness within a school context (see appendix L). Crafted to measure the extent to which kindness is modelled within schools and the frequency with which kindness is encouraged, this scale can provide a general indicator of how kind a school is. Scoring of the scale is straightforward, with higher scores indicating higher perceptions of school kindness. Normed on a sample of 1,753 students in grades four through eight (ages nine to fourteen years), several notable findings emerged from the administration of this scale to public school students.

Perceptions of school kindness across grades. Consistent with the finding that students' prosocial behaviour declines as they transition from pre-adolescence to adolescence (Caplan 1993; Hay 1994; Nantel-Vivier et al. 2009), students' perceptions of school kindness were found to decrease as they transition from fourth to eighth grade. When asked to rate their school in terms of how kind it is, younger students have significantly more positive views of their school than do their older counterparts. In light of this finding, there is need for additional kindness-themed interventions or the incorporation of kindness into students' school experience to help counter this declining trend.

Perceptions of school kindness by gender. When perceptions of school kindness were analysed by gender, it was discovered that, overall, girls have significantly more positive views of their schools than do boys. This pattern mirrors the research on the prevalence of prosocial behaviour by gender and is in concert with the research of Van der Graaff and colleagues (2018) and others (e.g., Carlo et al. 2015), who have found that girls demonstrate more prosocial behaviour than do boys. This difference in prosocial behaviour between genders may be explained by maturational differences in early adolescence (Van der Graaff et al. 2018) with girls' socio-cognitive functioning developing earlier than that of boys.

Future directions for the school kindness scale. Researchers have begun using the *school kindness scale* as an outcome measure in their research (e.g., Datu and Park 2019; Morgan and Cieminski 2020) and have also begun to assess its psychometric properties. In a study by Turkish researchers Yurdabakan and Bas (2018), the psychometric properties of the SKS were examined for use with ten- to sixteen-year-old students with the authors concluding, "The evidence suggests that scores from the Turkish version of the SKS are reliable and suitable to be used to assess school kindness in Turkish middle school students." Despite such promising initial findings, additional research employing rigorous scale validation techniques and the use of studies with cross-cultural designs are still required to expand the generalizability of this measure.

Table 8.2. School Kindness Checklist

Indicator	Description	Evidence?	
School mission statement	• Is reference to kindness made in the school's mission or vision statement? • Is kindness afforded importance and publicly declared important for all school and community stakeholders to see? • Are expectations to students clear on being kind?	Absent Weak Medium Strong	☐ ☐ ☐ ☐
Professional development on kindness	• Are faculty and staff given opportunities to learn how to foster kindness and the benefits of being kind?	Absent Weak Medium Strong	☐ ☐ ☐ ☐
Evidence of integration of kindness into curricula	• Are students given opportunities to learn about and discuss kindness as part of their routine learning experience? • Are students aware of the benefits of being kind?	Absent Weak Medium Strong	☐ ☐ ☐ ☐
Evidence of school-wide and classroom initiatives on kindness	• Beyond the integration of kindness into course curricula, is there evidence of classroom and school-wide kindness initiatives?	Absent Weak Medium Strong	☐ ☐ ☐ ☐
Implementation of kind discipline	• Are the principles of kind discipline evident in interactions with students who misbehave? • Are students who misbehave supported through a kind discipline approach?	Absent Weak Medium Strong	☐ ☐ ☐ ☐
Modelling of kindness by faculty and staff	• Are faculty and staff mindful of the importance of modelling kindness for students? • Do faculty and staff behave kindly toward one another?	Absent Weak Medium Strong	☐ ☐ ☐ ☐
Positive school and classroom climates	• From the perspective of students, staff, faculty, and parents, are the school culture and classroom climates characterized by kindness and described as being kind? • Is the "hidden curriculum" not so hidden?	Absent Weak Medium Strong	☐ ☐ ☐ ☐
Ecological evidence of the importance of kindness	• Is there evidence within the school that kindness is valued and celebrated? • Are reminders posted about the school that communicate to school stakeholders that kindness is valued and important?	Absent Weak Medium Strong	☐ ☐ ☐ ☐

How Kind Is Your School?

Many readers picked up this book to effect change within their students' learning communities. Consider the following checklist summarizing indicators of school kindness, presented here in a user-friendly format in the hope that it might facilitate discussion among faculty and staff (see table 8.2). It could be used launch a discussion on "where are we currently?" and "where do we want to go?" on the role of kindness within the school context.

Conclusion

As you think about determining just how kind your classroom or school context is, consider taking the "kindness temperature" rather than attempting to create a "kindness report card." Kindness is a complex and multidimensional concept. There will be areas of strength and of emerging strength, and areas that require attention when you evaluate the extent to which kindness is evident within your learning communities. Readers are reminded of the multiple benefits that arise from having young people enact kindness to those around them. In our next and last chapter, a review key elements of cultivating kindness is offered, as well as an examination of where the field of kindness might be headed.

Chapter Nine

Conclusion

Insights from a ninth-grader help put our discussion of kindness into perspective (see figure 9.1). In fact, it would be interesting to ask students, regardless of their grade level, "When you leave this school, how would you like to be remembered?" Many of us who mentor young people are motivated to pass along lessons to them that will make life a little easier – to reduce the road bumps in their journey. Helping to foster a *kindness regime* in the lives of young people can offer a buffer to the hiccups of life. As study after study informs us, being kind to others fosters well-being in the initiator, helps bridge connections to others and fortifies a sense of community, and can create a ripple effect of kindness. What follows is a review of key concepts and discoveries on kindness raised throughout the book, followed by a look at where the field of kindness might be headed.

Has Your Definition of Kindness Changed?

This book began with an examination of kindness definitions and, after reading an entire book on kindness, perhaps your own definition of kindness has morphed, changed, or evolved (see figure 9.2). Our definition of kindness from chapter 1 was "an act of emotional or physical support that helps build or maintain relationships with others" (Binfet and Gaertner 2015, 36–7). My sense is that this definition still holds but that our understanding of how young people bring it to life has deepened. Perhaps children and adolescents are much kinder than we think, and when we access their perceptions of kindness and how they enact kindness to others, we see that young people are kind in a variety of ways but not to a variety of recipients. The phrase "maintain relationships with others" captures our tendency to be kind to those with

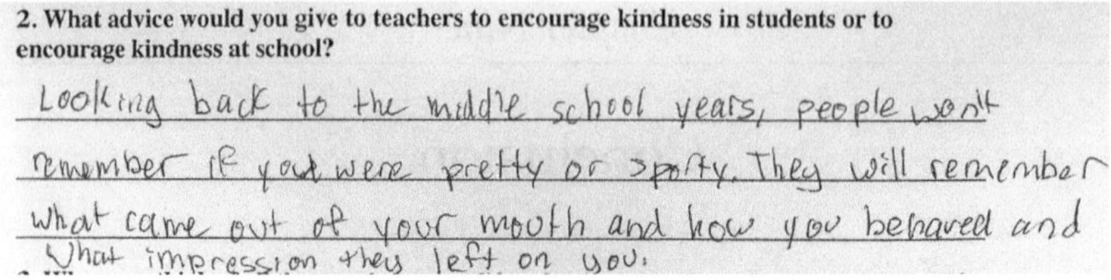

2. What advice would you give to teachers to encourage kindness in students or to encourage kindness at school?

> Looking back to the middle school years, people won't remember if you were pretty or sporty. They will remember what came out of your mouth and how you behaved and what impression they left on you.

Figure 9.1. A fourteen-year-old boy shares his advice to teachers on encouraging kindness.

Image credit: J.T. Binfet

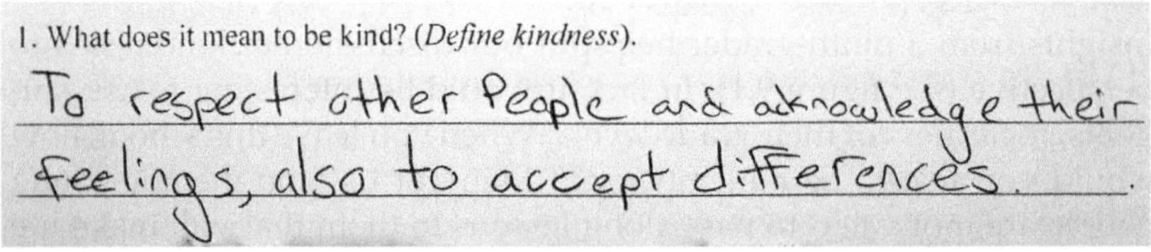

1. What does it mean to be kind? (*Define kindness*).

> To respect other People and acknowledge their feelings, also to accept differences.

Figure 9.2. A middle school student's definition of kindness.

Image credit: J.T. Binfet

whom we have pre-existing connections. That is, being kind to others fortifies our relationships to friends and family.

In chapter 5, in our discussion of intentional kindness, I tried to convey the importance of identifying a "bank of kindness recipients." It is at this preliminary planning stage of being kind to others that young people can expand their recipient range – practise perspective-taking to help identify who, around them and within their reach, could use an act of kindness. Here educators can encourage children and adolescents to reflect on their recipient bank and identify the recipients familiar to them and those they do not yet know well. Being kind to "unknown others" can foster rich intra- and inter-personal growth. It is by being kind to unfamiliar others that students will best learn about themselves and those around them.

Revisiting the Link between SEL and Kindness

In Chapter 2 we discussed the interconnections between social and emotional learning and kindness. There I raised the directional question: Does fostering social and emotional learning increase the likelihood young people will be kind, or does being kind to others foster social and emotional development? Likely a foundation of social and emotional competencies is required for children and adolescents to plan, deliver, and reflect upon their kind acts, but there is merit in the notion that planning, delivering, and reflecting on a series of kind acts holds ample potential to advance the social and emotional competencies of young people.

Recently, social and emotional learning has moved beyond the unique and bounded context of schools to include broader community and societal perspectives. We also see the possibilities for children's kind acts to broaden and include a wide and diversified range of recipients. Practising "arm's-length kindness," or kindness to those within one's immediate sphere or reach, is important. In doing so, young people can practise being kind within a safe climate or context. Moving beyond this comfortable recipient bank to include unknown others, the community, or even global issues such as climate change, are possibilities for young people seeking to expand their recipient bank. At the end of this chapter, an exploration of "kindness for climate change" is offered, inviting reflection on the potential it holds to engage young people in globally focused kindness.

Recall the Benefits to Well-Being Arising from Being Kind

Chapter 3 of this book was devoted to reviewing and understanding kindness research and the benefits to well-being that arise from being kind. It was evident that interest in kindness research is on the upswing, and more studies are being published on the role of kindness in the lives of children and adolescents and the benefits of being kind to others. Correspondingly, it is important for educators to keep abreast of these scientific discoveries, especially ones that illuminate our understanding of kindness within the school context – a unique applied learning laboratory where there are ample daily opportunities for students to be kind to those around them.

Recall that being kind is referred to in the psychological literature as a *happiness-increasing strategy* (Lyubomirsky et al. 2005). In light of the benefits that arise when children and adolescents have positive dispositions or are "happy," it is important for educators to be aware of the benefits to being kind, as being kind can help reduce rumination, create social capital, and foster a positive outlook on learning and students' school experience. Educators play particularly important roles in mentoring young people in understanding about, and enacting, kindness. Next, the three distinct ways that children and adolescents demonstrate kindness are revisited.

Children and Adolescents Are Kind in Different Ways

One takeaway after reading this book should be an awareness about the different and nuanced ways in which children and adolescents demonstrate kindness. This range of approaches to being kind can be very appealing and inviting for young people. There is not one right way to be kind, and children and adolescents can reflect on who around them needs kindness, the driving force behind their kindness (i.e., their time and energy versus material goods), how they would like to be kind (e.g., *responsive, intentional,* or *quiet*), and the impact on themselves and their recipients. There is ample leeway in how young people may go about being kind, and given their fascination with social media, they can be encouraged to creatively document their kindness – informally within the home context or more formally through class assignments and projects.

Alongside all of the kind acts done by young people is an opportunity for educators to guide, mentor, and encourage. In fact, as a starting point, I recommend that educators co-create and co-deliver kind acts. This close support in being kind to others not only serves to model kindness by adults for children but also helps create stronger links between the mentor and the child and, then in turn, between the team delivering kindness and their target recipients.

In chapter 7, the importance of guiding young people in the adoption of a kindness action plan or *kindness regime* was introduced. It can comprise setting expectations about being kind (i.e., the number of kind acts to be done weekly) and ample discussion on determining the bank of recipients for one's kind acts, the type of kind acts to be done, and post-delivery reflection and discussion about how it felt to be kind and how the recipient might have felt upon receiving these kind acts. Recall here too the normalization of kind acts: just as parents might ask a child, "Did you do your chores this week?," educators might also ask, "Have you done your kind acts for the week?" Related to the completion of kind acts is the reflection on the delivery of kindness to others. Here educators can engage young people in sharing their insights and perspectives on what it means to be kind, how it feels to be kind. Here they can practise perspective-taking and reflect on how their kind acts affected recipients. In short, a *kindness regime* provides ample opportunity for educators to engage young people in discussion. Reflect for a moment on the response of an eighth-grade girl from a kindness study I conducted who planned a series of kind acts (see figure 9.3). Her response presents insights into her thinking about herself and an opportunity for teachers to initiate discussion about the importance of kindness to self.

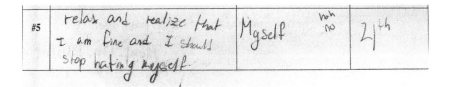

Figure 9.3. A middle school student's act of kindness for herself in response
to the prompt "Plan an act of kindness to be done over the course
of the next week."

Image credit: J.T. Binfet

Do You Have a Kindness Action Plan?

In chapter 7 the importance of educators modelling kindness for young
people was discussed. In that chapter, a young student recalled witnessing a teacher offer a colleague a cup of coffee. The power of modelling is not to be understated, and for adults who work with young
people, whether as a parent or a formal educator, having one's own
kindness regime provides ample examples of kindness for the children
and adolescents under our tutelage. Of course, having one's own *kindness regime* provides opportunities to invite or co-opt the talents and
efforts of the young people in our lives. Inviting them to lend a helping
hand in designing and delivering kind acts helps strengthen the bonds
between adults and children and creates new bonds with the targets
of your cooperative kindness. Thus, as a mentor to young people, my
question to educators is *How invested are you in* your *kindness action plan?*

Indicators of a Kind School

Chapter 8 explored a variety of kindness indicators that might characterize a school. Informal indicators such as student-teacher rapport and
class climate, and more formal ways to assess school kindness via the
school kindness scale (Binfet et al. 2016) were presented. Throughout this
chapter, it was emphasized that a school's kindness rating is gleaned
from a composite of factors. As outlined in the *school kindness checklist*
(see table 8.2), when a number of indicators are considered collectively,
they help determine just how kind a school is. Teasing apart these different factors helps educators target the components of school kindness.
They might consist of advocating for school-wide kindness initiatives,
professional development on the topic of kindness for educators, or
the integration of kindness within the curricula. In this chapter, the

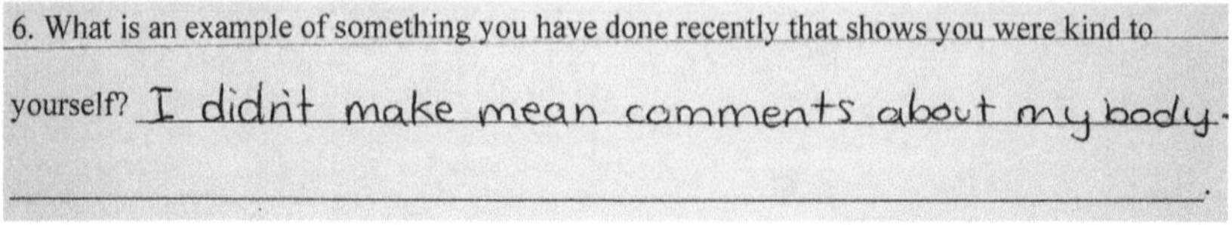

6. What is an example of something you have done recently that shows you were kind to
yourself? *I didn't make mean comments about my body.*

Figure 9.4. A middle school student shares how she is kind to herself.
Image credit: J.T. Binfet

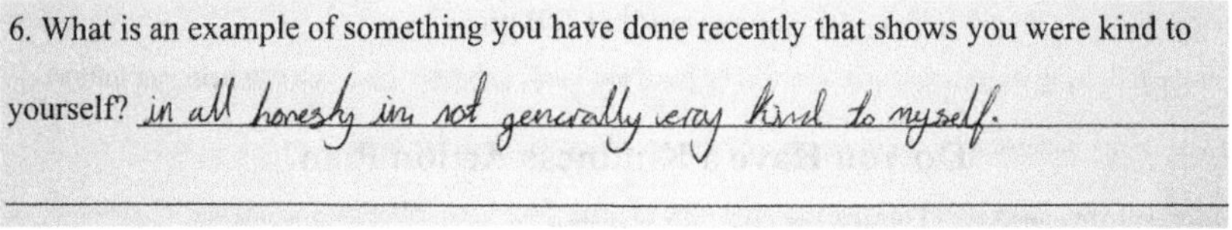

6. What is an example of something you have done recently that shows you were kind to
yourself? *in all honesty im not generally very kind to myself.*

Figure 9.5. A fourteen-year-old girl shares her thoughts on kindness to herself.
Image credit: J.T. Binfet

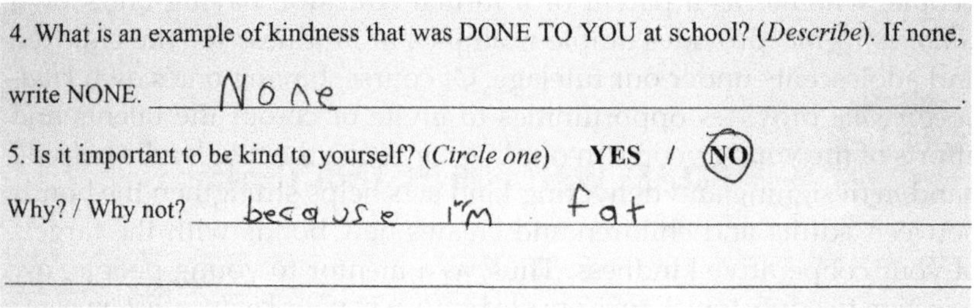

4. What is an example of kindness that was DONE TO YOU at school? (*Describe*). If none,
write NONE. *None*

5. Is it important to be kind to yourself? (*Circle one*)   YES / (NO)

Why? / Why not? *because i'm fat*

Figure 9.6. A twelve-year-old boy shares his views on being kind to himself.
Image credit: J.T. Binfet

importance of a school's mission statement allocating value to the role
of kindness was emphasized. Here a school is able to publicly declare
that being kind to one another is important and honoured.

The Importance of Kindness to Self

I often ask participants in my studies to describe something they have
done to show kindness to themselves. Children and adolescents can
struggle with this question, and their responses can provide insights into
self-loathing, a lack of self-worth, or a general hopelessness (see figures
9.4, 9.5, 9.6, and 9.7). Several student examples reveal such responses.

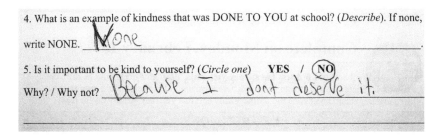

4. What is an example of kindness that was DONE TO YOU at school? (*Describe*). If none, write NONE. __None__

5. Is it important to be kind to yourself? (*Circle one*)   **YES** / (**NO**)

Why? / Why not? __Because I dont deserve it.__

Figure 9.7. A fourteen-year-old girl shares that she feels unworthy of kindness.

Image credit: J.T. Binfet

One subdivision of kindness research is devoted to "loving-kindness meditation," which is described as "an effective practice for promoting positive emotions" (Zeng et al. 2015, 1693). But a meta-analytic review of twenty-four empirical studies by Zeng and colleagues concluded that additional research is needed to fully understand the process and outcomes of this approach. It is often used within the context of therapy and has not had broad application within school contexts.

I share these examples here because it is important for educators to understand and be mindful that kindness to oneself might be a starting point for some students before they reach out to enact kindness to others. For example, you might see students list themselves on their "bank of recipients" planning sheet discussed in chapter 5. This would be a great entry point for discussion on feelings about oneself and the importance of kindness directed toward the self.

As was discussed in chapter 6 in our exploration of *quiet kindness*, because children's and adolescents' kind acts may fly beneath the radar of adults around them, they might resist kindness interventions and claim "But I'm already kind! Why do I have to do this?" Recognize too that asking children and adolescents to be kind to others might be met with resistance or outright opposition (see figure 9.8). Experience with prior kind acts going sideways (i.e., where a recipient refused the kindness) or being on the receiving end of their peers' bullying, can also make the idea of being kind to others unappealing. It is here that educators can educate young people about the benefits of being kind – that being kind to others is one way in which students can take care of themselves – to bolster their happiness and reorient their way of seeing the world. Even when unhappy and miserable, young people will often admit to wanting to change their emotional state, and informing them about the benefits of kindness helps increase their awareness of their situation and the control

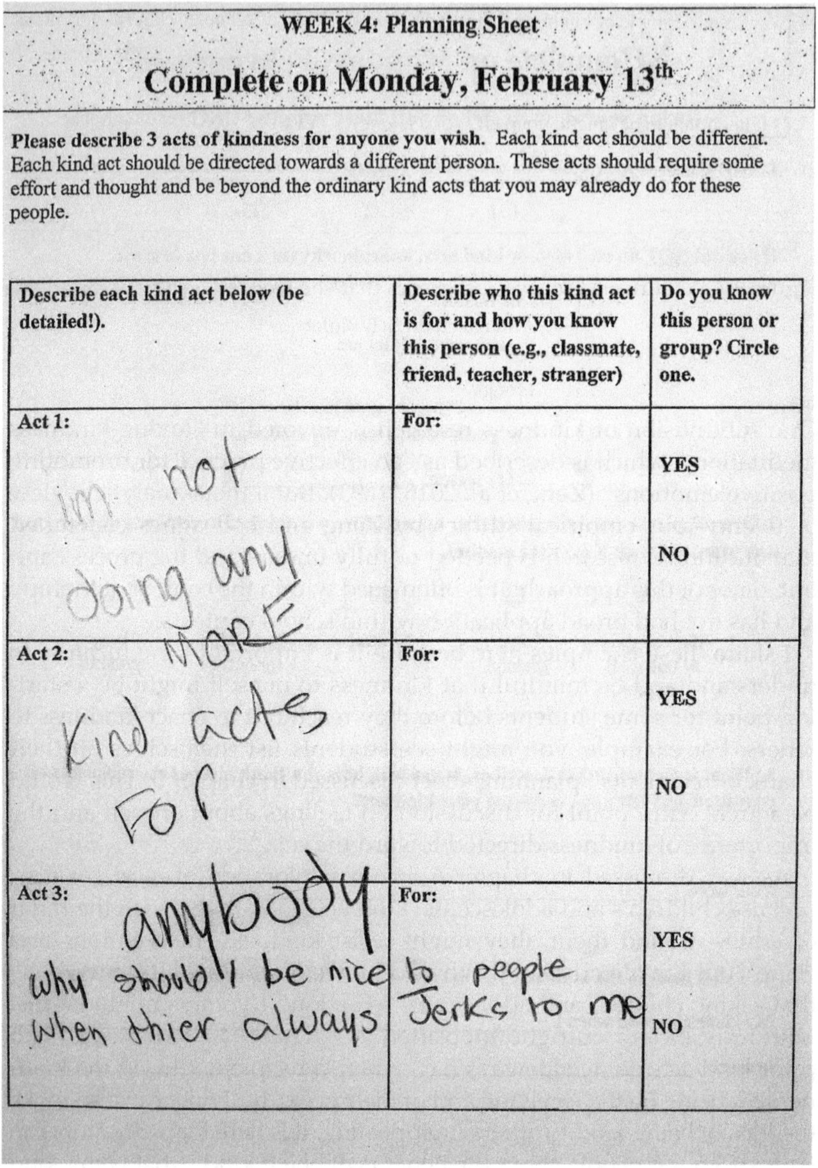

WEEK 4: Planning Sheet

Complete on Monday, February 13ᵗʰ

Please describe 3 acts of kindness for anyone you wish. Each kind act should be different. Each kind act should be directed towards a different person. These acts should require some effort and thought and be beyond the ordinary kind acts that you may already do for these people.

Describe each kind act below (be detailed!).	Describe who this kind act is for and how you know this person (e.g., classmate, friend, teacher, stranger)	Do you know this person or group? Circle one.
Act 1: *im not doing any MORE*	For:	YES NO
Act 2: *Kind acts For*	For:	YES NO
Act 3: *anybody why should I be nice to people when thier always Jerks to me*	For:	YES NO

Figure 9.8. A fourteen-year-old girl's reluctance to be kind to others.

Image credit: J.T. Binfet

they have over how they are feeling. Related to this, an appealing dimension of having young people engage in a *kindness regime* is that they determine the kind acts they will complete (within reason – ensuring safety for all). That is, they have ownership and "creative control" over how their kind acts are planned and delivered. For more socially and emotionally advanced students, they can be challenged to devise ways to be *"quietly"* kind – to plan and enact kindness anonymously.

Where Is the Field of School Kindness Research Headed?

Much of this book has been fuelled by research on kindness to help demystify the concept of kindness and inform and equip educators with strategies to foster kindness in the young people under their charge. Given the research-informed approach I have undertaken, researchers interested in the topic of kindness also stand to profit from the information amassed and shared here. There remain under-explored areas beneath the larger umbrella of kindness research that require further exploration. What follow are areas of research I foresee in need of additional empirical attention.

THE RELATION BETWEEN EDUCATOR WELL-BEING AND KINDNESS

While the link between student mental health and teacher stress is still being developed, teacher stress has been shown to influence school climate … and overall perception of student misbehavior. Therefore, in order to intervene for school mental health, it may be important to consider teacher wellness too.

von der Embse et al.

In chapter 3 we explored the benefits of being kind and discovered an array of well-being benefits that arise when kindness is practised. Recall from this chapter that planning and delivering a series of kind acts to others has been shown to boost one's happiness and life satisfaction and positively impact one's affect. The bulk of this research has examined the effects of being kind on the initiator of the kind acts, and in the case of kindness encouraged within the family or school context, no research could be found exploring the impact on the parent's or educator's well-being. How might mentoring young people in the completion of a series of kind acts – where mentors assist with the planning, organizing, delivering, and reflecting upon kindness with young people – affect the well-being of these adults? This is an area of research requiring additional exploration. My hunch is that there is a boost to well-being experienced by the adults who mentor young

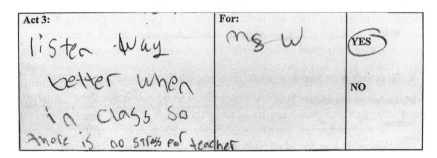

Act 3:	For:	
listen way better when in class so there is no stress for teacher	mrs w	YES NO

Figure 9.9. A fourteen-year-old boy links his in-class behaviour
to his teacher's well-being.

Image credit: J.T. Binfet

people in being kind by virtue of engaging in discussions about kindness and witnessing the completion of kind acts done by the young people around them.

There is a growing movement addressing teacher occupational stress and burnout (McCarthy 2019; Seton 2019; von der Embse et al. 2019). Concerns have been raised about stress thwarting teachers' abilities to establish positive rapport with students and stress compromising professional satisfaction – factors that contribute to teachers, especially new teachers, abandoning the profession. Certainly, teacher stress has been posited to compromise teachers' abilities to effectively manage learners and learning contexts (von der Embse et al. 2017). As a ninth-grader's description of his act of kindness illustrates, students are aware of teacher stress and the role they play in exacerbating teachers' working conditions (see figure 9.9).

Not to trivialize the complexities of teacher stress and burnout, but just as a kindness action plan holds benefits for students, there is potential in teachers enacting a kindness action plan within their professional duties to help bolster their mental health, ability to negotiate stressors, and create social capital to serve as a buffer against stress. In chapter 7 we discussed the notion of "pedagogical kindness," the idea that through teaching, students perceive teachers as kind agents within the school (see figure 9.10). Here I am speaking of teachers purposefully participating in a kindness regime to boost their well-being and help regulate their emotional experience within the school context. A teacher who, as part of his or her weekly professional duties, performed three acts of kindness to students, colleagues, or parents within the immediate school community would stand to reap well-being benefits. Such benefits would then serve to build resiliency to help navigate the professional stressors

<u>Step #2</u>: Draw a picture that shows a teacher doing something kind. What might a teacher do to show kindness at school?

WHO? teacher + self
WHAT? My teacher believed in me. She told me "You can do it!"

Figure 9.10. A nine-year-old boy recalls kindness from his teacher.
Image credit: J.T. Binfet

encountered each day. The role of *intentional kindness* as a stress-reducing and well-being boosting intervention for educators is a topic worthy of further exploration, and I suspect more research will be conducted examining the impact of kindness mentorship and kindness by educators on educator well-being as the field of kindness moves forward.

THE IMPORTANCE OF IMPLEMENTATION FIDELITY
IN KINDNESS INTERVENTION RESEARCH

Throughout several chapters of this book I have referenced two middle-school kindness studies (i.e., Binfet 2020; Binfet and Whitehead 2019). In both studies, I tracked the number of kind acts that adolescents actually completed as part of school-situated studies on kindness in middle school. Perhaps not surprisingly and in alignment with other school-centred tasks that young people are asked to complete, there was variability in the extent to which these adolescents completed their assigned kindness tasks. Researchers often make assumptions about participant engagement in the tasks comprising intervention research, and additional research is needed on the extent or degree to which participants in kindness-themed research actually complete the kind acts they are asked to do. Simply asking and expecting young people to be kind is not enough. They need structure, guidance, and support in their completion of kind acts, and researchers must avoid making assumptions about the completion rates of participants in their studies and dutifully report participant engagement as a component of a study's implementation fidelity (i.e., the degree to which a study was carried out as intended).

THE IMPORTANCE OF ASSESSING THE QUALITY OF KIND ACTS

It is increasingly popular in kindness research to ask that young people complete a series of kind acts as a means of determining the effect of being kind on any number of outcome variables. Assumptions can be made in kindness research that all kind acts are the same, and if anything has been learned from the research reported throughout this book, it is that children and adolescents are kind in varied and nuanced ways. Their acts of kindness vary in the preparatory time and organization, and in the sophistication of their delivery. In short, not all kind acts are of the same quality, and research is needed to examine just how the quality of kind acts is positioned within kindness intervention research. Might fewer high-quality acts elicit the same well-being benefits as several simple, less sophisticated acts of kindness? I have begun to explore this notion of "kindness quality" in some of my research with public

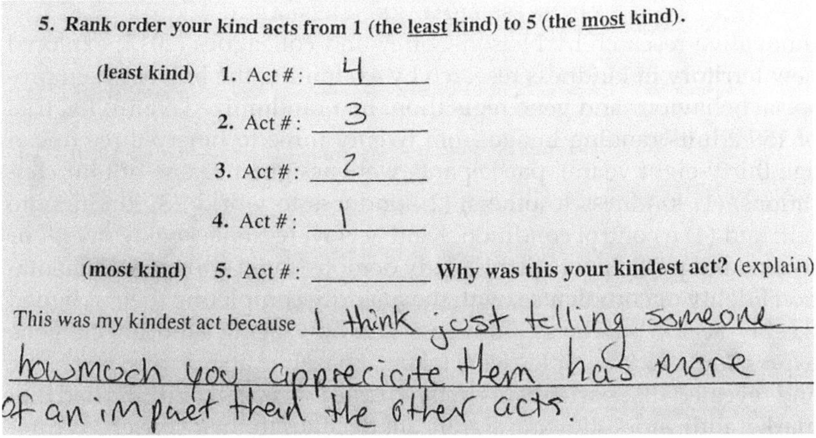

5. **Rank order your kind acts from 1 (the least kind) to 5 (the most kind).**

(least kind)   1. Act # : ___4___

2. Act # : ___3___

3. Act # : ___2___

4. Act # : ___1___

(most kind)   5. Act # : _____   **Why was this your kindest act?** (explain)

This was my kindest act because _I think just telling someone_ _howmuch you appreciate them has more_ _of an impact than the other acts._

Figure 9.11. A middle school student rank orders her kind acts
and justifies her kindest act.

Image credit: J.T. Binfet

school students and have incorporated rank-order tasks into my studies that require participants to reflect upon and rank (from most to least kind) the kind acts they complete (see figure 9.11).

CAPTURING THE VOICE OF YOUNG PEOPLE IN KINDNESS RESEARCH

As kindness research in schools advances, it will be important for researchers to capture the voice of students as their perspectives can help inform how educators think about encouraging kindness and how kindness initiatives might be situated within the context of the broader school community. As the student's insights at the outset of this chapter illustrated (see Figure 9.1 here), students have strong views regarding kindness and adolescents especially are able to think critically about this topic. They are, for example, quick to point out that adults who themselves are not perceived to be kind, are poorly positioned to try and encourage kindness in the students under their charge. Additionally, they are observant of the interactions they witness in school and recognize the importance of adults modelling kindness, especially in their interactions with students. In chapter 8 we discussed the concept of *Kind Discipline* and I suspect this will be a topic garnering the interest of educators as kindness continues to emerge as a topic of interest for those who work with young people.

KINDNESS BIOMARKER RESEARCH

Innovative research by Nelson-Coffey and colleagues (2017) explored new territory in kindness research by examining the link between pro-social behaviour and gene regulation. In a randomized controlled trial of 159 adults ranging in age from twenty-three to ninety-three (mean age thirty-eight years), participants were assigned to one of four conditions: (1) kindness to others; (2) kindness to world; (3) kindness to self; and (4) a control condition. Kind acts were done weekly over four weeks, and participants in this study demonstrated strong implementation fidelity or compliance, with the majority completing their assigned weekly acts of kindness. To assess just how being kind affects gene expression, blood samples were taken at baseline and during week five and revealed that participants in the *kindness to others* condition had biomarker indicators showing significant declines in their conserved transcriptional response to adversity (CTRA) or negative stress response to life adversity. Thus, it appears that being kind to others helps boost one's resiliency as reflected by biomarker indicators of well-being. It is likely we will see more research in this vein that explores the relation between being kind and physiological indicators of health.

In other biomarker research on the effects of being prosocial to others, Schreier and colleagues (2013) assigned tenth-graders to a prosocial (i.e., volunteering with younger students in an after-school program) or a waitlist control condition and examined biomarker indicators of cardiovascular health (e.g., risk markers of C-reactive protein level, interleukin 6 level, total cholesterol level, and body mass index). Adolescents in the intervention group had significantly lower levels of interleukin 6, cholesterol, and body mass when compared to control participants, thus suggesting that helping others is a way to improve one's physical health. I suspect more research exploring the biomarker effects of being kind, especially on stress reduction, is on the horizon.

KINDNESS FOR CLIMATE CHANGE

Looking ahead, I envision young people being motivated to enact kindness on behalf of larger, global issues such as climate change (see figure 9.12). Though relatively infrequent in their examples of kindness, there are students who, when asked for an example of their kindness, share acts of kindness that are ecologically themed – aimed at helping the environment, often their immediate school grounds. This is an example of where kindness, curriculum, and topics in the news can collide or intersect. It provides rich terrain for educators to incorporate kindness into the curriculum they teach. For example, "kindness for climate change" can challenge students to devise ways to counter climate change via their acts of kindness.

Step #1: In the box below, draw a picture of something you have done kind at school recently. What have you done to show kindness at school?

WHO? _____ Self _____

WHAT? _____ I'm picking up litter to help _____
the world.

Figure 9.12. A young student draws her act of kindness aimed
at helping the world.

Image credit: J.T. Binfet

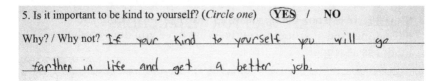

5. Is it important to be kind to yourself? (*Circle one*)   (YES) /   NO

Why? / Why not? If your kind to yourself you will go farther in life and get a better job.

Figure 9.13. A twelve-year-old boy shares his insights on why
it is important to be kind to oneself.

Image credit: J.T. Binfet

CYBER CIVILITY OR ONLINE KINDNESS

Another area in which I anticipate additional research and interest
from educators is cyber civility or cyber kindness (Sproull et al. 2013).
Rowland and Klisanin (2018) explore online prosocial behaviour. These
authors ask whether cyber kindness can counter cyber bullying, and in
light of the time we spend in digital worlds, how might cyber kindness
promote human flourishing? Additional research exploring the prosocial online lives and behaviour of young people is warranted, given the
influence the digital world has on intra- and interpersonal development.

KINDNESS DURING COVID

One last area that I foresee researchers addressing is the intersection of
the COVID-19 pandemic, virtual learning, and kindness. For example,
in learning within the context of online classes, how might students
show virtual kindness to teachers and to their classmates? Teachers can
lead discussions with students to help illustrate that being kind during
online classes is possible and might take the form of a "thumbs-up"
icon to show support for a classmate's shared idea, or an encouraging side-bar comment in praise of a presentation made by a classmate.
Researching the prevalence of kind acts and the nature of kind acts done
by students within virtual learning contexts is a research gap in need of
addressing, and doing so extends our understanding of how kindness
is situated within novel, technologically rich learning environments.

Conclusion

Throughout this book, I have leaned on the insights and examples from
over three thousand public school students who willingly shared with
me what and how they think about kindness. In writing this book, I, in
turn, share these examples with you to inform and challenge your thinking about kindness. Seeing what kindness means and how it is brought
to life by young people stands to inform our thinking as educators and

guide our efforts to foster kindness in the children and adolescents in our charge. Remember that participating in a series of kind acts is an accessible, low-cost, and high-reward endeavour. My hope in writing this book is that it will inspire educators to effect change – to be a "kindness catalyst" within their school communities. To continue your kindness education, I have compiled a list of curated kindness-themed online resources for you to consider (see appendix M). Throughout this book, I have relied heavily on examples from students on all facets of what it means to be kind, so I leave you with one last insightful and prophetic example. A sixth-grade student frankly summarizes the importance of self-directed kindness (figure 9.13).

List of Kindness Publications by the Author

Peer-Reviewed Articles

Binfet, J. T. (2015). Not-so random acts of kindness: A guide to intentional kindness in the classroom. *International Journal of Emotional Education, 7*, 35–51. https://doaj.org/article/3706dae6f26b427caf86 41d27d3f4983

Binfet, J. T. (2016). Kindness at school: What children's drawings reveal about themselves, their teachers, and their learning communities. *Journal of Childhood Studies, 41*, 29–42.

Binfet, J. T. (2020). Kinder than we might think: How adolescents are kind. *Canadian Journal of School Psychology, 35*, 87–99. https:// doi.org/10.1177/0829573519885802

Binfet, J. T., & Enns, C. (2018). Quiet kindness in school: Socially and emotionally sophisticated kindness flying beneath the radar of parents and educators. *Journal of Childhood Studies, 43*, 31–45.

Binfet, J. T., Gadermann, A. M., & Schonert-Reichl, K. A. (2016). Measuring kindness at school: Psychometric properties of a school kindness scale for children and adolescents. *Psychology in the Schools, 53*, 111–126. https://doi.org/10.1002/pits.21889

Binfet, J. T., & Gaertner, A. (2015). Children's conceptualizations of kindness at school. *Canadian Children, 40*, 27–39. https://doi.org /10.18357/jcs.v40i3.15167

Binfet, J. T., & Passmore, H. A. (2017). Teachers' perceptions of kindness at school. *International Journal of Emotional Education, 9*, 37–53. https://www.um.edu.mt/library/oar/bitstream/123456789/18277 /1/v1i9p3.pdf

Binfet, J. T., & Passmore, H. A. (2019). The who, what, and where of school kindness: Exploring students' perspectives. *Canadian Journal of School Psychology, 34*, 22–37. https://doi.org/10.1177 /0829573517732202

Binfet, J. T., & Whitehead, J. (2019). The effect of engagement in a kindness intervention on adolescents' well-being: A randomized controlled trial. *International Journal of Emotional Education, 11*, 33–49.

Binfet, J. T., Willis-Stewart, S., Lauze, A., Green, F. L. L., Draper, Z. A., & Calibaba, B. (in press). Understanding university students' conceptualizations and perceptions of kindness: A mixed methods study. *Journal of Further and Higher Education.* https://doi.org/10.10 80/0309877X.2021.1967895

Book Chapters

Binfet, J. T. (2016). Kindness: A mindful act of well-being. In K. Ragoonaden S. Bullock (Eds.), *Mindfulness and critical friendship: A new perspective on professional development for educators* (pp. 107–117). Lexington Books.

Paquet, A., Binfet, J. T., & Paquet, Y. (2019). La bienveillance à l'école: Essai de définition et exemples de la perception des élèves. In C. Martin-Krumm & C. Tarquinio (Eds.), *Psychologie positive: État des savoirs, champs d'application et perspectives* (pp. 133–148). Dunod.

Prisma Flow Chart

PRISMA flow chart indicating inclusion process for peer-reviewed articles included in Figure 1.8

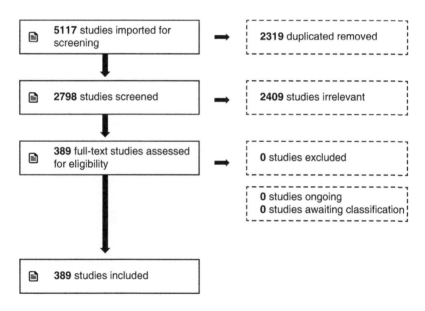

Search Process to Identify Bullying versus Kindness Publications across Databases

This literature review highlights the disequilibrium between academic journal articles published on the topic of kindness versus bullying. While this is not a systematic review of the literature, a systematic process was followed to ensure the accurate representation of the data taken from each indicated database. The measures include a structured and repeatable search operation with universally applied limiters, a de-duplication process conducted by Covidence, a manual review and screening of a randomly selected sample of titles and abstracts (of 20 per cent randomly selected subsample), as well as a presentation of the results which reflect journal article figures before and after the de-duplication process.

Methods

The databases in this review included ERIC (EBSCO), Education Source (EBSCO), Australian Education Index (ProQuest), APA PsychINFO (EBSCO), Academic Search Premier (EBSCO), CINAHL Complete (EBSCO), and Web of Science Core Collection (citation indexes utilized were the Science Citation Index Expanded, Social Sciences Citation Index, Arts & Humanities Citation Index, and the Emerging Sources Citation Index). These databases were selected to provide an inclusive and diverse range of sources from various disciplines.

The universally applied limiters began with excluding publications that were not peer-reviewed. The only database that did not contain a peer-reviewed limiter was the Web of Science Core Collection. The date range selected was 1 January 2000 to 31 December 2019. Any attempt at the inclusion of articles published in 2020 deteriorated the possibility of accurately recreating the search and would fail to represent a holistic view of publishing trends in 2020. Next, document and publication types were limited to "Journal Articles" or "Articles," depending on the database. To measure the effectiveness of this particular limiter, the searches were conducted twice: once with the limiter applied, and once without. The number of search results for both kindness and bullying were similarly affected, thus the limiter was applied universally across all search operations. Note that this limits the data to predominantly peer-reviewed publications.

Finally, the keywords chosen for the search operations were "Kindness" and "Bully*" respectively. "Kindness" was chosen over the truncated "Kind*" due to the wide range of words that were captured that did not apply to the subject matter at hand or were applied in a different context. Examples aree "*kind* of materials" or "*kind*ergarten class." The search term "Kindness" yielded consistent results related to social-emotional well-being and empathy studies and thus was chosen as the universal keyword. A similar problem did not arise with the truncated version of bullying, and so "Bully*" was applied as the universal keyword. These two keyword searches were performed for both the "title" and "abstract" parameters for all databases, and across all search operations.

The results from the search operations were exported to RIS files, which were then imported into Covidence to perform a de-duplication process. Pre-deduplication results were preserved in an effort to be able to accurately portray the individual databases' performance when requesting these articles, as well as avoid any unintended implications regarding the breadth of data available to users from database to database. Following the de-duplication process, a randomly selected set of 500 articles was screened manually to account for any applications of "Kindness" or "Bully*" that did not align with the expressed objective of this review. The eliminated results included any that did not have kindness or bullying as a specific research target, and instead captured either subject as a by-product of another focus, such as studies conducted with children who exhibit specific developmental disabilities, or a survey of children and their perspective on school playgrounds. In these examples, bullying and kindness is observed and noted as occurring in and around the specified environment, but the thesis or research goals are wholly unrelated to the literature review being conducted. In this review, 20 results out of the randomly selected 500 were removed, or a +/- 4 per cent margin for error overall. As a result of this finding, final results are presented with that margin for error included.

Social and Emotional Learning Resources

The following curated list of resources (presented in no particular order) is recommended to parents and educators seeking additional information on social and emotional learning.

Collaborative for Academic, Social, and Emotional Learning (CASEL)

A valuable resource for researchers and practitioners alike, the CASEL website is a well-respected and well-governed resource that serves as a repository for all things SEL.

www.casel.org

The Blue Dot

This is a UNESCO supported initiative that publishes an e-magazine on a variety of topics including education, peace, sustainable development, and global citizenship. Their special issue on social and emotional learning may be found at

https://mgiep.unesco.org/the-blue-dot-issue-10

The Future of Children

Out of Princeton University, this free resource compiles key findings in social and emotional learning and will serve as an informative information source for parents and educators.

https://www.wallacefoundation.org/knowledge-center/Documents/FOC-Spring-Vol27-No1-Compiled-Future-of-Children-spring-2017.pdf

Dalai Lama Centre for Peace and Education

This group's mission is to "educate the hearts of children by informing, inspiring and engaging the communities around them." They sponsor an annual "Heart-Mind Conference."
https://dalailamacenter.org/

Edutopia

This resource is supported by the George Lucas Educational Foundation and provides a repository of timely resources on social and emotional learning. It often features articles on kindness.
https://www.edutopia.org/social-emotional-learning

Social and Emotional Learning Resource Finder

Described as "a collection of social and emotional learning (SEL) resources for educators and other adults who work with children and youth," this site offers a rich repository of information for those interested in social and emotional learning. Published by the University of British Columbia.
http://www.selresources.com/

American Educational Research Association, Social and Emotional Learning, Special Interest Group

Known as AERA, this is the largest academic conference in North America and attracts researchers and practitioners keen on understanding and sharing information on SEL. The website links to newsletters that inform readers of new initiatives and upcoming events in SEL.
https://www.aera.net/SIG170/Social-and-Emotional-Learning-SIG-170

Committee for Children

Described as a site that "provides tools that help children thrive," this resource has a strong resiliency focus and offers a variety of resources on social and emotional learning.
https://www.cfchildren.org/what-is-social-emotional-learning/

Greater Good Magazine: Science-Based Insights
for a Meaningful Life

This well-known online resource is rich with social and emotional content and often features pieces dedicated to understanding the science behind kindness.

https://greatergood.berkeley.edu

Drawing Template for Early Elementary Students

In the box below, draw a picture of something kind *you* have done at school recently. What have you done to show kindness at school?

Who is in this drawing? _____

_____

What is happening? _____

_____

Drawing Template Teacher Kindness

In the box below, draw a picture of a *teacher* doing something kind at school. What has a teacher done to show kindness?

Who is in this drawing? _____

_____

What is happening? _____

_____

Kindness Scenarios to Facilitate Discussion

How Could You Respond with Kindness?

Student Scenarios

Scenario #1

Josh is a ninth-grade middle school student. He quickly learned that to survive in his school he has to be observant. This realization pays off by letting him know where to sit in the school cafeteria, whom to sit with, and whom to borrow notes from when he's been absent. Being observant also tells Josh a lot about his fellow students. Making his way through the school he notices Ben, a shy seventh-grader who seems to be the target of the school's bullies. Josh notices Ben wears mostly the same clothes each day. What could Josh do to show kindness to Ben? Is there someone in your school who needs kindness?

Scenario #2

Justine admits she can be selfish, but aren't most teenagers? She hears her mother's voice, "Think of somebody besides yourself for a change!" And as she anticipates going to college and "growing up," she wonders if it's time to change. What are small things that Justine could do to show she is thinking of others? What are small things you could do to show you think about, and care about, those around you?

Scenario #3

Fred likes to eat. He's the first to admit it. When there's food around, he goes into "competition mode" and can out-eat the best of them. His humanities teacher showed the class a film on food resources and food scarcity around the world and, as he sat in class, he felt the documentary was speaking directly to him. It was as if there was nobody else in the class. Fred thinks about changing how he thinks about food and how he could use food to help others. What could Fred do?

Scenario #4

Even though Elizabeth is only nine and in the fourth grade, she realizes that her life is pretty great. She gets a ride to school every day, her lunch always has a special treat or handwritten note in it from her mom, and her family eats out together at least once each weekend. While on her way to dance class, Elizabeth sees a line-up of people outside a store and asks her mom what's going on. Her mom explains that people are waiting in line at the local food bank. As a fourth-grader, what could Elizabeth do to help her local food bank?

Scenario #5

When she was told she was blunt, Mary-Ann just thought people were being too sensitive. Her favourite phrase was "Suck it up buttercup!" Her dad was always telling her, "Think before you speak," but she didn't really know what he meant as she just said what was on her mind. When her friend Emily said, "Ouch. You're brutal. That didn't feel good to hear that," Mary-Ann's first reaction was to use her favourite phrase. But seeing her friend Emily with tears in her eyes really caused her to stop. What does kindness in a friendship look like? What does truthful but kind feedback sound like?

Teacher and Administrator Scenarios

Scenario #1

After a long day teaching, Ms. Jones often found herself reflecting on the little victories she saw throughout her day. Admittedly, she did not find herself celebrating academic gains (e.g., higher test scores) but rather the moments when students showed gratitude, took another's perspective, or added positively to the class climate. She often thought she should have been a social worker, as she received a lot of joy from helping others. Even though she sometimes thought it a selfish act, Ms. Jones found herself wondering how to introduce kindness into her teaching. She knew celebrating students' kind acts would have benefits for students themselves and for the entire class but she wasn't sure how to *justify* this to school administrators. Where does kindness fit into the curriculum?

Scenario #2

As a high school principal, Mr. Jensen had seen it all. He was preparing paperwork to suspend Ted, a student who was repeatedly in fights at school when he thought, "There has to be another way. Clearly what we're doing isn't reducing his fighting." One of the school's new teachers had raised the notion of "kind discipline" in a faculty meeting and he remembered it getting a round of laughter. Mr. Jensen found himself wondering if kind discipline might be the solution for Ted. What might kind discipline look like?

Parenting Scenarios

Scenario #1

"It's not like he stole anything valuable from us!" argued Hannah. As a seventeen-year-old she realized how fortunate her family was in a society rife with inequity. Her mother professed to have an open-door policy and encouraged Hannah and her siblings to invite school friends over, especially for Sunday dinner. Hannah's mother caught Hannah's classmate Jacob taking canned goods from the cupboard and stuffing them into his backpack. She finds herself thinking, "Aren't I being kind enough with this kid by inviting him to dinner?" How might Hannah's mother respond to Jacob with kindness?

Scenario #2

As his children became teenagers, Jeff realized how quickly he was losing his connection to them. They seemed to come to him only when they needed money and it appeared that spending time with him was, from his children's perspective, painful or time to be tolerated. In a parenting book he'd picked up at his local bookstore, he read about parents who perform kind acts in their community alongside their children. It was argued that this approach would be beneficial for everyone – for Jeff himself, for his children, for their relationship, and for the recipients in their community. He was convinced it would be beneficial but he thinks his kids are too far gone and will see it as "lame" (their favourite word). How might Jeff introduce co-completing a series of kind acts with his children to them?

Appendix H

Kindness Planning Sheet

J.T. Binfet, Ph.D.
University of British Columbia

Name:_____

Class:_____

Intentional Kindness Planning Sheet

How kind are you currently? Indicate on the gas tank your current level of kindness. Is there room for impovement?

FULL

EMPTY

Brainstorm a list of all the people or places in your school or community you think could use some kindness.

	Steps	Questions and Cues
Recipient	**Step 1** Identify your recipient	Someone you know / familiar location *or* A stranger / unfamiliar location
Mechanism	**Step 2** Decide on the kind of kindness you will do	Materials (e.g., giving an object, making something) *or* Time or energy (e.g., helping someone)
Format	**Step 3** Decide if you want to be known or anonymous	Known *or* Anonymously (the recipient won't know it was you!)
Preparation	**Step 4** Figure out the details	What's involved? What do you need? Prepare your materials and gather supplies
Schedule	**Step 5** When is a good time?	When? When would be the best time to do your kind act?
Execution	**Step 6** Do your act of kindness	Execute
Evaluation	**Step 7** Assessment	How did it go? Did your act go as you planned? How do you think your recipient felt? How did *you* feel?

Directions: Plan five kindness activities (three that occur within school and two outside of school). Use the following grid to help you plan each activity. Do your best to plan *different* activities (don't repeat). Be creative!

		Kind act #1 in school	Kind act #2 in school	Kind act #3 in school
Recipient	**Step 1** Identify your recipient			
Mechanism	**Step 2** Decide on the type of kindness you will do			
Format	**Step 3** Decide if you want to be known or anonymous			
Preparation	**Step 4** Figure out the details			
Schedule	**Step 5** When is a good time?			
Execution	**Step 6** Do your act of kindness			
Evaluation	**Step 7** Assessment			

Kindness activities continued

		Kind act #4 outside of school	Kind act #5 outside of school
Recipient	**Step 1** Identify your recipient		
Mechanism	**Step 2** Decide on the type of kindness you will do		
Format	**Step 3** Decide if you want to be known or anonymous		
Preparation	**Step 4** Figure out the details		
Schedule	**Step 5** When is a good time?		
Execution	**Step 6** Do your act of kindness		
Evaluation	**Step 7** Assessment		

Name: _____

Post-Kindness Reflection

Directions: By now you have completed your intentional acts of kindness. It's time to reflect upon what you did, and the questions below will help you reflect on how you did and what impact doing kindness might have had on you. Answer honestly.

1. Revisiting the Kindness Self-Assessment

   How kind are you currently? Indicate your current level of kindness. Is there room for improvement?

2. Thinking back to the *recipients* of your kindness (the people who received kindness from you), *who* do you think was most appreciative or grateful? Why?

3. There are differences in the *quality* of the kind acts we do. That is, some acts are done more thoroughly and thoughtfully than others. When you think of the kind acts you did, which one had the highest quality? Why?

4. How did completing the acts of kindness impact you? Describe your feelings around being at school, about your classmates, and about yourself.

Curated List of Kindness-Themed Books

Presented in no particular order, here is a list of books for children and adolescents that parents and educators might consider using to initiate discussions about kindness and to provide examples of characters being kind.

Children

Enemy Pie, Derek Munson (2000)
> *Enemy Pie* is the story about how two young boys turn from "best enemies" to "best friends," thanks to a secret recipe for Enemy Pie (that includes spending an entire day with your enemy). For use in teaching children how to handle conflicts with kindness and respect.

If You Plant a Seed, Kadir Nelson (2015)
> This book opens with a question: "What happens if you plant a seed of kindness … or selfishness?" Using farmers and animals in his story, Kadir Nelson conveys the age-old message, "You reap what you sow," and illustrates how kindness toward others can contribute to a happier life.

Be Kind, Pat Zietlow Miller (2018)
> Growing from a small story set during a lunch break at school, Pat Miller develops a story that is focused upon examples of kindness on a global scale. Through acts of giving, paying attention to the needs of others, and helping out when you can, the examples in this book can aid in children's understanding of how they can positively affect those around them.

Little Blue Truck, Alice Schertle (2015)
A board book full of fun and engaging artwork along with opportunities to make a variety of sounds, this book aims to draw in the reader – or the parent and child together – while providing a message about being kind to others, even when they are not kind to you first.

Come with Me, Holly M. McGhee (2017)
Appropriate for children aged approximately five to eight years old and especially for children who have questions about what's happening in the world and shown on the news. The overall message of this book is that by being "brave, gentle, strong – and kind," one person can make a difference in the world, no matter what.

Most People, Michael Leannah (2017)
Most People is a story about how most people in the world just want to help one another through acts of kindness, compassion, and honesty. Filled with examples of how to be kind in the real world, *Most People* can provide a context for discussion for children who are curious about intentional acts of kindness.

How Kind! Mary Murphy (2004)
A board book for children, *How Kind!* shows that what goes around, comes around. Set in a barnyard full of happy and kind animals, this book is best shared with a younger child learning about what it means to be giving to others.

A Ball for Daisy, Chris Raschka (2011)
A wordless children's book that conveys a message of giving, forgiveness, and finding friendship through commonalities. Daisy the dog loses her favourite ball to another dog while on a walk. When that ball is popped, Daisy is distraught, but an unlikely act of kindness makes her feel better.

The Nice Book, David Ezra Stein (2013)
Using animals to demonstrate ways to be nice to others, *The Nice Book* is a wonderful way to introduce children to the concept of good manners toward others, and caring for the important people in your life.

Kindness Is Cooler, Mrs. Ruler, Margery Cuyler (2007)
When Mrs. Ruler's kindergarten class begins to misbehave, she chooses to correct their behaviour by teaching them all about

performing kindness acts in the classroom and in the world around them. They strive to reach 100 kind acts by the end of the year. This can serve as an example for teaching intentional kindness.

Albert the Fix-It Man, Janet Lord (2008)

Albert is the fix-it man for his community. He is always willing to lend a hand, rain or shine. But when Albert gets sick and isn't able to help his community, his community comes together to help him. Altruism, kindness, and loyalty are all key lessons in this feel-good book.

Each Kindness, Jacqueline Woodson (2012)

Chloe and her friends refuse to become friends with Maya, the new girl in school. Suddenly, Chloe notices that Maya has stopped coming to school, and the teacher begins to teach the students about being kind in order to change someone's world. Anti-bullying and inclusiveness are key messages in this story.

A Sick Day for Amos McGee, Philip C. Stead (2010)

Amos is a zookeeper and a reliable friend to all the animals. The animals that think of Amos as their best friend get worried when Amos fails to arrive for work one morning. They go on a mission to find their friend, teaching the reader about loyalty, kindness, and the meaning of friendship.

The Kindness Quilt, Nancy Elizabeth Wallace (2006)

When Minna is asked by her teacher to complete a kindness project, she struggles to come up with an idea that is just right. Once she starts to try out a few ideas, she decides to complete a kindness quilt as a collage of all her kind acts. Trying new things and being intentionally kind to others is clearly demonstrated in this book.

The Invisible Boy, Trudy Ludwig (2013)

Brian is a young boy who is so quiet that no one even seems to know he is there. A new friend in Justin helps to show Brian that he has a lot to contribute while still being himself. Inclusiveness and being a good friend are the foci of this book. Shows how people can be different but still be a great friend.

The Song of Delphine, Kenneth Kraeger (2015)

Delphine is a servant in Queen Theodora's palace and has no friends at all. All she has to keep her spirits up is singing, and this attracts an unlikely set of friends. This draws the attention of Princess Beatrice, and an unlikely friendship blossoms. Being kind even when others are unkind is a key and valuable lesson found in this book.

What Does It Mean to Be Kind? Rana DiOrio (2015)
When the new girl in class needs a friend, one girl is brave enough to step up and be kind. Her community notices her performing these kind acts and begins to follow her lead. Leading by example and recognizing the kindness of others are key takeaways from this book.

Adolescents

Random Acts, Valerie Sherrard (2015)
Zoey, Bean, and Jenna decide to make a pledge to perform anony-mous random acts of kindness around their community. Because they've never even thought about doing anything like this before, they think that *anything* they do will make a positive impact. This chapter book provides insight into how being kind to others can become a self-serving act when done for the wrong reasons.

Kindness Wins, Galit Breen (2015)
This book focuses on how we as a society are kind – or decidedly *un*kind – to one another online. Using ten chapters to illustrate the difference between kind and unkind, Breen provides the reader with the context and the tools to understand the role we play online, and how our online decisions have real world consequences.

Growing Up with a Bucket Full of Happiness: Three Rules for a Happier Life, Carol McCloud (2010)
A sequel to the children's book *Have You Filled a Bucket Today?*, this book aims to build on the concept of everyone in the world hav-ing a bucket that needs to be filled in order to feel happy. This book provides well-defined practices and chapters that directly ask readers to think about the people and the environment around them. Provides examples on how to speak about kindness, empa-thy, and positivity.

The Power of Kindness, Piero Ferrucci (2006)
A non-fiction book that champions kindness as the key to leading a happy and fulfilled life. With chapters focused on a range of topics

like "honesty," "forgiveness," "loyalty," and "service," as well as a collection of meditations and exercises, this book can serve as a resource for anyone looking to integrate acts of kindness into their life.

Kid President's Guide to Being Awesome, Robby Novak (2016)
From the history of "awesome" to treating everyone as if it is their birthday, Robby Novak is on a mission to provide tips, exercises, and practical guides on how to perform kindness acts out in the world. It is a casually written book, divided into understandable topics, which can allow for reading at one's own pace.

Inside Out & Back Again, Tanhha Lai (2011)
When Kim Há and her family are forced to leave their home in Vietnam, they must learn how to deal with the trauma they faced back home and the lack of kindness shown to them in their new home in Alabama. Learning the importance of family and being there for one another in a time of need are worthwhile lessons found in this story.

Lend a Hand, John Frank (2014)
Fourteen poems that explore different possible acts of kindness that people can do in everyday circumstances include examples such as giving up a bus seat, helping the elderly, and even training a puppy to become a guide dog. Positive messages and lessons are available for easy integration into reading programs, or sparking conversations with young readers.

Non-Random Acts of Kindness, Lauren Myracle (2014)
Part of a series, Ty confronts the difficulty of always committing to performing kind acts for others. He begins to worry himself about being kind enough and with a big act of kindness coming up in front of the whole class, he really starts to question what it takes to be kind. Intentionality and finding the drive to be kind are key takeaways from this story.

Just Mercy (adapted for young adults), Bryan Stevenson (2018)
Social justice advocate Brian Stevenson adapts this story for a young audience in order to provide his unique perspective on the wrongfully accused. His story fosters compassion and awareness of others for readers and introduces them to more mature themes that can serve as a larger call to action.

Jackpot: All Bets Are Off, Nic Stone (2019)

Rico works at a gas station and sells a winning lottery ticket. With the help of his friend Zan, he thinks that they can find the winner before they claim the prize. Explores themes of inequality, class, and privilege, this is a novel for a young reader learning about how to practise empathy for others.

Stargirl, Jerry Spinelli (2000)

Susan Caraway, who goes by the name "Stargirl," arrives at a new school and immediately stands out for her unique style, attitude, and nonconformity. Her friends pressure her to change her ways in order to fit in, leading to often disastrous results. With a series of complex and engaging messages for young readers, as well as a large online following of "Stargirl Societies," this is a useful book for readers developing their understanding of empathy and compassion. These themes can be used to explore ways in which children can be kind toward those who are different from themselves.

Wonder, R.J. Palacio (2012)

A story that centres upon August "Auggie" Pullman, who is inflicted with a disfiguring case of Treacher Collins syndrome. Complications begin to mount as Auggie attends public school, and the people that Auggie meets have to come to terms with his outward appearance and eventually see through to the inner beauty he possesses.

Resources in Support of Students with Special Needs

The following list of web-based resources, presented in no particular order, are resources readers might consult as they seek information about how best to support students with exceptionalities.

1. **Education Oasis**
   Provides a repository of resources "for teachers by teachers."
   http://www.educationoasis.com/visitor-resources/articles/adapting-special-needs/

2. **Teacher Vision**
   A collection of resources in support of modifying instruction to meet diverse student needs.
   https://www.teachervision.com/teaching-strategies/adaptations-modifications-students-special-needs

3. **Head Start: Early Childhood Learning & Knowledge Center**
   A static website containing presentations and information on strategies to "help to increase the participation of children who need more support or challenge."
   https://eclkc.ohs.acf.hhs.gov/children-disabilities/article/materials-adaptation

4. **Center for Parent Information and Resources**
   This resource is a hub of information for families of children with disabilities.
   https://www.parentcenterhub.org/accommodations/

Sample Teacher Survey of School Kindness

Though the survey below was designed for research purposes (see the associated publication Binfet & Passmore, 2017), it provides a framework to initiate discussion among school staff and faculty on kindness. The survey helps capture perceptions of kindness within the school context and may serve as a foundation upon which to build professional development opportunities for the school community.

Understanding Kindness - Teacher Survey

Binfet, J.T., & Passmore, H. A. (2017). Teacher perceptions of kindness at school.
The International Journal of Emotional Education, 9, 37-53.
(Reprinted with permission)

1. What does it mean to be kind? (define kindness).

_____

_____ .

2. If kindness happens in your school, <u>WHERE</u> does it happen most? (be specific)

Location: _____ (e.g., classroom, gym, hallways, etc.)

3. Are you generally kind at school?   **YES / NO** (circle one)

What is an example of kindness YOU have done recently at school? (describe)

_____

_____ .

Who was the recipient of your kindness? _____ (No names here - e.g., student, parent-

volunteer, noon-hour supervisor, teaching colleague, etc.)

4. How often is kindness done to you at school?

> **Not Very Often   Rarely   Sometimes   Pretty Often   All the Time**

What is an example of kindness that was DONE TO YOU at school? (describe)

_____

_____ .

Who did this?_____ (No names here - e.g., student, teacher, administrators, parent-

volunteer)

5. How often are <u>you</u> kind at SCHOOL? (circle one)

> **Not Very Often   Rarely   Sometimes   Pretty Often   All the Time**

6. When you think of the adults in your school, what is the <u>ROLE</u> of the adult who shows the most kindness? _____ (e.g., classroom teacher, resource teacher, principal, parent-volunteer, secretary, custodian, educational assistant)

What is an example of the kindness this person might do?

_____

_____.

7. Do you consider students to be generally kind?   **YES / NO**   (circle one)
Give of an example that shows a student was kind recently?

_____

_____.

8. Not all kind acts are the same. Some acts involve more investment of time, materials, thought, preparation, and effort, etc. Rate the overall QUALITY of kindness at your school (circle one response on the scale)

Poor   Fair   Good   Very Good   Excellent

9. How much <u>influence</u> do you believe you have on children's kindness?

No   Little   Some   Moderate   Strong

10. When you think of all of your professional responsibilities, how important is promoting kindness?

Not a Priority   Low Priority   Medium Priority   High Priority   Essential

School Kindness Scale

Directions: Circle the number that matches how you feel for each sentence

School Kindness Scale
(Binfet, Gadermann, & Schonert-Reichl, 2016)

How true is each statement for you?	Disagree a Lot	Disagree A Little	Don't Agree or Disagree	Agree a Little	Agree a Lot
1. The adults in my school model kindness.	1	2	3	4	5
2. Kindness happens regularly in my classroom.	1	2	3	4	5
3. Kindness happens regularly in my school.	1	2	3	4	5
4. My teacher is kind.	1	2	3	4	5
5. At my school, I am encouraged to be kind.	1	2	3	4	5

Scoring the School Kindness Scale

As there are no reverse items in this scale, the scoring of the *School Kindness Scale* is straight forward. Add the circled values for each item and divide this composite score by 5. Higher values indicate more positive perceptions of school kindness.

Citation

Binfet, J. T., Gadermann, A. M., & Schonert-Reichl, K. A. (2016). Measuring kindness at school: Psychometric properties of a School Kindness Scale for children and adolescents. *Psychology in the Schools, 53*, 111-126.

Curated List of Kindness Resources

The following curated list of web-based kindness resources is presented in no particular order and listed as resources readers might consult as they seek information about kindness.

Teaching Tolerance

www.tolerance.org

"Teaching Tolerance" is a robust online resource for educators that features an online lesson planner centred around the four pillars of social justice standards: identity, diversity, justice, action. These learning plans incorporate texts and actions that can enhance students' understanding of social and emotional well-being, diversity in the classroom/media, and increased recognition of opportunities for kindness and tolerance in the world.

Random Acts of Kindness

https://www.randomactsofkindness.org

Featuring thoroughly detailed, free, and downloadable lesson plans for grades K–8 – among a great deal of kindness-centred resources – Random Acts of Kindness provides online training and materials for teachers who hope to integrate kindness into their classrooms in a more meaningful way. The Random Acts of Kindness (RAK) foundation is a non-profit organization and provides materials free of charge.

Playful Learning

www.playfullearning.net

Founded in 2008, Playful Learning offers resources for parents, teachers, and children. Areas of focus include social and emotional learning, kindness instruction at home or in school, and a wealth of additional free resources on a wide variety of school-related subjects and relevant activities.

Making Caring Common

https://mcc.gse.harvard.edu/

A project of the Harvard Graduate School for Education, Making Caring Common is driven to helping children and young adults develop their capacity for kindness and empathy in their everyday lives. Conducting and publishing research, leading national initiatives, and collaborating with groups across multiple platforms is only the start. They also provide educational resources for teachers and families that can help in developing social and emotional well-being related to self-care and kindness.

Learning to Give

www.learningtogive.org

Learning to Give provides resources and lesson plans with a focus on volunteerism and philanthropy in an effort to foster caring habits in students from K to 12. Based on constructivist educational theory, Learning to Give break their lesson plans into themed units, or teachers can search for lessons in specific subjects to help bolster their curriculum or after-school programs.

The Be Kind People Project

www.thebekindpeopleproject.org

Kindness-focused education delivered through experience and project-based learning. Online resources provide lesson plans and activities in a wide range of academic and civil subjects including personal fitness, gardening, social and emotional wellness, and at-home activities for families to complete together.

Kindness.Org

www.kindness.org

An organization dedicated to the research and propagation of kindness acts worldwide. Focused on the data-driven research of kindness acts and stories curated from a global perspective, Kindness.org involves as many global citizens as possible through volunteer work, speaking engagements, online (viral) engagement, public works, and published research.

Collaborative for Academic, Social, and Emotional Learning (CASEL)

www.casel.org

With social and emotional learning as a cornerstone for their educational programs and resources, CASEL serves as a one-stop-shop for information about educating students K–12 with these principles in mind. CASEL also provides online training for teachers and school districts, as well as clear methodologies for parents to engage in social and emotional learning at home.

School Kindness Scale for Children and Adolescents

https://education.ok.ubc.ca/research-partnerships/school-kindness-scale-for-children-and-adolescents/

A practical tool to help measure kindness engagement and frequency in the classroom. Designed for research to quantify students' perceptions of school kindness.

References

Aknin, L. B., Barrington-Leigh, C. P., Dunn, E. W., Helliwell, J. F., Burns, J., Biswas-Diener, R., Kemeza, I., Nyende, P., Ashton-James, C. E., & Norton, M. I. (2013). Prosocial spending and well-being: Cross-cultural evidence for a psychological universal. *Journal of Personality and Social Psychology, 104*, 635–652. https://doi.org/10.1037/a0031578

Aknin, L. B., Dunn, E. W., Proulx, J., Lok, I., & Norton, M. I. (2020). Does spending money on others promote happiness? A registered replication report. *Journal of Personality and Social Development, 119*, e15–e26. https://doi.org/10.1037/pspa0000191

Aknin, L. B., Sandstrom, G. M., Dunn, E. W., & Norton, M. I. (2011). It's the recipient that counts: Spending money on strong social ties leads to greater happiness than spending on weak social ties. *PLOS ONE, 6*, 1–3. https://doi.org/10.1371/journal.pone.0017018

Algoe, S. B. (2019). Positive interpersonal processes. *Current Directions in Psychological Science, 28*(2), 183–188. https://doi.org/10.1177/0963721419827272

Allen, K., Kern, M. L., Vella-Brodrick, D., Hattie, J., & Waters, L. (2018). What schools need to know about fostering school belonging: A meta-analysis. *Educational Psychology Review, 30*, 1–34. https://doi.org/10.1007/s10648-016-9389-8

Anderson, N. B. (2003). *Emotional longevity: What really determines how long you live.* Viking.

Baldwin, C. P., & Baldwin, A. (1970). Children's judgments of kindness. *Child Development, 41*, 29–47. https://doi.org/10.2307/1127387

Bandura, A. (1977). *Social learning theory.* Prentice Hall.

Bandura, A., Ross, D., & Ross, S. A. (1961). Transmission of aggression through the imitation of aggressive models. *Journal of Abnormal and Social Psychology, 63*, 575–582.

Batson, C. D., Coke, J. S., Jasnoski, M. L., & Hanson, M. (1978). Buying kindness: Effect of an extrinsic incentive for helping on perceived altruism. *Personality and Social Psychology Bulletin, 4,* 86–91. https://doi.org /10.1177/014616727800400118

Biglan, A. (2003). Selection by consequences: One unifying principle for a transdisciplinary science of prevention. *Prevention Science, 4,* 213–232. https://evolution.binghamton.edu/evos/wp-content/uploads/2008/11 /Biglan_2003_Consequences.pdf

Binfet, J. T. (2015). Not-so random acts of kindness: A guide to intentional kindness in the classroom. *International Journal of Emotional Education, 7,* 35–51. https://doaj.org/article/3706dae6f26b427caf8641d27d3f4983

Binfet, J. T. (2016). Kindness at school: What children's drawings reveal about themselves, their teachers, and their learning communities. *Journal of Childhood Studies, 41,* 29–42.

Binfet, J. T. (2020). Kinder than we might think: How adolescents are kind. *Canadian Journal of School Psychology, 35,* 87–99. https://doi.org/10.1177 /0829573519885802

Binfet, J. T., & Enns, C. (2018). Quiet kindness in school: Socially and emotionally sophisticated kindness flying beneath the radar of parents and educators. *Journal of Childhood Studies, 43,* 31–45.

Binfet, J. T., Gadermann, A. M., & Schonert-Reichl, K. A. (2016). Measuring kindness at school: Psychometric properties of a School Kindness Scale for children and adolescents. *Psychology in the Schools, 53,* 111–126. https:// doi.org/10.1002/pits.21889

Binfet, J. T., & Gaertner, A. (2015). Children's conceptualizations of kindness at school. *Canadian Children, 40,* 27–39. https://doi.org/10.18357/jcs .v40i3.15167

Binfet, J. T., & Passmore, H. A. (2017). Teachers' perceptions of kindness at school. *International Journal of Emotional Education, 9,* 37–53.

Binfet, J. T., & Passmore, H. A. (2019). The who, what, and where of school kindness: Exploring students' perspectives. *Canadian Journal of School Psychology, 34,* 22–37. https://doi.org/10.1177/0829573517732202

Binfet, J. T., & Whitehead, J. (2019). The effect of engagement in a kindness intervention on adolescents' well-being: A randomized controlled trial. *International Journal of Emotional Education, 11,* 33–49.

Binfet, J. T., Willis-Stewart, S., Lauze, A., Green, F. L. L., Draper, Z. A., & Calibaba, B. (in press). Understanding university students' conceptualizations and perceptions of kindness: A mixed methods study. *Journal of Further and Higher Education.* https://doi.org/10.1080/03098 77X.2021.1967895

Blakey, K. H., Mason, E., Cristea, M., McGuigan, N., & Messer, E. J. E. (2019). Does kindness always pay? The influence of recipient affection and generosity on young children's allocation decisions in a resource distribution task. *Current Psychology, 38,* 939–949. https://doi.org/10.1007/s12144-019-00260-7

Bower, A. A., & Casas, J. F. (2016). What parents do when children are good: Parent reports of strategies for reinforcing early childhood prosocial behaviors. *Journal of Child and Family Studies, 25,* 1310–1324. https://doi.org/10.1007/s10826-015-0293-5

Bronfenbrenner, U. (2005). *Making human beings human: Bioecological approaches on human development.* Sage.

Campos, B., & Algoe, S. (2009). Kindness. In S. J. Lopez (Ed.), *The encyclopedia of positive psychology* (pp. 551–557). Wiley-Blackwell.

Canter, D., Youngs, D., & Yaneva, M. (2017). Towards a measure of kindness: An exploration of a neglected interpersonal trait. *Personality and Individual Differences, 106,* 15–20. https://doi.org/10.1016/j.paid.2016.10.019

Cantor, P., Osher, D., Berg, J., Steyer, L., & Rose, T. (2019). Malleability, plasticity, and individuality: How children learn and develop in context. *Applied Developmental Science, 23,* 307–337. https://doi.org/10.1080/10888691.2017.1398649

Caplan, M. (1993). Inhibitory influences in development: The case of prosocial behavior. In D. F. Hay & A. Angold (Eds.), *Precursors and causes in development psychopathology* (pp. 169–198). Wiley.

Carlo, G., Padilla-Walker, L. M., & Nielson, M. G. (2015). Longitudinal bidirectional relations between adolescents' sympathy and prosocial behavior. *Developmental Psychology, 51,* 1771–1777. https://doi.org/10.1037/dev0000056

Cataldo, C. Z. (1984). Assertive kindness and the support of early prosocial behavior. *Peace and Change, 10,* 13–22.

Chancellor, J., Margolis, S., Jacobs Bao, K., & Lyubomirsky, S. (2017). Everyday prosociality in the workplace: The reinforcing benefits of giving, getting, and glimpsing. *Emotion, 18,* 507–517. https://pubmed.ncbi.nlm.nih.gov/28581323/

Chatterjee Singh, N., & Duraiappah, A. K. (Eds.). (2020). *Rethinking learning: A review of social and emotional learning frameworks for education systems.* UNESCO MGIEP.

Clegg, S., & Rowland, S. (2010). Kindness in pedagogical practice and academic life. *British Journal of Sociology of Education, 31,* 719–735. https://doi.org/10.1080/01425692.2010.515102

Cohen, J. (2006). Social, emotional, ethical, and academic preparation: Creating a climate for learning, participation in democracy, and well-being. *Harvard Educational Review, 76*(2), 201–237. https://doi.org/10.17763/haer.76.2.j44854x1524644vn

Collaborative for Academic and Social and Emotional Learning. (2022). Fundamentals of SEL. https://casel.org/fundamentals-of-sel/

Comunian, A. L. (1998). The kindness scale. *Psychological Reports, 83,* 1351–1361. https://doi.org/10.2466/pr0.1998.83.3f.1351

Cotney, J. L., & Banerjee, R. (2019). Adolescents' conceptualizations of kindness and its links with well-being: A focus group study. *Journal of Social and Personal Relationships, 36,* 599–617. https://doi.org/10.1177/0265407517738584

Curry, O. S., Rowland, L. A., Van Lissa, C. J., Zlotowitz, S., McAlaney, J., & Whitehouse, H. (2018). Happy to help? A systematic review and meta-analysis of the effects of performing acts of kindness on the well-being of the actor. *Journal of Experimental Social Psychology, 76,* 320–329. https://doi.org/10.1016/j.jesp.2018.02.014

Dahl, A. (2015). The developing social context of infant helping in two U.S. samples. *Child Development, 86,* 1080–1093. https://www.ncbi.nlm.nih.gov/pmc/articles/PMC4575818/

Datu, J. A. D., & Bernardo, A. B. I. (2020). The blessings of social-oriented virtues: Interpersonal character strengths are linked to increased life satisfaction and academic success among Filipino high school students. *Social Psychological and Personality Science, 11*(7), 983–990. https://doi.org/10.1177/1948550620906294

Datu, J. A. D., & Park, N. (2019). Perceived school kindness and academic engagement: The mediational roles of achievement goal orientations. *School Psychology International, 40,* 456–473. https://doi.org/10.1177/0143034319854474

Davidov, M., Vaish, A., Knafo-Noam, A., & Hastings, P. D. (2016). The motivational foundations of prosocial behavior from a developmental perspective – Evolutionary roots and key psychological mechanisms: Introduction to the special section. *Child Development, 87,* 1655–1667. https://doi.org/10.1111/cdev.12639

Davis, A. N., Martin-Cuellar, A., & Luce, H. (2019). Life events and prosocial behaviors among young adults: Considering the roles of perspective taking and empathic concern. *The Journal of Genetic Psychology, 180,* 205–216. https://doi.org/10.1080/00221325.2019.1632785

Demanet, J., & Van Houtte, M. (2012). School belonging and school misconduct: The differing role of teacher and peer attachment. *Journal of Youth and Adolescence, 41,* 499–514. https://psycnet.apa.org/record/2012-06697-009

Denham, S. A. (2015). Assessment of social and emotional learning in educational contexts. In J. A. Durlak, C. E. Domitrovich, R. P. Weissberg, & T. P. Gullotta (Eds.), *Handbook of social and emotional learning: Research and practice* (pp. 285–300). Guilford.

de Vries, D. A., Moller, A. M., Wieringa, M. S., Eigenraam, A. W., & Hamelink, K. (2018). Social comparison as the thief of joy: Emotional consequences of

viewing strangers' Instagram posts. *Media Psychology, 21,* 222–245. https://
doi.org/10.1080/15213269.2016.1267647

de Waal, F. B. M. (2008). Putting altruism back into altruism: The evolution of
empathy. *Annual Review of Psychology, 59,* 279–300. https://doi.org/10.1146
/annurev.psych.59.103006.093625

Dewey, J. (1964). Need for a philosophy of education. In R. D. Archambault
(Ed.), *John Dewey on education: Selected writings* (pp. 3–14). Random House.

Diener, M. L., & Lucas, R. E. (2004). Adults' desires for children's emotions
across 48 countries. *Journal of Cross-Cultural Psychology, 35,* 525–547. https://
doi.org/10.1177/0022022104268387

Dolan, P., & Metcalfe, R. (2012). Measuring subjective wellbeing:
Recommendations on measures for use by national governments. *Journal of
Social Policy, 41,* 409–427. https://doi.org/10.1017/S0047279411000833

Downey, J. A. (2010). Recommendations for fostering educational resilience in
the classroom. *Preventing School Failure, 58,* 56–64. https://doi.org/10.3200
/PSFL.53.1.56-64

Dunfield, K. A. (2014). A construct divided: Prosocial behavior as helping,
sharing, and comforting subtypes. *Frontiers in Psychology, 5,* 1–13. https://
doi.org/10.3389/fpsyg.2014.00958

Dunn, E. W., Aknin, L. B., & Norton, M. I. (2008). Spending money on others
promotes happiness. *Science, 319,* 1687–1688. https://doi.org/10.1126
/science.1150952

Durlak, J. A., Weissberg, R. P., Dymnicki, A. B., Taylor, R. D., & Schellinger,
K. B. (2011). The impact of enhancing students' social and emotional
learning: A meta-analysis of school-based universal interventions. *Child
Development, 82,* 405–432. https://doi.org/10.1111/j.1467-8624.2010.01564.x

Einarsdottir, J., Dockett, S., & Perry, B. (2009). Prosocial development. In
W. Damon & N. Eisenberg (Eds.), *Handbook of child psychology: Social,
emotional, and personality development* (pp. 646–718). Wiley.

Eisenberg, N. (1986). *Altruistic emotion, cognition and behavior.* Erlbaum.

Eisenberg, N., Guthrie, I., Murphy, B. C., Shepard, S. A., Cumberland, A., &
Carlo, G. (1999). Consistency and development of prosocial dispositions:
A longitudinal study. *Child Development, 70,* 1360–1372. https://doi.org
/10.1111/1467-8624.00100

Ferber, R. (1977). Research by convenience. *Journal of Consumer Research,
4,* 57–58.

Fowler, J. H., & Christakis, N. A. (2008). Dynamic spread of happiness
in a large social network: Longitudinal analysis over 20 years in the
Framington Heart Study. *British Medical Journal, 337,* 1–9. https://doi
.org/10.1136/bmj.a2338

Frenzel, A. C., Becker-Kurz, B., Pekrun, R., Goetz, T., & Ludtke, O. (2018).
Emotion transmission in the classroom revisited: A reciprocal effects

model of teacher and student enjoyment. *Journal of Educational Psychology,* *110*(5), 628–639. https://doi.org/10.1037/edu0000228

Frydenberg, E., Martin, A. J., & Collie, R. J. (2017). *Social and emotional learning in Australia and the Asia-Pacific.* Springer.

Gherghel, C., Nastas, D., Hashimoto, T., & Takai, J. (2019). The relationship between frequency of performing acts of kindness and subjective well-being: A mediation model in three cultures. *Current Psychology,* early online publication. https://doi.org/10.1007/s12144-019-00391-x

Gibb, S., & Rahman, S. (2019). Kindness among colleagues: Identifying and exploring the gaps in employment contexts. *International Journal of Organizational Analysis, 27,* 582–595. https://doi.org/10.1108/IJOA-02-2018-1357

Gillham, J., Adams-Deutsch, Z., Werner, J., Reivich, K., Coulter-Heindl, V., ... Seligman, M. E. P. (2011). Character strengths predict subjective well-being during adolescence. *The Journal of Positive Psychology, 6*(1), 31–44. https://doi.org/10.1080/17439760.2010.536773

Goodenow, C., & Grady, K. E. (1993). The relationship of school belonging and friends' values to academic motivation among urban adolescent students. *Journal of Experimental Education, 62*(1), 60–71. https://doi.org/10.1080/00220973.1993.9943831

Greenberg, M. T., & Turksma, C. (2015). Understanding and watering the seeds of compassion. *Research in Human Development, 12,* 280–287.

Hammer, I. M., & Murray, J. P. (1979). Kindness in the kindergarten: The relative influence of role playing and prosocial television in facilitating altruism. *International Journal of Behavioral Development, 2,* 133–157.

Hamre, B. K., & Pianta, R. C. (2006). Student–teacher relationship. In G. G. Bear & K. M. Minke (Eds.), *Children's needs III: Development, prevention, and intervention* (pp. 59–72). National Association of School Psychologists.

Hanel, P. H. P., & Vione, K. C. (2016). Do student samples provide an accurate estimate of the general public? *PLOS ONE, 11,* e016834. https://doi.org/10.1371/journal.pone.0168354

Haslip, M. J., Allen-Handy, A., & Donaldson, L. (2019). How do children and teachers demonstrate love, kindness and forgiveness? Findings from an early childhood strength-spotting intervention. *Early Childhood Education Journal, 47,* 531–547. https://doi.org/10.1007/s10643-019-00951-7

Hay, D. F. (1994). Prosocial development. *Journal of Child Psychology and Psychiatry, 35,* 29–71.

Hay, D. F., Nash, A., & Pederson, J. (1981). Responses of six-month-olds to the distress of their peers. *Child Development, 52*(3), 1071–1075. https://doi.org/10.2307/1129114

Heffernan, L., & Wallace, J. (2016, 20 January). To get into college, Harvard report advocates for kindness instead of overachieving. *Washington Post.*

https://www.washingtonpost.com/news/parenting/wp/2016/01/20/to
-get-into-college-harvard-report-advocates-for-kindness-instead-of
-overachieving/?utm_term=.da11dcfbdcaf

Heintz, S., Kramm, C., & Ruch, W. (2019). A meta-analysis of gender
differences in character strengths and age, nation, and measure as
moderators. *The Journal of Positive Psychology, 14*(1), 102–112. https://doi.org
/10.1080/17439760.2017.1414297

Hendriks, T., Warren, M. A., Schotanus-Dijkstra, M., Hassankhan, A.,
Graafsma, T., Bohlmeijer, E., & de Jong, J. (2019). How WEIRD are positive
psychology interventions? A bibliometric analysis of randomized
controlled trials on the science of well-being. *The Journal of Positive
Psychology, 14*(4), 489–501. https://doi.org/10.1080/17439760.2018
.1484941

Henrich, J., Heine, S. J., & Norenzayan, A. (2010). The weirdest people in
the world? *Behavioral and Brain Science, 33*, 61–83. https://doi.org/10.1017
/S0140525X0999152X

Herbert, A. (1985). Random kindness and senseless acts of beauty. *Whole Earth
Review, 47*, 96.

Herbert, A., & Pavel, M. M. (1993). *Random kindness and senseless acts of beauty.*
Volcano Press.

Huber, A., Barber, A. L. A., Farago, T., Muller, C. A., & Huber, L. (2017).
Investigating emotional contagion in dogs (*Canis familiaris*) to emotional
sounds of humans and conspecifics. *Animal Cognition, 20*, 703–715. https://
doi.org/10.1007/s10071-017-1092-8

Humphrey, N. (Ed.). (2013). *Social and emotional learning: A critical appraisal.*
SAGE Publications.

Hyson, M., & Taylor, J. L. (2011, July). Caring about caring: What adults can
do to promote young children's prosocial skills. *Young Children, 66*, 74–83.
https://www.jstor.org/stable/42731285

Jackson, P. (1968). *Life in classrooms.* Holt, Rinehart, & Winston.

Jazaieri, H. (2018). Compassionate education from preschool to graduate
school: Bringing a culture of compassion into the classroom. *Journal of
Research in Innovative Teaching & Learning, 11*, 22–66.

Jennings, P. A., & Greenberg, M. T. (2009). The prosocial classroom: Teacher
social and emotional competence in relation to student and classroom
outcomes. *Review of Educational Research, 79*, 491–525. https://doi.org
/10.3102/0034654308325693

Jerald, C. D. (2006, December). School culture: The hidden curriculum. The
Center for Comprehensive School Reform and Improvement (pp. 1–8).
Journal of Social Issues, 44, 81–100.

Jones, D. E., Greenberg, M., & Crowley, M. (2015). Early social-emotional
functioning and public health: The relationship between kindergarten

social competence and future wellness. *American Journal of Public Health,* *105,* 2283–90. https://doi.org/10.2105/AJPH.2015.302630

Karris, M. A., & Craighead, W. E. (2012). Differences in character among U.S. college students. *Individual Differences Research, 10,* 69–80.

Keltner, D. (2009). *Born to be good: The science of a meaningful life.* W. W. Norton & Company.

Kerr, S. L., O'Donovan, A., & Pepping, C. (2015). Can gratitude and kindness interventions enhance well-being in a clinical sample? *Journal of Happiness Studies, 16,* 17–36. https://doi.org/10.1007/s10902-013-9492-1

Kim, H. R., Kim, S. M., Hong, J. S., Han, D. H., Yoo, S. K., Min, K. J., & Lee, Y. S. (2018). Character strengths as protective factors against depression and suicidality among male and female employees. *BMC Public Health, 18,* 1084. https://doi.org/10.1186/s12889-018-5997-1

Ko, K., Margolis, S., Revord, J., & Lyuobomirsky, S. (2019). Comparing the effects of performing and recalling acts of kindness. *The Journal of Positive Psychology.* Advance online publication. https://doi.org/10.1080/17439760.2019.1663252

Kosek, R. B. (1995). Measuring prosocial behavior of college students. *Psychological Reports, 77,* 739–742. https://doi.org/10.2466/pr0.1995.77.3.739

Krane, V., Ness, O., Holter-Sorensen, N., Karlsson, B., & Biner, P.-E., (2017). "You notice that there is something positive about going to school": How teachers' kindness can promote positive teacher–student relationships in upper secondary school. *International Journal of Adolescence and Youth, 22,* 377–389. https://doi.org/10.1080/02673843.2016.1202843

Laible, D., McGinley, M., Carlo, G., Augustine, M., & Murphy, T. (2014). Does engaging in prosocial behavior make children see the world through rose-colored glasses? *Developmental Psychology, 50,* 872–880. https://doi.org/10.1037/a0033905

Lamborn, S. D., Fischer, K. W., & Pipp, S. (1994). Constructive criticism and social lies: A developmental sequence for understanding honesty and kindness in social interactions. *Developmental Psychology, 30*(4), 495–508. https://doi.org/10.1037/0012-1649.30.4.495

Layous, K., Nelson, S. K., Kurtz, J. L., & Lyubomirsky, S. (2017). What triggers prosocial effort? A positive feedback loop between positive activities, kindness, and well-being. *The Journal of Positive Psychology, 12*(4), 385–398. https://doi.org/10.1080/17439760.2016.1198924

Layous, K., Nelson, S. K., Oberle, E., Schonert-Reichl, K. A., & Lyubomirsky, S. (2012). Kindness counts: Prompting prosocial behavior in preadolescents boosts peer acceptance and well-being. *PLOS ONE, 7,* e51380. https://doi.org/10.1371/journal.pone.0051380

Leahy, R. L. (1979). Development of conceptions of prosocial behavior: Information affecting rewards given for altruism and kindness.

Developmental Psychology, 15(1), 34–37. https://doi.org/10.1037/0012 -1649.15.1.34

Lee, C.-K. J., & Huang, J. (2021). The relations between students' sense of school belonging, perceptions of school kindness and character strength of kindness. *Journal of School Psychology, 84*, 95–108. https://doi.org/10.1016 /j.jsp.2020.12.001

Lickona, T. (2018, 2 May). Raising kind kids: 5 simple things you can do. *Psychology Today*. https://www.psychologytoday.com/us/blog/raising -kind-kids/201805/raising-kind-kids-5-simple-things-you-can-do

Long, N. J. (1997). The therapeutic power of kindness. *Reclaiming Children and Youth, 5*, 242–246.

Luks, A. (1988, October). Helper's high: Volunteering makes people feel good, physically and emotionally. And like "runner's calm," it's probably good for your health. *Psychology Today, 22*, 34–42.

Lynch, S. A., & Simpson, C. G. (2010). Social skills: Laying the foundation for success. *Dimensions of Early Childhood, 38*, 3–12.

Lyubomirsky, S., & Layous, K. (2013). How do simple positive activities increase well-being? *Current Directions in Psychological Science, 22*, 57–62. https://doi.org/10.1177/0963721412469809

Lyubomirsky, S., Sheldon, K. M., & Schkade, D. (2005). Pursuing happiness: The architecture of sustainable change. *Review of General Psychology, 9*, 111–131. https://doi.org/10.1037/1089-2680.9.2.111

Magen, Z., & Aharoni, R. (1991). Adolescents' contributing toward others: Relationship to positive experiences and transpersonal commitment. *Journal of Humanistic Psychology, 31*, 126–143.

Magnani, E., & Zhu, R. (2018). Does kindness lead to happiness? Voluntary activities and subjective well-being. *Journal of Behavioral and Experimental Economics, 77*, 20–28. https://doi.org/10.1016/j.socec.2018.09.009

Mahoney, J. L., Durlak, J. A., & Weissberg, R. P. (2018-2019). An update on social and emotional learning outcome research. *Phi Delta Kappan, 100*, 18–23. https://doi.org/10.1177/0031721718815668

McCarthy, C. J. (2019, November). Teacher stress: Balancing demands and resources. *Phi Delta Kappan, 101*(3): 8–14. https://doi.org/10.1177 /0031721719885909

McGrath, R. E. (2015). Character strengths in 75 nations: An update. *The Journal of Positive Psychology, 10*, 41–52. https://doi.org/10.1080/17439760.2014.888580

Mehus, C. J., Watson, R. J., Eisenberg, M. E., Corliss, H. L., & Porta, C. M. (2017). Living as an LGBTQ adolescent and a parent's child: Overlapping or separate experiences. *Journal of Family Nursing, 23*(2), 175–200. https://doi.org /10.1177/1074840717696924

Merriam-Webster. (2020). Compassion. https://www.merriam-webster.com /dictionary/compassion

Mesurado, B., Guerra, P., Richaud, M. C., & Rodriguez, L. M. (2019). Effectiveness of prosocial behavior interventions: A meta-analysis. In P. A. Gargiulo & H. L. Arroyo (Eds.), *Psychiatry and neuroscience update: From translational research to a humanistic approach: Vol. 3* (pp. 259–271). Springer.

Midlarsky, E. (1991). Helping as coping. In M. S. Clark (Ed.), *Review of Personality and Social Psychology: Vol. 12. Prosocial Behavior* (pp. 238–264). Sage Publications.

Miles, A., Andiappan, M., Upenieks, L., & Orfanidis, C. (2021). Using prosocial behavior to safeguard mental health and foster emotional well-being during the Covid-19 pandemic: A registered report protocol for a randomized controlled trial. *PLOS ONE, 16*(1), e0245865. https://doi.org/10.1371/journal.pone.0245865

Mongrain, M., Barnes, C., Barnhart, R., & Zalan, L. B. (2018). Acts of kindness reduce depression in individuals low on agreeableness. *Translational Issues in Psychological Science, 4*, 323–334. https://doi.org/10.1037/tps0000168

Morgan, T. L., & Cieminski, A. B. (2020). Exploring mechanisms that influence adolescent academic motivation. *Journal of Educational Studies.* Early online edition. https://doi.org/10.1080/03055698.2020.1729102

Morrish, L., Rickard, N., Chin, T. C., & Vella-Brodrick, D. A. (2018). Emotion regulation in adolescent well-being and positive education. *Journal of Happiness Studies, 19*, 1543–1564. https://doi.org/10.1007/s10902-017-9881-y

Nantel-Vivier, A., Kokko, K. Caprara, G. V., Pastorelli, C., Gerbino, M. G., Paciello, M., … Tremblay, R. E. (2009). Prosocial development from childhood to adolescence: A multi-informant perspective with Canadian and Italian longitudinal studies. *Journal of Child Psychology and Psychiatry, 505*, 590–598.

Nantel-Vivier, A., Pihl, R., O., Cote, S., & Tremblay, R. E. (2014). Developmental association of prosocial behaviour with aggression, anxiety and depression from infancy to preadolescence. *Journal of Child Psychology & Psychiatry, 55*, 1135–1144. https://doi.org/10.1111/jcpp.12235

Nelson-Coffey, S. K., Fritz, M. M., Lyubomirsky, S., & Cole, S. W. (2017). Kindness in the blood: A randomized controlled trial of the gene regulatory impact of prosocial behavior. *Psychoneuroendocrinology, 81*, 8–13. https://doi.org/10.1016/j.psyneuen.2017.03.025

Noddings, N. (1995). Teaching themes of care. *Phi Delta Kappan, 76*(9), 675–679.

Oberle, E., & Schonert-Reichl, K. A. (2016). Stress contagion in the classroom? The link between classroom teacher burnout and morning cortisol in elementary school students. *Social Science & Medicine, 159*, 30–37. https://doi.org/10.1016/j.socscimed.2016.04.031

Oliner, S. P. (2005). Altruism, forgiveness, empathy, and intergroup apology. *Humbolt Journal of Social Relations, 29*, 8–39. https://www.jstor.org/stable/pdf/23262795

Organisation for Economic Co-operation and Development. (2015). *Skills for social progress: The power of social and emotional skills*. OECD Publishing.

Organization for Economic Co-operation and Development. (2018). *The future of education and skills: Education 2030*. E2030 Position Paper. OECD Publishing.

Otake, K., Shimai, S., Tanaka-Matsumi, J., Otsui, K., & Fredrickson, B. L. (2006). Happy people become happier through kindness: A counting kindness intervention. *Journal of Happiness Studies, 7*, 361–375. https://doi.org/10.1007/s10902-005-3650-z

Padilla-Walker, L. M., Memmott-Elison, M. K., & Coyne, S. M. (2018). Associations between prosocial behavior and problem behavior in early to late adolescence. *Journal of Youth and Adolescence, 47*, 961–975. https://doi.org/10.1007/s10964-017-0736-y

Padilla-Walker, L. M., Memmott-Elison, M. K., & Nielson, M. G. (2018). Longitudinal change in high-cost prosocial behaviors of defending and including during the transition to adulthood. *Journal of Youth and Adolescence, 47*, 1853–1865. https://doi.org/10.1007/s10964-018-0875-9

Padilla-Walker, L. M., Stockdale, L. A., Son, D., Coyne, S. M., & Stinnett, S. C. (2020). Associations between parental media monitoring style, information management, and prosocial and aggressive behaviors. *Journal of Social and Personal Relationships, 37*, 180–200. https://doi.org/10.1177/0265407519859653

Paquet, A., Binfet, J. T., & Paquet, Y. (2019). La bienveillance à l'école: Essai de définition et exemples de la perception des élèves (pp. 131–150). In C. Martin-Krumm & C. Tarquino (Eds.), *Psychologie positive: État des savoirs, champs d'application et perspectives*. Dunod. https://www.dunod.com/sites/default/files/atoms/files/9782100794072/Feuilletage.pdf

Park, N., Peterson, C., & Seligman, M. E. (2006). Character strengths in fifty-four nations and fifty US states. *The Journal of Positive Psychology, 1*(3), 118–129. https://doi.org/10.1080/17439760600619567

Pastorelli, C., Lansford, J. E., Luengo Kanacri, B. P., Malone, P. S., Di Giunta, L., ... Sorbring, E. (2016). Positive parenting and children's prosocial behavior in eight countries. *Journal of Child Psychology and Psychiatry, 57*, 824–834. https://doi.org/10.1111/jcpp.12477

Pekel, K., & Scales, P. C. (2018, February). Remember the relationships: The missing link that makes SEL measures more understandable and actionable. https://measuringsel.casel.org/remember-relationships-missing-link-makes-sel-measures-understandable-actionable/

Peterson, C., & Seligman, M. E. (2004). *Character strengths and virtues: A handbook and classification*. Oxford University Press.

Peterson, R. A., & Merunka, D. R. (2014). Convenience samples of college students and research reproducibility. *Journal of Business Research, 67*, 1035–1041. https://doi.org/10.1016/j.jbusres.2013.08.010

Piaget, J. (1932/1964). Development and learning. *Journal of Research in Science Teaching, 2,* 176–186. https://psychscenehub.com/wp-content/uploads/2021/03/Piaget-Cognitive-Development-in-Children.pdf

Poll, Z. (2019, 9 October). In France, elder care comes with the mail. *The New Yorker.* https://www.newyorker.com/culture/annals-of-inquiry/in-france-elder-care-comes-with-the-mail

Pommier, E., Neff, K. D., & Tosh-Kiraly, I. (2020). The development and validation of the Compassion Scale. *Assessment, 27,* 27–39. https://doi.org/10.1177/1073191119874108

Post, S. G. (2005). Altruism, happiness, and health: It's good to be good. *International Journal of Behavioral Medicine, 12,* 66–77. https://doi.org/10.1207/s15327558ijbm1202_4

Post, S. G. (2011). *The hidden gifts of helping: How the power of giving, compassion, and hope can get us through hard times.* Jossey-Bass.

Post, S. G. (2017). Rx It's good to be good (G2BG) 2017 commentary: Prescribing volunteerism for health, happiness, resilience, and longevity. *American Journal of Health Promotion, 31,* 164–172.

Raposa, E. B., Laws, H. B., & Ansell, E. B. (2016). Prosocial behavior mitigates the negative effects of stress in everyday life. *Clinical Psychological Sciences, 4,* 691–698. https://doi.org/10.1177/2167702615611073

Riley, K. (2019). Agency and belonging: What transformative actions can schools take to help create a sense of place and belonging? *Educational & Child Psychology, 36,* 91–103.

Roeser, R. W., Colaianne, B. A., & Greenberg, M. A. (2018). Compassion and human development: Current approaches and future directions. *Research in Human Development, 15,* 238–251.

Rogers, S., & Renard, L. (1999). Relationship-driven teaching. *Educational Leadership, 57,* 34–37.

Rowland, L. (2018). Kindness: Society's golden chain? *The Psychologist, 31,* 30–35. https://thepsychologist.bps.org.uk/volume-2018/february-2018/kindness-societys-golden-chain

Rowland, L., & Curry, O. S. (2018). A range of kindness activities boost happiness. *The Journal of Social Psychology.* Advance online publication. https://doi.org/10.1080/00224545.2018.1469461

Rowland, L., & Klisanin, D. (2018). Cyber-kindness: Spreading kindness in cyberspace. *Media Psychology Review, 12*(1). https://mprcenter.org/review/cyber-kindness-spreading-kindness-in-cyberspace/

Ryan, R. M., & Deci, E. L. (2000). Self-determination theory and the facilitation of intrinsic motivation, social development, and well-being. *American Psychologist, 55*(1), 68–788. https://doi.org/10.1037//0003-066x.55.1.68

Schachter, R. (1999). Can kindness be taught? *Instructor, 120,* 58–63.

Schonert-Reichl, K. A. (2019). Advancements in the landscape of social and emotional learning and emerging topics on the horizon. *Educational Psychologist, 54,* 222–232.

Schonert-Reichl, K. A., Kitil, M. J., & Hanson-Peterson, J. (2017). *To reach the students, teach the teachers: A national scan of teacher preparation and social and emotional learning.* University of British Columbia Press.

Schonert-Reichl, K. A., Oberle, E., Lawlor, M. S., Abbott, D., Thomson, K., Oberlander, T. F., & Diamond, A. (2015). Enhancing cognitive and social-emotional development through a simple-to-administer mindfulness-based school program for elementary school children: A randomized controlled trial. *Developmental Psychology, 51,* 52–66.

Schonert-Reichl, K. A., & O'Brien, M. U. (2012). Social and emotional learning and prosocial education: Theory, research, and programs. In A. Higgins-D'Alessandro, M. Corrigan, & P. Brown (Eds.), *The case for prosocial education: Developing caring, capable citizens* (Vol. 1, pp. 311–345). Rowman & Littlefield.

Schonert-Reichl, K. A., Smith, V., Zaidman-Zait, A., & Hertzman, C. (2012). Promoting children's prosocial behaviors in school: Impact of the "Roots of Empathy" program on the social and emotional competence of school-aged children. *School Mental Health, 4,* 1–21.

Schreier, H. M. C., Schonert-Reichl, K. A., & Chen, E. (2013). Effect of volunteering on risk factors for cardiovascular disease in adolescents. *Journal of American Medical Association, 167,* 327–332. https://doi.org/10.1001/jamapediatrics.2013.1100

Seligman, M. E. P., & Csikszentmihalyi, M. (2000). Positive psychology: An introduction. *American Psychologist, 55,* 5–14.

Seligman, M. E. P., Ernst, R. M., Gillham, J., Reivich, K., & Linkins, M. (2009). Positive education: Positive psychology and classroom interventions. *Oxford Review of Education, 35,* 293–311. https://doi.org/10.1080/03054980902934563

Seton, H. (2019, October). The elephant in the classroom. *Educational Leadership, 77,* 80. https://eric.ed.gov/?id=EJ1231158

Shapiro, J., Youm, J., Kheriaty, A., Pham, T., Chen, Y., & Clayman, R. (2019). The human kindness curriculum: An innovative preclinical initiative to highlight kindness and empathy in medicine. *Education for Health, 32,* 53–61.

Shin, L. J., Margolis, S. M., Walsh, L. C., Kwok, S. Y. C. L., Yue, X., Chan, C.-K., Siu, N., Sheldon, K. M., & Lyubomirsky, S. (2021). Cultural differences in the hedonic rewards of recalling kindness: Priming cultural identify with language. *Affective Science, 2,* 80–90. https://doi.org/10.1007/s42761-020-00029-3

Shoshani, A. (2019). Young children's character strengths and emotional well-being: Development of the Character Strengths Inventory for Early

Childhood (CSI-EC). *The Journal of Positive Psychology, 14*(1), 86–102. https://doi.org/10.1080/17439760.2018.1424925

Shoshani, A., & Slone, M. (2013). Middle school transition from the strengths perspective: Young adolescents' character strengths, subjective well-being, and school adjustment. *Journal of Happiness Studies, 14,* 1163–1181. https://doi.org/10.1007/s10902-012-9374-y

Smeets, E., Neff, K., Alberts, H., & Peters, M. (2014). Meeting suffering with kindness: Effects of a brief self-compassion intervention for female college students. *Journal of Clinical Psychology, 70*(9), 794–807. https://doi.org/10.1002/jclp.22076

Sparks, A. M., Fessler, D. M. T., & Holbrook, C. (2019). Elevation, an emotion for prosocial contagion, is experienced more strongly by those with greater expectations of the cooperativeness of others. *PLOS ONE, 14,* e0226071. https://doi.org/10.1371/journal.pone.0226071

Sproull, L., Conley, C. A., & Moon, J. Y. (2013). The kindness of strangers: Prosocial behavior on the internet. In Y. Amichai-Hamburger (Ed.), *The social net: Understanding our online behavior* (pp. 140–153). https://doi.org/10.1162/daed_a_00120

Staub, E. (1988). The evolution of caring and nonaggressive persons and societies. *Journal of Social Issues, 44*(2), 81–100. https://doi.org/10.1111/j.1540-4560.1988.tb02064.x

Staub, E. (2005). The roots of goodness: The fulfillment of basic human needs and the development of caring, helping and nonaggression, inclusive caring, moral courage, active bystandership, and altruism born of suffering. In G. Carlo & C. P. Edwards (Eds.), *Moral motivation through the lifespan* (Vol. 51, pp. 33–72). University of Nebraska Press.

Stiff, C., Rosenthal-Stott, H. E. S., Wake, S., & Woodward, A. (2019). Student pro-sociality: Measuring institutional and individual factors that predict pro-social behaviour at university. *Current Psychology, 38,* 920–930. https://doi.org/10.1007/s12144-019-00256-3

Suldo, S. M., Hearon, B. V., Bander, B., McCullough, M., Garofano, J., Roth, R. A., & Tan, S. Y. (2015). Increasing elementary school students' subjective well-being through a classwide positive psychology intervention: Results of a pilot study. *Contemporary School Psychology, 19,* 300–311. https://doi.org/10.1007/s40688-015-0061-y

Taylor, R. D., Oberle, E., Durlak, J. A., & Weissberg, R. P. (2017). Promoting positive youth development through school-based social and emotional learning interventions: A meta-analysis of follow-up effects. *Child Development, 88*(4), 1156–1171. https://doi.org/10.1111/cdev.12864

Thomas, A. G., Jonason, P. K., Blackburn, J. D., Ottensen Kennair, L. E., Lowe, R., … Li, N. P. (2019). Mate preference priorities in the East and West:

A cross-cultural test of the mate preference priority model. *Journal of Personality, 88*(3), 606–620. https://doi.org/10.1111/jopy.12514

Torrente, C., Alimchandani, A., & Aber, J. L. (2015). International perspectives on social and emotional learning. In J. A. Durlak, C. E. Domitrovich, R. P. Weissberg, & T. P. Gullotta (Eds.), *Handbook on social and emotional learning: Research and practice* (pp. 566–587). Guilford Publications.

Trew, J. L., & Alden, L. E. (2015). Kindness reduces avoidance goals in socially anxious individuals. *Motivation and Emotion, 39*(6), 892–907. https://doi.org/10.1007/s11031-015-9499-5

Van der Graaff, J., Carlo, G., Crocetti, E., Koot, H. M., & Branje, S. (2018). Prosocial behavior in adolescence: Gender differences in development and links with empathy. *Journal of Youth and Adolescence, 47*(5), 1086–1099. https://doi.org/10.1007/s10964-017-0786-1

Vella-Brodrick, D. A., Chin, T.-C., & Rickard, N. S. (2019). Examining the processes and effects of an exemplar school-based well-being approach on student competency, autonomy and relatedness. *Health Promotion International, 35*(5), 1190–1198. https://doi.org/10.1093/heapro/daz115

von der Embse, N. P. (2017). The psychological and instructional consequences of high-stakes accountability. *Psychology of Education Review, 41*, 45–50.

von der Embse, N., Ryan, S. V., Gibbs, T., & Mankin, A. (2019). Teacher stress interventions: A systematic review. *Psychology in the Schools, 56*, 1328–1343. https://doi.org/10.1002/pits.22279

Wang, S., & Tamis-Lemonda, C. S. (2003). Do child-rearing values in Taiwan and the United States reflect cultural values of collectivism or individualism? *Journal of Cross-Cultural Psychology, 34*, 629–642. https://doi.org/10.1177/0022022103255498

Warneken, F., & Tomasello, M. (2006). Altruistic helping in human infants and young chimpanzees. *Science, 311*, 1301–1303. https://doi.org/10.1126/science.1121448

Warneken, F., & Tomasello, M. (2011). The roots of human altruism. *British Journal of Psychology, 100*(3), 455–471. https://doi.org/10.1348/000712608X379061

Warneken, F., & Tomasello, M. (2014). Extrinsic rewards undermine altruistic tendencies in 20-month olds. *Motivation Science, 1*, 43–48. https://doi.org/10.1037/2333-8113.1.S.43

Watson, A., & McCathren, R. (2009, March). Including children with special needs: Are you and your early childhood program ready? *Young Children*, 20–26.

Weissberg, R. P. (2019). Promoting the social and emotional learning of millions of school children. *Perspectives on Psychological Science, 14*, 65–69. https://doi.org/10.1177/1745691618817756

Weissberg, R. P., Durlak, J. A., Domitrovich, C. E., & Durlak, J. A. (2015). Social and emotional learning: Past, present, and future. In J. A. Durlak, C. E. Domitrovich, R. P. Weissberg, & T. P. Gullotta (Eds.), *Handbook of social and emotional learning: Research and practice* (pp. 3–19). Guilford.

Wentzel, K. R. (1993). Does being good make the grade? Social behavior and academic competence in middle school. *Journal of Educational Psychology, 85*(2), 357–364.

Whillans, A. V., Dunn, E. W., Sandstrom, G. M., Dickerson, S. S., & Madden, K. M. (2016). Is spending money on others good for your heart? *Health Psychology, 35,* 574–583. https://doi.org/10.1037/hea0000332

Winkler, J. L., Walsh, M. E., de Blois, M., Mare, J., & Carvajal, S. C. (2017). Kind discipline: Developing a conceptual model of a promising school discipline approach. *Evaluation and Program Planning, 62,* 15–24. https://doi.org/10.1016/j.evalprogplan.2017.02.002

Yurdabakan, I., & Bas, A. U. (2019). Factor structure, measurement invariance, criterion validity, and reliability of the School Kindness Scale: Turkish middle school sample. *Journal of Psychoeducational Assessment, 37*(8), 1002–1015. https://doi.org/10.1177/0734282918803500

Zeng, X., Chiu, C. P. K., Wang, R., Oei, T. P. S., & Leung, F. Y. K. (2015). The effect of loving-kindness meditation on positive emotions: A meta-analytic review. *Frontiers in Psychology, 6,* 1693. https://doi.org/10.3389/fpsyg.2015.01693

Zinsser, K. M., Denham, S. A., Curby, T. W., & Shewark, E. A. (2015). "Practice what you preach": Teachers' perceptions of emotional competence and emotionally supportive classroom practices. *Early Education and Development, 26,* 899–919. https://doi.org/10.1080/10409289.2015.1009320

Index

Abbott, D., 29, 207
Aber, J.L., xvii, 209
active lifestyle, 49
Adams-Deutsch, Z., 47, 200
adjustment, 45
administrator, xx, xxiii, 26, 127, 130, 168–9
adolescents, xvii, xx, 3, 7–13, 16–20, 23, 25–6, 28–9, 31–3, 35, 37, 45–7, 49, 51–5, 58–9, 61–2, 64–5, 67, 69, 71–3, 75–6, 79, 81, 83–6, 89, 92, 95–7, 99–101, 105, 107–9, 112, 114–16, 118–19, 131, 135–7, 139–41, 146–8, 151, 153–4, 177, 180, 193, 196–8, 200, 202–4, 207–8; mid-, 11; pre-, 54
adult, xvii–xviii, xx, 18, 23, 29, 49–51, 69, 77, 81–3, 89, 97, 99–101, 104, 112, 116, 128–31, 138–9, 141, 143, 147–8, 160, 181, 192, 198–9, 201, 205; adulthood, xvii–xviii, 10–11, 23, 205; caregiver, 11, 83, 89, 99, 104; participants, 12; perspectives, 7
adversity, 96, 148
advocating, 42, 139
affect, 5, 12, 23–4, 27, 30, 35, 45–9, 56, 58, 61, 64, 97, 104, 108, 124, 138, 143, 148, 158, 177, 196, 202, 207; negative, 45–7, 56; positive, 45, 47–9, 58, 108, 177
agencies, 76, 78, 95, 130
agency, 206
aggressive, 59, 107, 208; behaviours, xviii, 36, 59, 61–2, 107–8, 205; models, 36, 195

Aharoni, R., 52, 99, 203
Aknin, L.B., 12, 38, 53, 195, 199
Alberts, H., 13, 208
Alden, L.E., 12, 209
Algoe, S.B., 5, 13, 195, 197
Alimchandani, A., xvii, 209
Allen, K., 124, 195
Allen-Handy, A., 12, 200
alliance, 96
altruism, xvi, xviii, xxi, 3, 5–6, 13, 51, 179, 196, 199–200, 202, 204, 206, 208–9
Amichai-Hamburger, Y., 150, 208
Anderson, N.B., 56, 195
Andiappan, M., 12, 204
anger, 103, 106
Angold, A., 132, 197
animal shelter, 78, 95
Ansell, E.B., 49, 51, 206
anxiety, 81, 84, 204
appreciation, 6
Archambault, R.D., xvi, 199
Arroya, H.L., 61–2, 204
Ashton-James, C.E., 12, 38, 195
attitudes, 26–8
audience, 18, 89, 181
Augustine, M., 61, 202
autonomy, 108, 209
awareness, 18, 52, 76, 79, 86, 89, 118, 133, 137–8, 141, 144, 181; global, xvi; self, 18, 30; social, 18, 30;

Baldwin, A., 7, 11, 195
Baldwin, C.P., 7, 11, 195
Bander, B., 14, 208
Bandura, A., 36, 195

Banerjee, R., 5, 12, 37, 39, 198
Barber, A.L.A., 101, 201
Barnes, C., 56, 204
Barnhart, R., 56, 204
Barrington-Leigh, C.P., 12, 38, 195
Bas, A.U., 12, 132, 210
Batson, C.D., 13, 196
Becker-Kurz, B., 103, 199
behaviour, xi–xii, xvii, 5, 7, 9, 14–15,
    23–4, 26, 29–32, 35–6, 39, 49–50,
    52, 59, 62, 64, 71, 81, 83–4, 89–90,
    105–7, 109, 112, 124, 127, 130, 144,
    178; adolescent, 16; aggressive,
    xviii, 36, 61–2, 107; altruistic,
    107; child, 16, 90; comforting, 5;
    defending, 91; desired, 127, 129;
    externalizing, 59; goal-directed,
    5; helping, 5, 49; including,
    91; mindful, 31; negative, 100;
    positive, 26; problems, xviii;
    prosocial (see under prosocial);
    sharing, 5; student, 16, 26, 39, 105;
    voluntary, 61
belonging, 12, 45, 106, 123–4, 195,
    198, 200, 203, 206
benefits, vii, x, xvii, 5, 7, 11–12, 26–8,
    33, 49, 50–1, 54, 58, 61–2, 84, 97,
    100, 124, 134, 137, 144, 168, 197;
    kindness (see under kindness)
Berg, J., 62, 101, 197
Bernardo, A.B.I., 6, 198
Biglan, A., 90, 196
Biner, P.E., 104–5, 202
Binfet, J.T., iii, v, xv, xvi, xvii, xviii,
    xix, 12, 153–4, 196, 205
biomarker, 104, 148
Biswas-Diener, R., 12, 38, 195
Blackburn, J.D., 17, 208
Blakey, K.H., 12, 38, 196
Bohlmeijer, E., 34, 38, 201
Bower, A.A., 91, 197
brainstorm, ix–x, 8, 65, 75–6, 78, 130,
    171
Branje, S., 63, 132, 309
bravery, 81
Bronfenbrenner, U., xx, 197
Brown, P., xvi, 207
bullying, vii, xviii, 15–16, 91, 141,
    157–8; anti-, 15, 179; cyber-, 150
burnout, 103–4, 144, 204
Burns, J., 12, 38, 195

Calibaba, B., 12, 39, 154, 196
Campos, B., 5, 197
Canter, D., 5, 12, 131, 197
Cantor, P., 62, 101, 197
Campos, B., 197
Caplan, M., 132, 197
Caprara, G.V., 11, 61,
    132, 204
care, xv–xvi, xix, 7, 9, 17, 30–1, 70–1,
    83, 96, 99, 119, 122–3, 167, 204, 206;
    giver, 11, 83, 89, 99, 104; for others,
    xv, xx, 8, 20, 22, 31, 33, 128, 141
Carlo, G., 5, 11, 61, 63, 132, 197, 199,
    202, 208–9
Carvajal, S.C., xiii, 128–30, 210
Casas, J.F., 91, 197
case study, 37
Cataldo, C.Z., 7, 197
Chan, C.K., 12, 207
Chancellor, J., 12, 39, 103, 197
character, 6, 14, 17, 32, 129–30, 202;
    strengths, 6–7, 45, 47, 198, 200–2,
    205, 207–8
characteristics, xiii, xvi, 130; activity,
    35; individual, 35
Chatterjee Sing, N., 17, 197
Chen, E., xvii, 148, 207
Chen, Y., 12, 207
children, xv, xvii–xx, 3, 7–8, 10–15,
    17–20, 23, 25–6, 28–9, 33, 35, 37,
    39–40, 45, 49, 51–6, 58–9, 61–2,
    64–5, 67, 69, 71–3, 75–6, 79, 81–6,
    89–92, 95–7, 99–101, 104–5, 107–9,
    112, 114–16, 118–19, 131, 135–41
Chin, T.C., 15, 204, 209
Chiu, C.P.K., 141, 210
Christakis, N.A., 35, 103, 199
Cieminski, A.B., 132, 204
Clark, M.S., 49, 204
class, 46, 65, 70, 73, 79, 81, 99, 101,
    105–6, 109, 114, 117–18, 123–4, 138,
    144, 150, 158, 168, 171, 178, 180–2;
    climate, 123–4, 139, 168; online, 150
classmates, 28, 47, 63, 69–70, 88, 101,
    109, 117–18, 124, 150, 175
classroom, xv, xvii–xx, 15, 17, 28,
    30, 32, 36–7, 39–40, 42, 53, 55,
    70, 79, 97, 101, 104–6, 109, 112,
    114, 117–19, 121–2, 124, 127–9,
    133–4, 153, 179, 191, 193, 196, 199,
    201, 204, 207, 210; behaviour, 39;

climate, 30, 100, 106, 124, 133;
    community, 112; instruction, 129;
    management, 39
Clayman, R., 12, 207
Clegg, S., 13, 39, 197
climate change, 137, 148
coding, 40, 46
cognitive, xviii, 23–4, 64, 100, 132,
    206–7
Cohen, J., 28, 197
Coke, J.S., 13, 196
Colaianne, B.A., xvi–xvii, 206
Cole, S.W., 61, 204
Collaborative for Academic, Social,
    and Emotional Learning (CASEL),
    22–4, 27, 29, 123, 159, 193, 197
Collie, R.J., xvii, 200
communication, 61, 77, 130
community, 14–15, 19, 29, 33, 49, 58,
    65, 67, 77–8, 83, 91, 95–6, 101, 112,
    114, 116, 118, 120–1, 124, 127–30,
    133, 135, 137, 144, 147, 169, 171,
    179–80, 185
commitment, xx, 53, 99–100, 127,
    160, 181, 203
compassion, xv–xix, xxi, 3, 5–7, 13,
    56, 65, 130, 178, 181–2, 200–1, 203,
    206, 208; scale, 131, 206
competencies, xiii, xv–xviii, xiii,
    20–6, 28–32, 36, 49, 116, 120, 137,
    201–2, 207, 209–10
compliment, 77, 84
Comunian, A.L., 131, 198
conceptual models, xxi, 210
confidence, 56, 61, 81, 83, 95, 117
conflict management, 130
Conley, C.A., 150, 208
connection, xv, 6, 22, 39, 45, 53–4, 79,
    103–8, 119, 123–4, 130, 135–6, 169
control conditions, 13, 27, 38, 51, 54,
    107–8, 148
Corliss, H.L., 17, 203
Corrigan, M., xvi, 207
Cote, S., 61, 204
Cotney, J.L., 5, 12, 37, 39, 198
Coulter-Heindl, V., 47, 200
COVID-19, 150
Covidence, 157–8
Coyne, S.M., 7, 51, 107–8, 205
Craighead, W.E., 17, 202
creativity, 17

Cristea, M., 12, 38, 196
Crocetti, E., 63, 132, 309
Crowley, M., xvii, 201
Csikszentmihalyi, M., 14–15, 207
cultural diversity, 35
culture, 14, 200–1, 206; peer, 105, 119;
    school, 15, 123, 128–9, 133
Cumberland, A., 5, 11, 61, 199
Curby, T.W., 29, 210
curriculum, 12–13, 26, 28–9, 45, 47,
    51, 114, 118–19, 128–9, 133, 139,
    148, 169, 192, 201, 207; course, 133;
    hidden, 128–9, 133
Curry, O.S., 12, 38, 47,
    198, 206
cyber bullying/kindness, 150

Dahl, A., 90, 198
Damon, W., 5, 11, 61, 199
database, vii, ix, 13–16, 157–8
Datu, J.A.D., 6, 12, 34, 46, 132, 198
Davidov, M., 90, 198
Davis, A.N., 64, 79, 100, 198
de Blois, M., xiii, 128–30, 210
Deci, E.L., 35–6, 206
decisions, xvi, 18, 22–4, 26, 31, 72, 97,
    180, 197
deep-breathing, 106
defending, 91, 205
de Jong, J., 34, 38, 201
delinquency, 62
delivery, 11, 27, 52, 82–5, 88, 92, 116,
    118, 121, 138, 146
Demanet, J., 124, 198
Denham, S.A., 28–9, 198, 210
depression, 6, 20, 47, 56, 103, 202, 204
development, xiii–xvi, xvii–xviii, 3,
    8, 10, 15, 18, 20, 22–4, 26, 28–30, 32,
    36, 39, 45, 59, 61–2, 65, 77, 79, 81–2,
    89, 96–7, 100–1, 112, 114–20, 127,
    133, 137, 139, 150, 154, 158–9, 185,
    195, 197–200, 202–10
de Vries, D.A., 108, 198
de Wall, F.B.M., 64, 199
Dewey, J., xvi, 199
Diamond, A., 29, 207
Dickerson, S.S., 12, 38, 210
Diener, M.L., 14, 199
Di Giunta, L., 10–11, 39, 205
disability, 116, 158, 183
disappointment, xix

discipline, xiii, 30, 114, 128–30, 133, 147, 157, 169, 210
dispositions, 6, 15, 105, 137, 199
Dockett, S., 40, 199
Dolan, P., 47, 199
Domitrovich, C.E., xvi–xvii, 28, 198, 209–10
Donaldson, L., 12, 200
Downey, J.A., 15, 199
Draper, Z.A, 12, 39, 154, 196
drawing-telling methodology, 40
Dunfield, K.A., 5–6, 199
Dunn, E.W., 12, 38, 53, 76, 195, 199, 210
Duraiappah, A.K., 17, 197
Durlak, J.A., xvii, 8, 15, 26, 28, 198–9, 203, 208–10
Dymnicki, A.B., xvii, 8, 15, 26, 199

early childhood, 10, 116, 183, 197, 200; education, 116, 200
education, xv–xvii, xx, 13–16, 18, 45, 90–1, 116, 130, 151, 153–4, 157, 159–60, 183, 192–3, 196–7, 199–201, 204–5, 207, 209–10
educators, v, xvi, xviii, xx, 3, 7, 13–19, 21–3, 25, 27–30, 32, 35–6, 39, 49, 52–5, 62, 65, 69, 71–3, 75–6, 78, 81, 83–5, 89–92, 96–7, 99–101, 104–5, 108–9, 112, 114–16, 119, 121–4, 126, 130, 136–9, 141, 143, 146–8, 150–1, 153–4, 159–60, 177, 191, 196
Edwards, C.P., xvii, 208
egocentric, 31
Eigenraam, A.W., 108, 198
Einarsdottir, J., 40, 199
Eisenberg, M.E., 17, 203
Eisenberg, N., 5, 7, 11, 40, 61, 199
emotion, vii, xiii, xv–xviii, xxi, 5–8, 10, 13–15, 18–32, 36, 40, 45–8, 50, 56, 58, 63–5, 67, 71–2, 86, 90–2, 96, 99, 100–1, 103–4, 106, 108–9, 112, 114, 116, 123, 126–7, 130–1, 135–7, 141, 143–4, 153–4, 158–61, 191–3, 195–9, 201, 203–5, 207–10; contagion, 30, 36, 101, 103, 109, 201; crossover, 103; distress, 27; experience, 144; spillover, 30, 103; support, 20, 99, 109, 131; transmission, 103, 114; vocabulary, 112

empathy, xv–xvi, xviii, xxi, 23–4, 61–2, 64–5, 67, 69, 71, 79, 86, 114, 116, 126, 158, 180, 182, 192, 199, 204, 207, 209
employment, xviii, 95, 200
encourage, xi, 9, 17–8, 22–4, 27, 36, 38, 40, 50–1, 54, 56, 61, 65, 69, 71, 75–6, 84, 89–91, 95, 97, 100–1, 108, 115, 117–19, 127–30, 132, 136, 138, 143, 147, 169
energy, 81–2, 91, 100, 138, 172
engaged citizenship, xvi
engagement, 25, 36, 46, 52, 91–2, 96, 108, 146, 153, 193, 196, 198
Enns, C., 88, 153, 196
environment, xvi, 29, 36, 63, 67, 97, 108, 119, 148, 158, 180; education, 18; emotion, 90; family, 55; helping, xvi, 67; home, 91; learning, 62, 106, 150; low-stimulus, 62; school, xviii, 69; social, xviii, 91, 124; stimulating, 62, 124
Ernst, R.M., 14–15, 207
evaluations, xviii, 84, 172–4, 210
excellence, v, 6, 127

faculties of education, 13
faculty, 81, 128–30, 133–4, 169, 185
fairness, 17, 39
familiar others, 46, 53, 78–9, 136
family, 9, 14–15, 19, 29, 48, 51, 54–6, 58, 70, 82, 115, 136, 143, 168–9, 181, 197, 203; cohesion, 48, 54; context, 15, 19, 51, 115; life, 24, 54; member, 54–6, 58
Farago, T., 101, 201
feedback, 28, 53, 81, 83, 89, 92, 99, 168, 202
feelings, xix, 6, 24–5, 31, 62, 65, 83, 106, 117, 126–7, 141, 175
Ferber, R., 35, 199
Fessler, D.M.T., 103, 208
Fischer, K., 11, 202
follow through, 46
food insecurity, 95
formal reasoning, 10
Fowler, J.H., 35, 103, 199
Fredrickson, B.L., 7, 51, 205
Frenzel, A.C., 103, 199
friendship, 8, 22, 31, 40, 53, 78–9, 82, 105, 154, 168, 178–80; friends, x–xi,

9, 31, 40, 45, 63, 72, 76, 78, 82, 91, 107, 136, 168–9, 177, 179–80, 182, 200
Fritz, M.M., 61, 204
Frydenberg, E., xvii, 200

Gadermann, A.M., 12, 19, 42, 128, 131, 139, 153, 196
Gaertner, A., 7–8, 15, 40, 135, 153, 196
Gargiulo, P.A., 61–2, 204
Garofano, J., 14, 208
gender, 6, 8–9, 11, 132, 201, 209; differences, 11, 201, 209
gene, 204; expression, 148; regulation, 148
Gerbino, M.G., 11, 61, 132, 204
Gherghel, C., 12, 131, 200
Gibb, S., 39, 200
Gibbs, T., 143–4, 209
Gillham, J., 14–15, 47, 200, 207
givers, 54, 59
giving, xix, 5, 10, 40, 42, 46, 77, 81–2, 99, 127, 172, 177–8, 181, 197, 206
goal, xvii, 22–4, 31, 129, 158, 209; setting, 31, 130
Goetz, T., 103, 199
Goodenow, C., 124, 200
Graafsma, T., 34, 38, 201
grade, xvii, 32, 39–40, 42, 45–7, 53–4, 69, 72, 75, 81–2, 86, 109, 132, 135, 138, 151, 167–8, 191, 210
Grady, K.E., 124, 200
grateful, xxiii, 51, 106, 175
gratitude, 13, 63, 83, 92, 106, 168, 202
Green, F.L.L., 12, 39, 154, 196, 196
Greenberg, M.A., xvi–xvii, 206
Greenberg, M.T., xvi–xvii, 23, 29, 91, 200–1
growth, xvi, 14, 23–4, 29, 32, 62, 84, 115, 123, 130, 136
guardian. See parent
Guerra, P., 61–2, 204
guidance, 53, 69, 82, 96–7, 146
Gullotta, T.P., 28, 198, 209–10
Guthrie, I., 5, 11, 61, 199

Hamelink, K., 108, 198
Hammer, I.M., 107–8, 200
Hamre, B.K., 112, 200
Han, D.H., 6, 34, 202
Hanel, P.H.P., 35, 200

Hanson, M., 13, 196
Hanson-Peterson, J., 29, 207
happy, xvii, 7, 12, 38, 47–53, 58, 61, 83, 99, 103–6, 137, 141, 178, 180, 195, 198–9, 200, 202–6, 208
harm, 20, 22, 71, 83
Hashimoto, T., 12, 131, 200
Haslip, M.J., 12, 200
Hassankhan, A., 34, 38, 201
Hastings, P.D., 90, 198
Hattie, J., 124, 195
Hay, D.F., 132, 197, 200
health, xvi–xvii, 18, 24, 49, 51, 56, 69, 101, 104, 122, 143–4, 148, 201–4, 206–7, 209–10
Hearon, B.V., 14, 208
Heffernan, L., 200
Heine, S.J., 34, 201
Heintz, S., 6, 201
Helliwell, J.F., 12, 38, 195
helping, ix–x, xii, xix, 4–5, 8, 10–11, 33, 35–6, 39–40, 42, 45–6, 49, 54, 58, 61, 63–4, 66–8, 75, 77, 81, 91, 105, 114–16, 119, 126, 135, 139, 148–9, 168, 172, 177, 181, 192, 196, 198–9, 204, 206, 208–9, 126; academically, 45; at home, 46; emotionally, 45–6, 67, 72; generic, 8, 45–6
helpers, 54; high, 47–8, 83; physically, 45–6, 72; others, 10, 33, 40, 42, 45, 49, 61, 64, 148, 168
Hendriks, T., 34, 38, 201
Henrich, J., 34, 201
Herbert, A., 62–3, 201
Hertzman, C., xviii, 207
Higgins-D'Alessandro, A., xvi, 207
history, xv, 45, 181
Holbrook, C., 103, 208
Holter-Sorensen, N., 104–5, 202
homeless, 22, 71, 81, 83, 95
honesty, 17, 178, 181, 202
Hong, J.S., 6, 34, 202
hopelessness, 140
Huang, J., 34, 203
Huber, A., 101, 201
Huber, L., 101, 201
human behaviour, 14
humanity, xv, 6
Human Society, 78, 95
human traits, xvi, 17
humour, 17, 130

Humphrey, N., xvii, 201
Hyson, M., 112, 201

identity, 106, 191
implementation fidelity, 146, 148
incentives, 35, 196
initiator, 5, 18, 31, 33, 47, 53, 79, 84,
    86, 88–9, 91–2, 121, 135, 143
in situ coding, 40
instructional practice, 28
interpersonal relations, 8, 122
intervention, xviii, 16, 26–8, 37–9,
    45–6, 49–51, 56, 58, 62, 132, 141,
    146, 148, 154, 196, 199–202, 204–5,
    207–9; studies, 27, 38
interviews, 37, 39, 104
introspection, 24, 55, 75
isolate, 53, 79, 106, 124

Jackson, P., 128, 201
Jacobs Bao, K., 12, 39, 103, 197
Jasnoski, M.L., 13, 196
Jazaieri, H., xvi, 201
Jennings, P.A., 23, 29, 91, 201
Jerald, C.D., 128–9, 201
Jonason, P.K., 17, 208
Jones, D.E., xvii, 201
joy, 36, 101, 103, 106, 116, 168, 198,
    200; contagion, 101, 103–6, 108

Karlsson, B., 104–5, 202
Karris, M.A., 17, 202
Keltner, D., xvii, 202
Kemeza, I., 12, 38, 195
Kern, M.L., 124, 195
Kerr, S.L., 7, 50, 54, 99, 202
keyword, 158
Kheriaty, A., 12, 207
Kim, H.R., 6, 34, 202
Kim, S., 6, 34, 202
kindergarten, xvii–xviii, 27, 40, 109,
    158, 178, 200–1
kindness, v, x–xi, xv–xxi, 3–22, 25–6,
    30–9, 40–61, 63–4, 67, 69–73, 75–9,
    81–9, 91–4, 96–101, 103–5, 107, 109,
    111–12, 114–19, 121–2, 124, 126,
    127–35, 137–41, 143–51, 153, 157–8,
    167, 171–4, 176, 186–7, 189; action
    plan, 85, 114–15, 138–9, 144; acts,
    ix–xii, 5–8, 11–14, 17–18, 20–2,
    25–6, 31–3, 35–42, 45–59, 64–7, 72–9,
    81–101, 103, 109, 115–18, 123–5,
    128, 136–9, 141, 143–51, 153, 174–5;
    additional, 75; adolescents, xx, 8,
    12, 18, 32, 37, 45–6, 53, 55, 59, 62, 67,
    69, 72, 75, 79, 85, 96, 100, 116, 138,
    151, 153; aspects, 37; assess, 131,
    173–4; assignments, 52; awareness,
    17–18; bank, 136; barriers, 122;
    behaviour, 52, 83, 107, 127; being,
    xv, xvii–xviii, xxiii, 3–5, 8–12, 14,
    17–22, 24, 32–3, 35–45, 47, 49–51,
    53–6, 58–9, 61, 63, 69, 71–2, 76, 78–9,
    81, 83–6, 89–90, 92, 95–9, 102, 105,
    109–11, 113–19, 121–2, 124, 126,
    128, 131, 133, 135–8, 140–4, 146–8,
    150–1, 177; benefits, 18, 24, 33, 48,
    58, 99, 124, 133, 141; calling out, 118;
    capacity, xix; catalyst, 151; catching,
    114; celebrate, 119; children, xvii–
    xviii, xx, 8, 12, 14, 18, 39, 55, 59,
    61–2, 67, 69, 72, 75, 79, 84–5, 91,
    95–6, 100, 116, 137–8, 151, 187;
    classmate, 124; classroom, 97, 114,
    117–19; climate change, 137, 148;
    coaching, 114; community, 77–8,
    114, 127; complex, 9, 91; confidence,
    81, 83, 95, 117; cultivation, v, xvii,
    xv–xvi, xx, 14, 97, 103, 122, 134;
    cyber, 150; definition, ix, 3–5, 7–10,
    20, 42, 86, 126, 135–6, 186; deliver,
    18, 22, 50, 59, 62–3, 77, 83–5, 88,
    95, 116–17, 124, 137–9, 143, 146;
    demonstrates, 3, 11–12, 31, 37,
    46, 72, 87–8, 138; design, 62, 100,
    116, 118, 139; developmentally
    appropriate, 77; differentiating,
    5, 59, 91; dimensions, 13, 16;
    discipline, 128–30, 133; education,
    151; educator, 109; effects, 13, 38, 50,
    59; emotional, 40, 63, 71; employee,
    17; enact, 3, 6–8, 11–12, 18, 20–2,
    25, 30, 33, 42, 45–6, 50, 52–4, 56, 59,
    61–3, 70, 72, 75, 79, 84, 92, 96–7, 100,
    118, 121, 124, 126, 134–5, 137, 141,
    143–4, 148; encouraged, xi, 18–19,
    90, 105, 119, 136, 143, 147; energy,
    81 2; engage, 90; environmental,
    63; expressed, 11, 17; extending,
    78, 114–15; face to face, x, 46, 73–5;
    family, 39, 54–5, 58, 115; field of,
    xx, 134; forms of, 92; fostering, 3,

17–18, 20, 37, 39, 55, 59, 71, 75, 96–7,
100, 104, 106, 121, 126–7, 133, 143,
150–1; frequency questionnaire,
131; friendship as, 8; gas tank, x,
75; identify, 127; implementation,
19, 78, 119, 133; importance, 17–18,
127; incorporate, 17, 51, 118, 132;
indicators, 19, 120, 139; information,
114; initiate, 31, 33, 78–9, 81, 84, 88,
116, 119, 122, 128, 147; institutional,
17; integrate, xx, 118, 133, 139;
intentional, x, 18, 71–2, 76–7, 84–5,
88, 92, 96, 116, 129, 136, 138, 146,
171, 175; interpersonal aspects,
5–6, 18, 124; intervention, 38, 46,
49–51, 56, 58, 71, 124, 132, 141,
146; intrapersonal aspects, 5, 18;
leadership, 78; level, 73; literature,
129; loving-kindness-mediation,
141; manifested, 8; material driven,
8, 117; means to be, 10; measuring,
12, 19, 121–2, 130–1; media, 118;
modelling, 14, 61–2, 105, 114, 117,
119, 128, 132–3, 138–9, 147; needing,
76; nurture, 8, 14; oneself, 56;
online, x, 46, 73–5, 150; opportunity,
xix, 19, 95; organization, 95, 118,
143, 146; others, 15, 21, 49, 56,
67, 69, 71, 78, 97, 105, 118, 142,
148; pedagogical, 109, 112, 144;
perception, 12, 46, 121–2, 126, 135;
performing, 92; physical, 40, 63, 71;
plan, 50, 52, 55–6, 62, 84–5, 88, 92,
118, 124, 137, 139, 143; practising,
18, 20, 55, 61–2; previous acts, 17;
professional development, 114, 133;
profile, 73; promoting, xvii–xviii,
xx, 13, 15, 37, 79, 120, 127, 133, 187;
quality, 75, 146, 187; quiet, xi, 18,
85–6, 88–9, 91–2, 95–6, 115–16, 118,
129, 138, 141, 143; random, 62–3;
random acts of, 62–3; recipient,
x, 33, 46, 50, 53, 75–6, 79, 81, 84,
88, 114–15, 124, 136, 173–5, 186;
recognizing, 3, 89; reflect, 50, 62, 84,
115, 118, 137–8, 143, 175; regime,
99, 115, 135, 138–9, 143–4; reinforce,
83, 90; report card, 134; research,
11–15, 19, 32–4, 38–9, 45, 50, 58,
109, 137, 143, 146, 148; responsive,
xxiii, 18, 58–9, 62–5, 67, 69, 70–2,

83, 85, 88, 92, 96, 115–16, 129, 135,
138, 144; role, 33, 140; routine, x,
62; scale, 131–2; scenarios, 167;
School Kindness Checklist, 133,
139; School Kindness Scale, 19,
42, 131–2, 139; schools, x, 12, 25,
31, 38–9, 42, 45–7, 53–4, 60, 62–4,
77–8, 104, 109, 120–2, 124, 126–8,
131–4, 139, 143, 153, 185; self, 21, 38,
105, 139–41, 148, 150–1, 175; self-
evaluate, 73, 75, 84; simple, 9; skills,
23–4; social, 63; societal importance,
17; students, xv, 9, 13, 18, 46–7, 53,
95, 104, 124, 147; studies on, ix–xi,
3, 12–13, 18, 33–7, 48, 104, 121, 126,
129, 146; task, xi, 98, 146; teacher,
xi, 42–4, 102, 105, 109–13, 126–7,
145, 165; teaching, 37, 112, 128;
team, 138; temperature, 121–2, 134;
time, 81–2, 146; toward others, 21;
toward self, 21, 141; understands, 3,
11–12, 37, 40, 58–9, 114–15, 137, 186;
university, 39; unworthy of, 141;
value, 14–15, 17; virtual, 150; visual,
128; wheelhouse, 116; world, 148;
workplace, 17, 39
Kitil, M.J., 29, 207
Klisanin, D., 150, 206
Knafo-Noam, A., 90, 198
Ko, K., 12–13, 38, 50, 202
Kokko, K., 11, 61, 132, 204
Koot, H.M., 63, 132, 309
Kosek, R.B., 39, 202
Kramm, C., 6, 201
Krane, V., 104–5, 202
Kurtz, J.L., xvii, 7, 11–12, 39, 54, 202
Kwok, S.Y.C.L., 12, 207

Laible, D., 61, 202
Lamborn, S.D., 11, 202
language arts, 79
Lansford, J.E., 10–11, 39, 205
Lauze, A., 12, 15, 39, 154, 196
Lawlor, M.S., 29, 207
Laws, H.B., 49, 51, 206
Layous, K., xvii, 7, 11, 12, 35, 39, 47,
54, 59, 99, 116, 202–3
Leahy, R.L., 13, 202
learning, xvi, xviii, xix–xx, 18, 24, 36,
47, 101, 105, 119, 123, 133, 137, 150,
178, 181–3, 191–2, 196–7, 201, 206;

learning (*continued*)
  climate, 28; community, 18–19,
  120, 133–4, 153; conditions, 32,
  114; context, xix, 29, 122, 124, 144,
  150; enable, 123; environment,
  62, 106, 150; foundation of, xviii;
  from others, 61; observational, 36;
  opportunities, 45, 61; social and
  emotional learning (*see* social and
  emotional learning); virtual, 150
Lee, C.K.J., 12, 203
Lee, Y., 6, 34, 202
lessons, xviii, 27–8, 30, 106, 114, 117,
  129–30, 135, 179, 181, 192
Leung, F.Y.K., 141, 210
LGTBTQ+, 55, 203
Li, N.P., 17, 208
Lickona, T., 14, 203
life adversity, 148
life satisfaction, 45, 48, 58, 143, 198
lifespan development, 3, 23–4, 208
Linkins, M., 14–15, 207
lived experience, 37
Lok, I., 38, 195
loneliness, 17
Long, N.J., 7, 37, 203
longitudinal studies, xvii, 11, 13, 45,
  47, 62, 103, 197, 199, 204–5
Lopez, S.J., 5, 197
love, 6, 9, 13, 56, 200
Lowe, R., 17, 208
Lucas, R.E., 14, 199
Luce, H., 64, 79, 100, 198
Ludtke, O., 103, 199
Luengo Kanacri, B.P., 10–11, 39, 205
Luks, A., 49, 203
Lynch, S.A., 116, 203
Lyubomirsky, S., xvii, 7, 11–13, 35,
  38–9, 47, 49, 50, 52, 54, 59, 99, 103,
  116, 137, 148, 197, 202–4, 207

Madden, K.M., 12, 38, 210
Magnani, E., 12–13, 47, 203
Magon, Z., 52, 99, 203
Mahoney, J.L., 14, 27, 203
maladjusted, 79
malleability. *See* plasticity
Malone, P.S., 10–11, 39, 205
management, 18, 24, 65, 112, 128,
  130, 205

Mankin, A., 143–4, 209
Mare, J., xiii, 128–30, 210
Margolis, S., 12, 39, 103, 197, 202, 207
Martin, A.J., xvii, 200
Martin-Cueller, A., 12, 64, 79, 100,
  154, 198, 205
Mason, E., 12, 38, 196
materials, 76–7, 81–4, 91, 100, 106,
  117–8, 138, 158, 172, 191
mathematics, 45
McAlaney, J., 12, 38, 47, 198
McCarthy, C.J., 144, 203
McCathren, R., 116, 209
McCullough, M., 14, 208
McGingley, M., 61, 202
McGrath, R.E., 17, 203
McGuigan, N., 196
meaningfulness, 49, 161, 191, 202
media, 90, 107–8, 118, 191, 199,
  205–6; access, 108; class, 114;
  consumption, 108; literacy, 109;
  monitoring, 108, 205; prosocial,
  107–9, 119; social (*see* social
  media); studies, 108, 114
Mehus, C.J., 55, 203
Memmott-Elison, M.K., 61–2, 91, 205
mental health, 49, 51, 69, 143–4, 204,
  207
mentoring, 51–2, 69, 82, 84, 97,
  115–16, 120, 124, 128, 130, 135,
  137–9, 143, 146
Merriam-Webster, 6, 203
Merunka, D.R., 35, 205
Messer, E.J.E., 12, 38, 196
Mesurado, B., 61–2, 204
Metcalfe, R., 47, 199
Midlarsky, E., 49, 204
Miles, A., 12, 204
Min, K.J., 6, 34, 202
mindful, 31, 70, 104, 106, 108, 133,
  141, 154, 207
MindUp, xviii
modelling, 14, 62, 105, 109, 114,
  116–17, 133, 139, 147
Moller, A.M., 108, 198
money, 38, 53, 71, 91, 169, 195, 199, 210
Mongrain, M., 56, 204
mood, 49, 105
Moon, J.Y., 150, 208
Morgan, T.L., 132, 204

Morrish, L., 15, 204
motivation, xx, 7, 36, 46–7, 79, 90, 96, 105, 116, 198, 200, 204, 206, 208–9
Muller, C.A., 101, 201
Murphy, B.C., 5, 11, 61, 199
Murphy, T., 61, 202
Murray, J.P., 107–8, 200

Nantel-Vivier, A., 11, 61, 132, 204
Nastas, D., 12, 131, 200
needs of others, 20, 64, 79, 84, 177
Neff, K.D., 13, 131, 206, 208
Nelson, S.K., xvii, 7, 11–12, 39, 54, 202
Nelson-Coffey, S., 12, 148, 204
Ness, O., 104–5, 202
Nielson, M.G., 132, 197, 199, 202, 105, 208–9
Noddings, N., xv–xvi, 204
Norenzayan, A., 34, 201
normative, 108
Norton, M.I., 12, 38, 53, 195, 199
numerical data, 38
nurture, 8, 14–15, 23, 47, 81, 97, 114, 123, 127
Nyende, P., 12, 38, 195

Oberlander, T.F., 29, 207
Oberle, E., xvii, 7, 11–12, 15, 27, 39, 54, 104, 202, 204, 207–8
O'Brien, M.U., xvi, 207
observation, xi, 11, 36, 61, 98, 109, 122
O'Donovan, A., 7, 50, 54, 99, 202
Oei, T.P.S., 141, 210
Oliner, S.P., 13, 204
Orfanidis, C., 12, 204
Organisation for Economic Co-operation and Development, xvii, 205
organizations, xvii, 22, 95–6, 118; non-profit, 96, 191
organized, 27–9, 72, 77, 85, 118, 143, 146
Osher, D., 62, 101, 197
Otake, K., 7, 51, 205
Otsui, K., 7, 51, 205
Ottensen Kennnair, L.E., 17, 208
outcomes, xvii, 22, 27, 33, 35, 38, 47, 49, 108, 141, 146, 201,

203; negative, 6, 100, 108–9, 132; positive, 26–7, 32–3, 58; psychological, 6

Paciello, M., 11, 61, 132, 204
Padilla-Walker, L.M., 61–2, 91, 107–8, 197, 205
Paquet, A., 12, 154, 205
Paquet, Y., 12, 154, 205
parents, xvi, xxiii, 13–14, 17, 22, 32, 54, 58, 90, 97, 104, 108, 112, 115–16, 121, 127–8, 130, 133, 138, 144, 153, 159, 169, 177, 191, 193, 196–7
participants, xviii, 6, 11–13, 17–18, 27, 34–40, 45, 47, 49–53, 56, 58–9, 103, 108, 115, 123, 131, 140, 146–8
Park, N., 12, 17, 34, 46, 132, 198, 205
Passmore, H.A., 5, 9, 11–2, 42, 109, 126, 153, 185, 196
Pastorelli, C., 10–11, 20, 39, 61, 132, 204–5
Pavel, M.M., 62–3, 201
pedagogy, 8, 89, 109, 112, 121, 144, 197
peer, 61, 76–7, 84, 90–1, 107, 124, 127, 130–1, 141, 198, 200, 202; acceptance, xvii, 54; bullying, 141; culture, 96, 105, 119; microclimates, 105; modelling, 105; reviewed, 13, 16, 22, 33–4, 58, 116, 153, 155, 157–8
Pekel, K., 123, 205
Pekrun, R., 103, 199
Pepping, C., 7, 50, 54, 99, 202
perception, 12, 45–6, 48–9, 63, 73, 89, 121–2, 126, 131–2, 135, 143, 153–4, 185, 193, 196, 203, 205, 210; educator, 126, 153, 196, 210; self, 48, 51, 73; student, 72, 126, 131–2, 154, 193, 196, 203
Perry, B., 40, 199
perseverance, 47
person activity fit, 35
personality trait, 131
personal skills, 54
perspective, 3, 64, 71, 77, 126, 135, 137–8, 168, 181, 192, 198, 204–5, 208–9, 136, 138; adult, 7; children and adolescents, 3, 7, 8, 18, 37, 61, 64, 112, 158; students, 3, 30, 39, 42,

perspective (*continued*)
   64, 76, 96, 117, 133, 147, 153, 196;
   taking, 6, 8, 10, 15, 20, 22, 25, 30–1,
   34, 37, 46, 54–6, 61–5, 67, 69, 71–2,
   76–7, 79, 84, 86, 96, 115, 117, 126, 138
Peterson, C., 6–7, 17, 35, 205
Peterson, M., 13, 208
Peterson, R.A., 35, 205
Pham, T., 12, 207
physiology, 12, 101–2, 148
Piaget, J., 2–6, 10, 206
Pianta, R.C., 112, 200
Pihl, R.O., 61, 204
Pipp, S., 11, 202
planning, viii–x, xii, 11, 18, 20, 22,
   30–1, 45–6, 50, 52–6, 62, 65, 72–4,
   77, 79, 81, 83–5, 88, 92, 95–6, 99,
   115–16, 118, 124, 128, 136–9, 141,
   143–4, 171–3, 191–2, 210
plasticity, 62, 197
play skills, 116
politics, xvi, 91
Poll, Z., 17, 206
Pommier, E., 131, 206
popularity, 11, 13–14, 22, 26, 49, 54,
   62, 101, 103, 146
Porta, C.M., 17, 203
positive, 7–9, 15, 18, 26, 28, 36, 39,
   42, 54, 75, 81, 83–4, 96, 99, 101,
   105, 108, 119, 122, 127, 130, 132,
   137, 144, 154, 168, 180–1, 195,
   197, 200–5, 207–8; activity model,
   35, 99, 116; affect, xvi, 45, 47–9,
   58, 99, 108, 143, 177; attitude, 28;
   behaviour, 14, 26; benefits, 22;
   change, xx; classroom, 15, 100,
   133; education, 14–15, 18, 207;
   emotions, 22, 56, 90, 101, 103–4,
   141, 210; feedback, 28; goals, 22–3,
   31; health practices, xvi; human
   qualities, xvi–ii; outcomes (*see
   under* outcomes); psychology,
   14–15, 207–8; relationships, xvi,
   7, 22–4, 31; social interactions, 54;
   well-being, 50, 52, 58, 100
Post, S.G., xvii, 33, 49, 51, 56, 83, 206
post-test, design, 38, 58; measures,
   13, 38, 45, 58; survey, 115
poverty, 95
power, 38, 52, 97, 109, 117, 120, 123,
   130, 139, 180, 203, 205–6

practice, v, xiii, xvi, xx, 8, 13, 16,
   28–30, 45, 61–2, 69, 71, 79, 81, 84–5,
   91, 112, 117, 124, 129–30, 141, 180,
   197–8, 209–10
praise, 89–90, 150
predicting, xviii, 20, 29, 47, 59, 63,
   104, 200, 208
pre-service teacher education
   programs, 15, 38
pre-test measures, 13, 45, 58
principle, 129
principles, 130, 133, 193, 196
PRISMA, vii, 13, 155
professional, competence, 120;
   development, 15, 22, 100, 114, 120,
   133, 139, 154, 185; duties, 112, 144;
   responsibility, 15; satisfaction, 144;
   stressors, 144
prompt, ix–xii, 25, 31, 40, 50, 55, 64–5,
   73, 78, 88–9, 95, 116–17, 128, 139, 202
prosocial, xvii, 5, 11, 15, 53, 61–2, 89,
   103, 114–15, 118, 120, 130, 148; act,
   61, 91, 103; behaviours, xvii–xviii,
   3, 5–6, 10, 11, 13, 18, 39, 49, 52, 59,
   62–4, 81, 86, 90–1, 100, 107–9, 112,
   116, 118, 121, 124, 127–8, 131, 148;
   children, 108, 112; competencies,
   xvii; confidence, 55–6, 61; contagion,
   103–4, 128; emotional reactions, 6;
   expectations, 112; interactions, 114;
   low, 59; lowers, xvii; media, 107–8,
   119; online, 150; online lives, 89;
   skills, xviii, 6, 116; spending, 38,
   53; students, 132; television,
   107–8; themes, 107, 128;
   YouTube, 114
Proulx, J., 38, 195
puppetry, 116

qualitative, 37; design, 13;
   methodology, 37; research, 37–8, 58
quantitative, 37; approach, 37–8;
   framework, 37; research, 38
question, xii, 3, 12, 17, 20–1, 36–7, 39,
   40, 53, 65, 73, 75–6, 78–9, 84, 95, 99,
   115, 118, 131, 136, 139–40, 172, 175,
   177 8, 181

Rahman, S., 39, 200
randomized controlled trials, 38, 54,
   148, 154, 196, 201, 204, 207

Raposa, E.B., 49, 51, 206
reactionary, 63, 72
recipient, x, 22, 31, 33, 46, 48, 50,
  53–4, 59, 75–9, 81, 83–6, 88–9, 91–2,
  95, 99, 115–16, 118, 124, 126, 135–8,
  141, 169, 172–5, 195–6; bank, 75–6,
  84–5, 95, 136–8, 141
reflect, ix–x, xiii, xv, 3, 7, 10, 13, 20,
  22–4, 34, 50, 55–5, 59, 62, 64–5,
  69, 70, 72–3, 77–9, 84–5, 90–2, 96,
  88–100, 104, 106, 112, 115, 117–18,
  123–4, 126–8, 130, 136–8, 143,
  147–8, 157, 168, 175, 209
reinforce, 47, 78, 81, 86, 89–91, 124,
  130
Reivich, K., 14–15, 47, 200, 207
relationships, xvi, xx, 7–8, 15, 18,
  22–5, 30–1, 33, 48, 53–4, 56, 72,
  77, 79, 91, 96, 105, 112, 122–4, 129,
  135–6, 169, 198, 200–3, 205–6
Renard, L., 105, 122–3, 206
repository, 76, 118, 159–60, 183
respect, xii–xviii, xx, 9, 40, 42, 46,
  63, 69, 75, 101, 123–4, 126–7, 130,
  158–9, 177
resilience, xix, 6, 32, 49, 96, 144, 148,
  199, 206
resistance, 107, 141
resource, vii–viii, 5, 19, 21–2, 26,
  38, 95, 99, 101–1, 105–6, 119, 151,
  159–61, 168, 181, 183, 191–3, 197,
  203; distribution strategies, 38, 197
responsible, 18, 39, 126; civic, 91;
  decision making, xvi, 18, 26, 31, 224
restorative justice, 130
Revord, J., 12–13, 38, 50, 202
reward, 7, 11, 35, 90, 118, 129, 151,
  202, 207, 209
Richaud, M.C., 61–2, 204
Rickard, N., 15, 204, 209
Riley, K., 124, 206
Rodriquez, L.M., 61–2, 204
Roeser, R.W., xvi–xvii, 206
Rogers, S., 105, 122–3, 206
roleplaying, 65, 84
Roots of Empathy, xviii, 207
Rose, T., 62, 101, 197
Rosenthal-Stott, H.E.S., 131, 208
Ross, D., 36, 195
Ross, S.A., 36, 195
Roth, R.A., 14, 208

Rowland, L., 5, 12–13, 38–9, 47, 59,
  150, 197–8, 206
Rowland, S., 13, 39, 197
Ruch, W., 6, 201
Ryan, R.M., 35–6, 206
Ryan, S.V., 143–4, 209

sad, 31, 61
safety, 31, 83, 122, 143
sample, 26, 34–5, 38, 51, 72, 104,
  131–2, 148, 157, 185, 187, 198, 200,
  202, 205, 210
Sandstrom, G.M., 12, 38, 195, 210
satisfaction, 90; life, 45, 47–8, 58, 143,
  198; professional, 144
Scales, P.C., 123, 205
science, xv–xvi, xviii, xx, xxiii, 15–16,
  18–19, 23, 35, 45, 47, 79, 82, 97, 101,
  157, 161, 195–9, 201–7, 209
Schachter, R., 114, 206
schedule, 52, 84, 172–4
Schellinger, K.B., xvii, 8, 15, 26, 199
Schkade, D., 49, 203
Schonert-Reichl, K.A., vii–xxi, 7,
  11–12, 15, 19, 27, 29, 39, 42, 54, 104,
  128, 131, 139, 153, 196, 202, 204, 207
school, vii–xii, xv–xvi, xix–xx, xxiii,
  3, 9, 13, 25, 27–33, 39, 40–4, 46–7,
  49, 51, 53–4, 60, 62–3, 68, 70, 72,
  77–8, 81–2, 86–7, 91, 93–7, 99,
  100–1, 105, 112, 114, 116, 118–19,
  121–2, 124, 126–30, 132–5, 138–40,
  143–4, 147–8, 153, 173, 175,
  185, 187, 200; administrators,
  xxiii, 26; based curriculum, 12,
  26; belonging, 124; career, 20;
  climate, 122–3, 127–30, 143; code
  of conduct, 127; community,
  17–19, 67, 101, 114, 118, 121, 124,
  127, 129, 144, 147, 151, 185–6;
  context, xviii, 3–4, 7, 14, 19, 29,
  33, 39, 45, 54, 105, 114, 116, 121,
  124, 126–7, 131–2, 134, 137–8, 141,
  144; counsellor, 42, 99; culture,
  15, 123, 129, 133; discipline, 129;
  duty, 127; elementary, xvii, 32,
  77–8, 126–7; environments, xviii,
  69, 124; experience, 15, 64, 114,
  126–7, 132, 137; high school, xviii,
  xix, 9, 27, 32, 46–7, 70, 77–8, 83, 99,
  104; kindness (see under kindness);

school (*continued*)
mental health, 143; middle, ix–xii, xvii–xviii, 9, 32, 45–6, 52–5, 70, 74, 76–8, 86, 88, 104–5, 126, 129, 132–3, 139–40, 146–7; mission statement, 127, 129, 133, 140; personnel, 127; playground, 158; preschool, 11, 107–8; programs, 27, 64; public school, 3, 54, 76, 91, 109, 126, 132, 150; resources, 26; school success, xvi, xviii, 39; situated tasks, 46, 52; skills, 45; social environment, 124; stakeholders, 129
Schotanus-Dijkstra, M., 34, 28, 201
Schreier, H.M.C., xvii, 148, 207
secrecy, 108
self, ix, 7, 9, 18, 22, 56, 84, 107, 116, 126, 138, 140–1, 208; administer, 99; assess, 84, 175; awareness, 18, 30; care, 192; conscious, 70; determination theory, 35, 206; efficacy, 49, 84; esteem, 84; evaluate, 73; focused, 10, 31; kindness (*see under* kindness); loathing, 140; management, 18; perception, 48, 51, 73; rating, x, 45–6, 49, 51, 74–5; reflection, 130; regulating, 25, 29, 47, 86, 127; reporting, 35, 56; selection, 35; serving, 78, 180; worth, 140
selfish, 33, 75, 167–8, 177
Seligman, M.E.P., 6–7, 14–15, 17, 47, 200, 205, 207
service, xxiii, 15, 99, 181
Seton, H., 144, 207
Shapiro, J., 12, 207
sharing, xviii, 5–6, 8, 10–11, 23, 39, 61, 69, 77, 82, 101, 123, 138, 160, 199
Sheldon, K.M., 12, 38, 49, 52, 99, 116, 137, 203, 207
Shepard, S.A., 5, 11, 61, 199
Shewark, E.A., 29, 210
Shimai, S., 7, 51, 205
Shoshani, A., 6, 34, 45, 207–8
shy, 81, 92, 96, 167
Simpson, C.G., 116, 203
Siu, N., 12, 207
Slone, M., 6, 34, 45, 208
smart phones, 49
Smeets, E., 13, 208
smile, xix, 101, 105–6

Smith, V., xviii, 207
social: awareness, 18; behaviours, 39; bonds, 53–4, 78; capital, 49, 54, 58, 61, 96, 137, 144; challenge, xvi; comparison, 108, 198; competence, xviii, 202; connections, 45, 79, 103, 119; conventions, 6; environment, 91, 124; exchanges, 61; expectations, 92; integration, 48–9; interaction, 54, 92, 95, 100, 202; isolates, 53, 79, 124; learning theory, 36, 195; media, 103–4, 108–9, 138; networks, 103, 105; norms, 90; phenomenon, 64; praise, 90; responsibility, 127; settings, 61; skills, 116, 203; support, 105
social and emotional, 86, 89, 91, 143; competencies, xv, xvii–xviii, 20–6, 28–32, 116, 137, 201, 207; content, 20, 30–1, 161; development, 23–4, 30, 96, 137; dimensions, xvi; environments, 90; growth, 24, 29; learning, vii, xiii, xvi, xxi, 8, 14–15, 18–29, 31–2, 45, 50, 64–5, 86, 112, 123, 127, 130, 136–7, 159–61, 191, 193, 197–201, 203, 207–10; measurement, 123; recalibration station, 106; research, 27; SEL, xvi, xvii, xviii, 18–19, 136; SEL approaches, xvii; SEL competencies, xvi; SEL programs, xvii, xviii, 26–9; SEL Wheel of Competencies, 23, 28; skills, xiii, 8, 20, 23–8, 45, 86, 91–2; support, 99–100; teaching practices, 30; well-being, xvii, 191–2
socialization, 90
socio-cognitive functioning, 132
Son, D., 107–8, 205
Sorbring, E., 10–11, 39, 205
Sparks, A.M., 103, 208
special needs, viii, x, 73, 116–19, 183, 209
Sproull, L., 150, 208
staff, xxiii, 122, 127–8, 130, 133–4, 185
stakeholders, 114, 121, 128–9, 133
Staub, E., xvii, 2008
stereotype, 31
Steyer, L., 62, 101, 197
Stiff, C., 131, 208
Stinnett, S.C., 107–8, 205

Stockdale, L.A., 107–8, 205
storytelling, 116, 118
strain, 103
stranger, xi, 11, 22–3, 38, 53, 88, 107, 172, 199, 208
strengths, xix, 6–7, 15, 45, 47, 79, 117, 134, 139, 198, 200–3, 205, 207–8
stress, xvi, 6, 11, 27, 30, 36, 42, 48–9, 55, 100–1, 103–6, 108, 117, 119, 122, 143–4, 146, 148, 200, 203–4, 206, 209; contagions, 101, 103–4, 108, 204; experiences, 100; indicators, 102; reduction, 117, 146; response, 148; teacher, 143–4
students, v, vii–x, xii–xx, xxiii, 3, 5, 9–10, 13, 15–16, 18–19, 21–4, 26–30, 32–3, 36–7, 39–40, 42, 45–7, 51–4, 63–70, 72–3, 75–6, 78–9, 81–3, 86–7, 92, 95–7, 99–101, 104–6, 108–9, 112, 114–19, 121–4, 126–9, 130–44, 147–51, 167–9, 179, 187, 191–3, 199–200; accountability, 130; attendance, 96; behaviour, 16, 22, 26, 39, 65, 105, 124, 130; development, 15, 26, 30, 127; early elementary, 77–8; elementary, vii, ix, x, xi, xvii, 4, 9, 37, 40, 42, 64, 69–70, 109, 112, 163, 204, 208; engagement, 96; governing, 127; high school, 27, 32, 46–7, 70, 77–8, 99, 104–5, 198; infractions, 15, 130; introverted, 92, 95–6; isolated, 124; mental health, 143; misbehaviour, 65, 130, 133, 143; middle school, ix–xii, xvii, 9, 16, 32, 45–6, 52–5, 70, 73–4, 76–8, 86, 88, 105–6, 126, 132, 136, 139–40, 147, 167; motivation, 96, 122; perception, 72, 131, 193, 196; perspectives of, 3, 39, 126, 133, 153; pro-sociality scale, 131; public, 3, 54, 76, 109, 124, 132, 146–7, 150; publications, 153; school achievement, 26, 39; school experience, 39, 137; sense of belonging, 124; shy, 92; special needs, viii, 73, 116–19, 183; teacher relationships, 112, 122–4, 130, 139, 200, 202; to student cohesion, 124; upper elementary, 9, 32, 42, 77–8; undergraduate, 131; university, 34–5, 108, 154, 196, 202, 205, 208

studies, design and sample size, 34
studies, participants, 34
success, 124
suicide, 6
Suldo, S.M., 14, 208
support, 65
suspension, 129
sympathy, 13, 107

Takai, J., 12, 131, 200
Tamis-Lemonda, C.S., 14, 209
Tan, S.Y., 14, 208
Tanaka-Matsumi, M.K., 7, 51, 205
Tarquino, C., 12, 154, 205
Taylor, J.L., 112, 201
Taylor, R.D., xvii, 8, 15, 26–7, 199, 208
teacher, vii–viii, x–xx, xxiii, 13–15, 27–30, 37, 40, 42–7, 53, 65–7, 69–70, 79, 82–4, 90, 93, 95, 97–102, 104–6, 109–14, 119, 121–4, 126–7, 129–30, 136, 138–9, 143–5, 150, 153, 165, 168–9, 179, 183, 185, 187, 189, 191–3, 196, 198, 200–3, 207, 209–10; behaviour, 127; curricula, 13; high school, 126; kindness survey, 126; middle school, 126; perspective, 126; public school, 126; ratings, xvii; student rapport, 122–4, 139; student relationships, 30; teacher training, xviii; well-being, 143
teaching, xi, xiii, xvi, xix–xx, 29–30, 37, 42, 105, 108–9, 112, 117, 119, 122–4, 126, 128, 144, 168, 177–9, 183, 191, 201, 204, 206; method, 123; relationship driven, 105, 122, 126; strategy, 117, 123
teamwork, 47
technology, 101, 108, 117
temperance, 47
temptation, 107
textual data, 38
thanks, xxiii, 40, 92, 101, 103, 117, 177
therapy, 141
thinking, 25
thinking out loud, 65
Thomas, A.G., 17, 208
Thomson, K., 29, 207
thoughtful, 70, 72, 97, 99, 175
time, xv–xvi, xviii–xix, 7, 13, 17, 23, 30, 35, 38, 42, 46, 50, 54, 62, 69,

time (*continued*)
    71–2, 79, 81–2, 86, 91, 99–100, 106,
    108, 114–15, 118, 122, 130, 138, 146,
    150, 160, 167–9, 172–5, 181, 206
toddler, 10, 90
Tomasello, M., 10–11, 90, 209
Torrente, C., xvii, 209
Tosh-Kiraly, I., 131, 206
transient housing, 95
treatment, 13, 38, 51, 54, 99
Tremblay, R.E., 11, 61, 132, 204
Trew, J.L., 12, 209
trust, 30, 54, 130
Turksma, C., xvi, 200

Upenieks, L., 12, 204

Vaish, A., 90, 198
values, 35, 122–3, 200, 209
Van der Graaff, J., 63, 132, 209
Van Houtte, M., 124, 198
Van Lissa, C.J., 12, 38, 198
variability, 23, 25, 46, 52–3, 64, 90,
    146
Vella-Brodrick, D., 15, 124, 195, 204,
    209
violence, 95, 107
Vione, K.C., 35, 200
voice of students, xvii, xix, xx, 19,
    147
vulnerability, xix
volunteering, 51, 148, 203, 207
von der Embse, N.P., 143–4, 209

Wake, S., 131, 208
Wallace, J., 200
Walsh, L.C., 12, 207
Walsh, M.E., xiii, 128–30, 210
Wang, R., 141, 210
Wang, S., 14, 209
Warneken, F., 10–11, 90, 209
Warren, M.A., 34, 28, 201
Waters, L., 123, 195
Watson, A., 116, 209

Watson, R.J., 17, 203
well-being, x, xii, xvii–xviii, xx, 6,
    11–13, 18, 33, 35–8, 46–8, 50–2, 54,
    56, 58–9, 61, 92, 95, 99, 100–1, 103–
    4, 108, 114–15, 117–19, 121, 135–7,
    143–4, 146, 148, 154, 158, 191–2,
    195–8, 200–4, 206–9; benefits, x,
    12, 35, 46, 48, 50, 52, 61, 115, 117,
    121, 143–4, 146; framework, 35, 58;
    individual, 95; positive, 50, 52, 58
welfare. *See* safety
Weissberg, R.P., xvi–xvii, 27–8,
    198–9, 203, 209–10
Wentzel, K.R., xvii, 39, 210
Werner, J., 47, 200
WEIRD, 34, 45, 201
Whillans, A.V., 12, 38, 210
Whitehead, J., 12, 15, 27, 45, 52–3, 79,
    146, 154, 196
Whitehouse, H., 12, 38, 47, 198
Wieringa, M.S., 108, 198
Willis-Stewart, S., 12, 39, 154, 196
Winkler, J.L., xiii, 128–30, 210
Woodward, A., 131, 208

Yaneva, M., 5, 12, 131, 197
Yoo, S.K., 6, 34, 202
Youm, J., 12, 207
young adulthood, 10, 100
Youngs, D., 5, 12, 131, 197
young people, 3, 8, 18, 20, 49,
    51–2, 54–5, 58–9, 62–3, 65, 71–2,
    85, 88, 90–2, 96–7, 99, 101, 104, 115,
    119–20, 124, 131, 134–9, 141, 143–4,
    146–8, 150
Yue, X., 12, 207
Yurdabakan, I., 12, 132, 210

Zaidman-Zait, A., xviii, 207
Zalan, L.B., 56, 204
Zeng, X., 141, 210
Zhu, R., 12–13, 47, 203
Zinsser, K.M., 29, 210
Zlotowitz, S., 12, 38, 47, 198

Printed and bound by CPI Group (UK) Ltd, Croydon, CR0 4YY

09/06/2025

14685785-0001